CALIFORNIA History–Social Science

myWorld INTERACTIVE

4

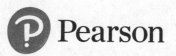

Pearson

Boston, Massachusetts   Chandler, Arizona
Glenview, Illinois   New York, New York

Pearson would like to extend a special thank you to all of the California teachers who helped guide the development of this program. We gratefully acknowledge your efforts to realize the possibilities of elementary Social Studies teaching and learning. Together, we will prepare California students for college, careers, and civic life.

Cover: Santa Barbara Mission
       Credit: Mitch Diamond/Stockbyte/Getty Images

Excerpts from the History-Social Science Content Standards for California Public Schools Grades K–5. Copyright © California Department of Education.

Credits appear on pages R63–R65, which constitute an extension of this copyright page.

ISBN-13: 978-0-328-95168-0
ISBN-10: 0-328-95168-4

10 19

Program Authors

Dr. Linda B. Bennett
Faculty, Social Studies Education
College of Education
University of Missouri
Columbia, MO

Dr. James B. Kracht
Professor Emeritus
Departments of Geography and
   Teaching, Learning, and Culture
Texas A&M University
College Station, TX

Reviewers and Consultants

Program Consultants

ELL Consultant
Jim Cummins Ph.D.

Professor Emeritus,
Department of
   Curriculum, Teaching,
   and Learning
University of Toronto
Toronto, Canada

**Differentiated Instruction
Consultant**

Kathy Tuchman Glass
President of Glass
   Educational Consulting
Woodside, CA

Reading Consultant
Elfrieda H. Hiebert Ph.D.

Founder, President and
   CEO, TextProject, Inc.
University of California
   Santa Cruz

Inquiry and C3 Consultant

Dr. Kathy Swan
Professor of Curriculum
   and Instruction
University of Kentucky
Lexington, KY

Academic Reviewers

Paul Apodaca, Ph.D.

Associate Professor,
American Studies
Chapman University
Orange, CA

Warren J. Blumenfeld, Ed.D.

Former Associate
Professor, Iowa State
University, School
of Education
South Hadley, MA

Dr. Albert M. Camarillo

Professor of History,
Emeritus
Stanford University
Palo Alto, CA

Steven Hackel, Ph.D.

Professor, History
Department of History
University of California
   at Riverside
Riverside, CA

Xiaojian Zhao

Professor, Department
   of Asian American
   Studies
University of California,
   Santa Barbara
Santa Barbara, CA

Teacher Reviewers

Stephanie Fortunato
Teacher
Inglewood USD
Inglewood, CA

Mercedes Kirk
First grade teacher
Folsom Cordova USD
Folsom, CA

Janet Mulder
Educational Consultant
San Diego, CA

Doris Sterling
Teacher
Sacramento City USD
Sacramento, CA

Kristin Sullens
Teacher, Grade 4
Chula Vista ESD
San Diego, CA

Program Partner

Campaign for the Civic Mission of Schools is a coalition of
over 70 national civic learning, education, civic engagement,
and business groups committed to improving the quality and
quantity of civic learning in American schools.

CAMPAIGN FOR THE CIVIC MISSION OF SCHOOLS

Educating for Democracy

Celebrating California and the Nation

Analysis HI.2

Geography Skills Handbook

HSS 4.1.1, 4.1.2, 4.1.3, 4.1.4, 4.3.3, 4.4.2 **Analysis** CST.4, CST.5

Writing Workshop

HSS 4.4.1

Using Primary and Secondary Sources

HSS 4.1.1, 4.5.2 **Analysis** RE.1, RE.2

Chapter 1

California's Geography

GO ONLINE FOR
DIGITAL RESOURCES

📖 ETEXT

▶ VIDEO

- **Field Trip Video**
  Giants in the Mist
- **Digital Skill Practice**
  Interpret Physical Maps
  Summarize

🔊 AUDIO

Rap About It lyrics and music

👆 INTERACTIVITY

- **Big Question Activity**
  How does geography affect our lives?
- **Quest Interactivities**
  Quest Kick Off
  Quest Connections
  Quest Findings
- **Lesson Interactivities**
  Lesson Introduction
  Key Ideas
  Lesson Review

🎮 GAMES

Vocabulary Practice

☑ ASSESSMENT

Lesson Quizzes and Chapter Tests

The **BIG** Question How does geography affect our lives?

Chapter 2
California's Early History

GO ONLINE FOR
DIGITAL RESOURCES

📖 ETEXT

▶ VIDEO

- **Field Trip Video**
  Using the Past to
  Inform our Future
- **Digital Skill
  Practice**
  Compare and
  Contrast
  Analyze Images

🔊 AUDIO

Rap About It lyrics
and music

👆 INTERACTIVITY

- **Big Question
  Activity**
  How do people
  adapt to where they
  live?
- **Quest
  Interactivities**
  Quest Kick Off
  Quest Connections
  Quest Findings
- **Lesson
  Interactivities**
  Lesson Introduction
  Key Ideas
  Lesson Review

🎮 GAMES

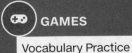
Vocabulary Practice

✅ ASSESSMENT

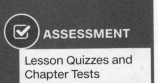
Lesson Quizzes and
Chapter Tests

The BIG Question How do people adapt to where they live?

GO ONLINE FOR
DIGITAL RESOURCES

📖 ETEXT

▶ VIDEO

• **Field Trip Video**
A Window into the
Past

• **Digital Skill
Practice**
Compare
Viewpoints
Distinguish Fact
From Opinion

🔊 AUDIO

Rap About It lyrics
and music

👆 INTERACTIVITY

• **Big Question
Activity**
How does the past
shape our present
and future?

• **Quest
Interactivities**
Quest Kick Off
Quest Connections
Quest Findings

• **Lesson
Interactivities**
Lesson Introduction
Key Ideas
Lesson Review

🎮 GAMES

Vocabulary Practice

☑ ASSESSMENT

Lesson Quizzes and
Chapter Tests

The **BIG** Question How does the past shape our present and future?

The Gold Rush and Statehood

GO ONLINE FOR DIGITAL RESOURCES

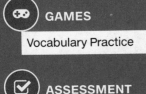 **ETEXT**

▶ **VIDEO**
- **Field Trip Video**
  A Gold Rush Experience
- **Digital Skill Practice**
  Distinguish Fact From Fiction
  Interpret Timelines

◀)) **AUDIO**

Rap About It lyrics and music

👆 **INTERACTIVITY**
- **Big Question Activity**
  How can change create opportunities?
- **Quest Interactivities**
  Quest Kick Off
  Quest Connections
  Quest Findings
- **Lesson Interactivities**
  Lesson Introduction
  Key Ideas
  Lesson Review

🎮 **GAMES**

Vocabulary Practice

☑ **ASSESSMENT**

Lesson Quizzes and Chapter Tests

The **BIG** Question How can change create opportunities?

Chapter 5 California After Statehood

GO ONLINE FOR DIGITAL RESOURCES

📖 **ETEXT**

▶ **VIDEO**
- **Field Trip Video** Exploring the Legacy of Chinese in America
- **Digital Skill Practice** Interpret Graphs Draw Inferences

🔊 **AUDIO**

Rap About It lyrics and music

👆 **INTERACTIVITY**
- **Big Question Activity** Why do some people leave their homelands?
- **Quest Interactivities** Quest Kick Off Quest Connections Quest Findings
- **Lesson Interactivities** Lesson Introduction Key Ideas Lesson Review

🎮 **GAMES**

Vocabulary Practice

☑ **ASSESSMENT**

Lesson Quizzes and Chapter Tests

The BIG Question Why do some people leave their homelands?

California in a Time of Expansion

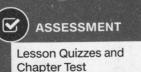
The BIG Question How do people respond to good times and bad?

The **BIG Question** How can change create opportunities?

Chapter 8
California's Government

GO ONLINE FOR DIGITAL RESOURCES

 **ETEXT**

VIDEO
- **Field Trip Video** Government at the Golden State Capitol
- **Digital Skill Practice** Identify Main Idea and Details Use and Interpret Evidence

AUDIO
Rap About It lyrics and music

INTERACTIVITY
- **Big Question Activity** What should the goals of government be?
- **Quest Interactivities** Quest Kick Off Quest Connections Quest Findings
- **Lesson Interactivities** Lesson Introduction Key Ideas Lesson Review

GAMES
Vocabulary Practice

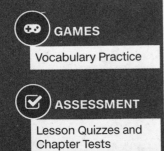 **ASSESSMENT**
Lesson Quizzes and Chapter Tests

Quests

Ask questions, explore sources, and cite evidence to support your view!

Maps

Where did this happen? Find out on these maps in your text.

Maps continued

Graphs and Charts

Find these charts, graphs, and tables in your text. They'll help you pull it together.

Primary Sources

Read primary sources to hear voices from the time.

Primary Sources continued

People to Know

Read about the people who made history.

Citizenship

Biographies Online

Abigail Adams   Elsie Allen

John Adams   James Armistead

Samuel Adams   Benedict Arnold

People to Know continued

Clara Barton

Delilah Beasley

James Beckwourth

William Bradford

Chaz Bono

Sergey Brin

Jerry Brown

Edmund Burke

Juan Rodriguez Cabrillo

Tani Gorre Cantil-Sakauye

Christopher "Kit" Carson

César Chávez

Louise Clappe

Thomas Clifford

Christopher Columbus

Hernán Cortés

Juan Crespi

Charles Crocker

Hallie M. Daggett

Juan Bautista de Anza

Pedro Menéndez de Avilés

Samuel de Champlain

Gaspar de Portolá

Antonio Lopez de Santa Anna

María Angustias de la Guerra

Bartolomeu Dias

John Dickinson

Walt Disney

Frederick Douglass

Ralph Waldo Emerson

William Fargo

Wong Chin Foo

Benjamin Franklin

John C. Fremont

Eric Garcetti

John Gast

Nathan Hale

Alexander Hamilton

John Hancock

Kamala D. Harris

Patrick Henry

Mark Hopkins

Henry Hudson

Dolores Huerta

Collis P. Huntington

Anne Hutchinson

Daniel Inouye

Joseph James

Thomas Jefferson

Hiram Johnson

Billie Jean King

Martin Luther King Jr.

King Charles III

King George III

Dorothea Lange

Lewis and Clark

Abraham Lincoln

Henry Wadsworth Longfellow

Mary Ludwig Hays

Lord Dunmore

Ferdinand Magellan

Wilma Mankiller

People to Know continued

James Wilson Marshall

John Marshall

Biddy Mason

Louis B. Mayer

Sylvia Mendez

Metacom

Harvey Milk

James Monroe

Samuel Morse

John Muir

José Nicolás

Pat Nixon

Thomas Paine

Charley Parkhurst

William Penn

William Pitt

James K. Polk

Prince Henry the Navigator

Edmund Randolph

Ronald Reagan

Paul Revere

Sally Ride

Jackie Robinson

Eleanor Roosevelt

Sarah Royce

Bernarda Ruiz

Sacagawea

Haym Salomon

Deborah Sampson

José Julio Sarria

Dalip Singh Saund

Junípero Serra

Roger Sherman

Sir Francis Drake

John Drake Sloat

Jedediah Smith

John Smith

Leland Stanford

John Steinbeck

Levi Strauss

John A. Sutter

Mary Tape

Archie Thompson

Tisquantum

Harriet Tubman

Mariano Guadalupe Vallejo

Earl Warren

Mercy Otis Warren

George Washington

Henry Wells

Phillis Wheatley

Narcissa Whitman

Mary Williams

Roger Williams

Sarah Winnemucca

John Winthrop

Jerry Yang

Skills

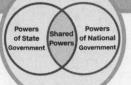

Practice key skills in these skills lessons.

Literacy Skills

Critical Thinking Skills

Map and Graph Skills

Skills continued

Build Historical and Social Sciences Analysis Skills.

Gold found at Sutter's Mill.   Calif beco

48 1849 1850 1

Analysis Skills

Skills Online

Analyze Cause and Effect   Ask and Answer Questions

Analyze Costs and Benefits   Classify and Categorize

Analyze Images   Compare and Contrast

Skills continued

Compare Viewpoints

Conduct Research

Create Charts

Deliver an Effective Presentation

Distinguish Fact From Opinion

Distinguish Fact From Fiction

Draw Conclusions

Draw Inferences

Evaluate Media Content

Generalize

Generate New Ideas

Identify Bias

Identify Main Idea and Details

Interpret Cultural Data on Maps

Interpret Economic Data on Maps

Interpret Graphs

Interpret Physical Maps

Interpret Timelines

Make Decisions

Predict Consequences

Resolve Conflict

Sequence

Solve Problems

Summarize

Use and Interpret Evidence

Use Latitude and Longitude

Use Primary and Secondary Sources

Use the Internet Safely

Work in Cooperative Teams

Standards at a Glance

History-Social Science Content Standards

4.1	Students demonstrate an understanding of the physical and human geographic features that define places and regions in California.
4.1.1	Explain and use the coordinate grid system of latitude and longitude to determine the absolute locations of places in California and on Earth.
4.1.2	Distinguish between the North and South Poles; the equator and the prime meridian; the tropics; and the hemispheres, using coordinates to plot locations.
4.1.3	Identify the state capital and describe the various regions of California, including how their characteristics and physical environments (e.g., water, landforms, vegetation, climate) affect human activity.
4.1.4	Identify the locations of the Pacific Ocean, rivers, valleys, and mountain passes and explain their effects on the growth of towns.
4.1.5	Use maps, charts, and pictures to describe how communities in California vary in land use, vegetation, wildlife, climate, population density, architecture, services, and transportation.
4.2	Students describe the social, political, cultural, and economic life and interactions among people of California from the pre-Columbian societies to the Spanish mission and Mexican rancho periods.
4.2.1	Discuss the major nations of California Indians, including their geographic distribution, economic activities, legends, and religious beliefs; and describe how they depended on, adapted to, and modified the physical environment by cultivation of land and use of sea resources.
4.2.2	Identify the early land and sea routes to, and European settlements in, California with a focus on the exploration of the North Pacific (e.g., by Captain James Cook, Vitus Bering, Juan Cabrillo), noting especially the importance of mountains, deserts, ocean currents, and wind patterns.
4.2.3	Describe the Spanish exploration and colonization of California, including the relationships among soldiers, missionaries, and Indians (e.g., Juan Crespi, Junipero Serra, Gaspar de Portola).
4.2.4	Describe the mapping of, geographic basis of, and economic factors in the placement and function of the Spanish missions; and understand how the mission system expanded the influence of Spain and Catholicism throughout New Spain and Latin America.
4.2.5	Describe the daily lives of the people, native and nonnative, who occupied the presidios, missions, ranchos, and pueblos.
4.2.6	Discuss the role of the Franciscans in changing the economy of California from a hunter-gatherer economy to an agricultural economy.
4.2.7	Describe the effects of the Mexican War for Independence on Alta California, including its effects on the territorial boundaries of North America.
4.2.8	Discuss the period of Mexican rule in California and its attributes, including land grants, secularization of the missions, and the rise of the rancho economy.
4.3	Students explain the economic, social, and political life in California from the establishment of the Bear Flag Republic through the Mexican-American War, the Gold Rush, and the granting of statehood.
4.3.1	Identify the locations of Mexican settlements in California and those of other settlements, including Fort Ross and Sutter's Fort.

4.3.2	Compare how and why people traveled to California and the routes they traveled (e.g., James Beckwourth, John Bidwell, John C. Fremont, Pio Pico).
4.3.3	Analyze the effects of the Gold Rush on settlements, daily life, politics, and the physical environment (e.g., using biographies of John Sutter, Mariano Guadalupe Vallejo, Louise Clapp).
4.3.4	Study the lives of women who helped build early California (e.g., Biddy Mason).
4.3.5	Discuss how California became a state and how its new government differed from those during the Spanish and Mexican periods.
4.4	Students explain how California became an agricultural and industrial power, tracing the transformation of the California economy and its political and cultural development since the 1850s.
4.4.1	Understand the story and lasting influence of the Pony Express, Overland Mail Service, Western Union, and the building of the transcontinental railroad, including the contributions of Chinese workers to its construction.
4.4.2	Explain how the Gold Rush transformed the economy of California, including the types of products produced and consumed, changes in towns (e.g., Sacramento, San Francisco), and economic conflicts between diverse groups of people.
4.4.3	Discuss immigration and migration to California between 1850 and 1900, including the diverse composition of those who came; the countries of origin and their relative locations; and conflicts and accords among the diverse groups (e.g., the 1882 Chinese Exclusion Act).
4.4.4	Describe rapid American immigration, internal migration, settlement, and the growth of towns and cities (e.g., Los Angeles).
4.4.5	Discuss the effects of the Great Depression, the Dust Bowl, and World War II on California.
4.4.6	Describe the development and locations of new industries since the turn of the century, such as the aerospace industry, electronics industry, large-scale commercial agriculture and irrigation projects, the oil and automobile industries, communications and defense industries, and important trade links with the Pacific Basin.
4.4.7	Trace the evolution of California's water system into a network of dams, aqueducts, and reservoirs.
4.4.8	Describe the history and development of California's public education system, including universities and community colleges.
4.4.9	Analyze the impact of twentieth-century Californians on the nation's artistic and cultural development, including the rise of the entertainment industry (e.g., Louis B. Meyer, Walt Disney, John Steinbeck, Ansel Adams, Dorothea Lange, John Wayne).
4.5	Students understand the structures, functions, and powers of the local, state, and federal governments as described in the U.S. Constitution.
4.5.1	Discuss what the U.S. Constitution is and why it is important (i.e., a written document that defines the structure and purpose of the U.S. government and describes the shared powers of federal, state, and local governments).
4.5.2	Understand the purpose of the California Constitution, its key principles, and its relationship to the U.S. Constitution.

4.5.3	Describe the similarities (e.g., written documents, rule of law, consent of the governed, three separate branches) and differences (e.g., scope of jurisdiction, limits on government powers, use of the military) among federal, state, and local governments.
4.5.4	Explain the structures and functions of state governments, including the roles and responsibilities of their elected officials.
4.5.5	Describe the components of California's governance structure (e.g., cities and towns, Indian rancherias and reservations, counties, school districts).

Historical and Social Sciences Analysis Skills

Chronological and Spatial Thinking

CST.1	Students place key events and people of the historical era they are studying in a chronological sequence and within a spatial context; they interpret time lines.
CST.2	Students correctly apply terms related to time, including *past, present, future, decade, century,* and *generation*.
CST.3	Students explain how the present is connected to the past, identifying both similarities and differences between the two, and how some things change over time and some things stay the same.
CST.4	Students use map and globe skills to determine the absolute locations of places and interpret information available through a map's or globe's legend, scale, and symbolic representations.
CST.5	Students judge the significance of the relative location of a place (e.g., proximity to a harbor, on trade routes) and analyze how relative advantages or disadvantages can change over time.

Research, Evidence, and Point of View

RE.1	Students differentiate between primary and secondary sources.
RE.2	Students pose relevant questions about events they encounter in historical documents, eyewitness accounts, oral histories, letters, diaries, artifacts, photographs, maps, artworks, and architecture.
RE.3	Students distinguish fact from fiction by comparing documentary sources on historical figures and events with fictionalized characters and events.

Historical Interpretation

HI.1	Students summarize the key events of the era they are studying and explain the historical contexts of those events.
HI.2	Students identify the human and physical characteristics of the places they are studying and explain how those features form the unique character of those places.
HI.3	Students identify and interpret the multiple causes and effects of historical events.
HI.4	Students conduct cost-benefit analyses of historical and current events.

Welcome to Your Book!

Your textbook is made up of chapters and lessons.
Each lesson starts with pages like this.

Look for these words as you read.

Words with yellow highlight are important social studies words. The sentence with the word will help you understand what the word means.

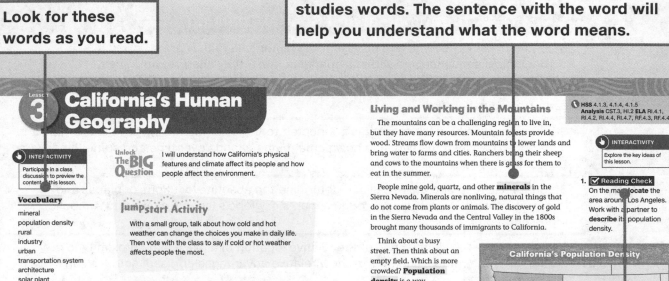

Lesson

3 California's Human Geography

INTERACTIVITY

Participate in a class discussion to preview the content of this lesson.

Vocabulary

mineral
population density
rural
industry
urban
transportation system
architecture
solar plant

Academic Vocabulary

community
service

Unlock The BIG Question

I will understand how California's physical features and climate affect its people and how people affect the environment.

JumpStart Activity

With a small group, talk about how cold and hot weather can change the choices you make in daily life. Then vote with the class to say if cold or hot weather affects people the most.

You have studied California's physical features. Now you will learn about its human geography. This means studying where people live and how they make a living in different places. You will see that California's landforms and climate strongly affect its people.

This road in a rural community (left) is different from the highway in an urban community (right). You can see how they are different in their population density, land use, and transportation.

26   Chapter 1 • California's Geography

Living and Working in the Mountains

The mountains can be a challenging region to live in, but they have many resources. Mountain forests provide wood. Streams flow down from mountains to lower lands and bring water to farms and cities. Ranchers bring their sheep and cows to the mountains when there is grass for them to eat in the summer.

People mine gold, quartz, and other **minerals** in the Sierra Nevada. Minerals are nonliving, natural things that do not come from plants or animals. The discovery of gold in the Sierra Nevada and the Central Valley in the 1800s brought many thousands of immigrants to California.

Think about a busy street. Then think about an empty field. Which is more crowded? **Population density** is a way geographers measure how crowded an area is. They compare how many people live in one square mile of a city, for example, to how many people live in one square mile in the country. The city will have many more people in the same amount of land. This means it has a higher population density.

The mountain region has a low population density. It is less dense than the coast or the Central Valley. Physical features such as steep, rocky cliffs make many areas difficult to reach. Snow and ice also make mountain passes hard to drive through in the winter.

HSS 4.1.3, 4.1.4, 4.1.5 **Analysis** CST.3, HI.2 **ELA** RI.4.1, RI.4.2, RI.4.4, RI.4.7, RF.4.3, RF.4.4

INTERACTIVITY

Explore the key ideas of this lesson.

1. ☑ **Reading Check** On the map **locate** the area around Los Angeles. Work with a partner to **describe** its population density.

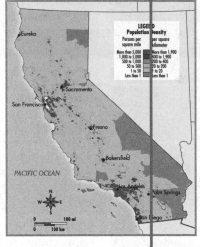

California's Population Density

LEGEND
Population Density
Persons per square mile
Persons per square kilometer

More than 5,000 / More than 1,900
1,000 to 5,000 / 400 to 1,900
500 to 1,000 / 200 to 400
50 to 500 / 20 to 200
1 to 50 / 1 to 20
Less than 1 / Less than 1

Eureka
Sacramento
San Francisco
Fresno
Bakersfield
PACIFIC OCEAN
Los Angeles
Palm Springs
San Diego

0   100 mi
0   100 km

Lesson 3 • California's Human Geography   27

Reading Checks will help you make sure you understood what you read.

Your Turn!

Flip through your book with a partner.

1. Find the start of another lesson.
   What do you see on the page?

This book will give you a lot of chances to figure things out. Then you can show what you have figured out and give your reasons.

The Quest Kick Off will tell you the goal of the Quest.

Watch for Quest Connections all through the chapter.

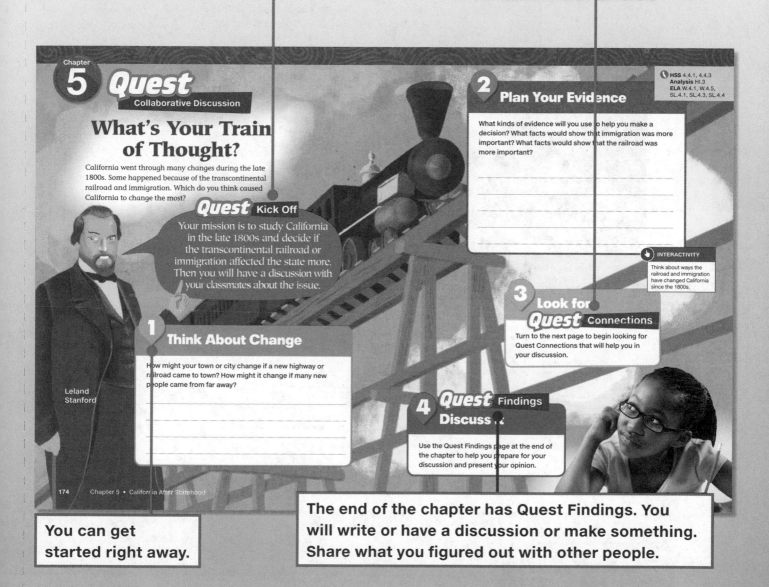

Chapter
5 *Quest*
Collaborative Discussion

What's Your Train of Thought?

California went through many changes during the late 1800s. Some happened because of the transcontinental railroad and immigration. Which do you think caused California to change the most?

Quest Kick Off

Your mission is to study California in the late 1800s and decide if the transcontinental railroad or immigration affected the state more. Then you will have a discussion with your classmates about the issue.

Leland Stanford

1 Think About Change

How might your town or city change if a new highway or railroad came to town? How might it change if many new people came from far away?

174   Chapter 5 • California After Statehood

HSS 4.4.1, 4.4.3
Analysis HI.3
ELA W.4.1, W.4.5, SL.4.1, SL.4.3, SL.4.4

2 Plan Your Evidence

What kinds of evidence will you use to help you make a decision? What facts would show that immigration was more important? What facts would show that the railroad was more important?

INTERACTIVITY
Think about ways the railroad and immigration have changed California since the 1800s.

3 Look for *Quest* Connections

Turn to the next page to begin looking for Quest Connections that will help you in your discussion.

4 *Quest* Findings
Discuss It

Use the Quest Findings page at the end of the chapter to help you prepare for your discussion and present your opinion.

You can get started right away.

The end of the chapter has Quest Findings. You will write or have a discussion or make something. Share what you figured out with other people.

2. Find two words with yellow highlight. What page are they on?

3. Find another Reading Check. What does it ask you to do?

4. Find another Quest. What is it called?

Learn to use important skills.

Read the explanation. Look at all the text and pictures.

Practice the skill. You'll be ready to use it whenever you need it.

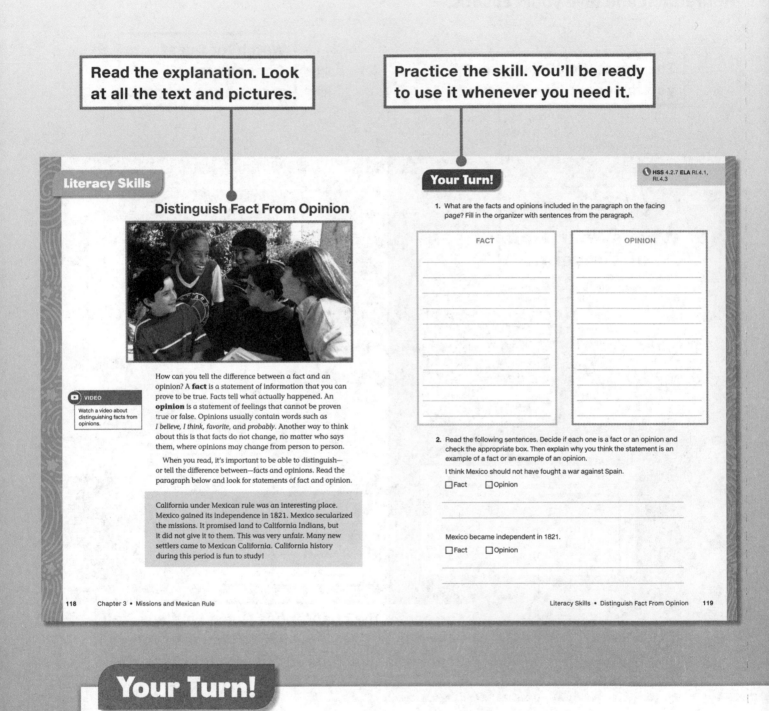

Literacy Skills

Distinguish Fact From Opinion

▶ VIDEO
Watch a video about distinguishing facts from opinions.

How can you tell the difference between a fact and an opinion? A **fact** is a statement of information that you can prove to be true. Facts tell what actually happened. An **opinion** is a statement of feelings that cannot be proven true or false. Opinions usually contain words such as *I believe, I think, favorite,* and *probably.* Another way to think about this is that facts do not change, no matter who says them, where opinions may change from person to person.

When you read, it's important to be able to distinguish— or tell the difference between—facts and opinions. Read the paragraph below and look for statements of fact and opinion.

California under Mexican rule was an interesting place. Mexico gained its independence in 1821. Mexico secularized the missions. It promised land to California Indians, but it did not give it to them. This was very unfair. Many new settlers came to Mexican California. California history during this period is fun to study!

Your Turn!

HSS 4.2.7 ELA RI.4.1, RI.4.3

1. What are the facts and opinions included in the paragraph on the facing page? Fill in the organizer with sentences from the paragraph.

FACT	OPINION

2. Read the following sentences. Decide if each one is a fact or an opinion and check the appropriate box. Then explain why you think the statement is an example of a fact or an example of an opinion.

I think Mexico should not have fought a war against Spain.

☐ Fact   ☐ Opinion

_____

Mexico became independent in 1821.

☐ Fact   ☐ Opinion

_____

Your Turn!

Work with a partner.

1. Find another Skill lesson. What skill will you learn? Talk about another time you might need that skill.

Every chapter has Primary Source pages. You can read or look at these sources to learn right from people who were there.

Find out what this source is about and who wrote it.

These questions help you think about the source.

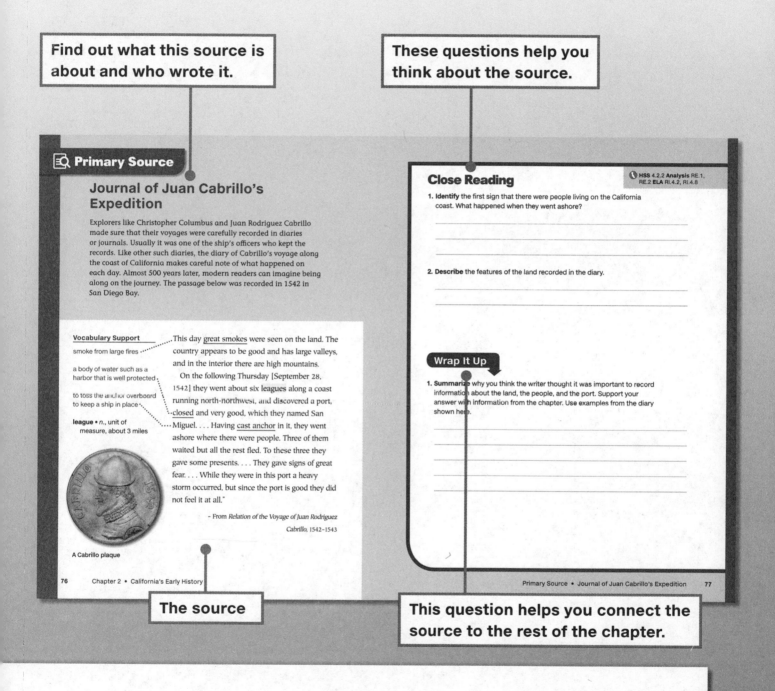

Primary Source

Journal of Juan Cabrillo's Expedition

Explorers like Christopher Columbus and Juan Rodriguez Cabrillo made sure that their voyages were carefully recorded in diaries or journals. Usually it was one of the ship's officers who kept the records. Like other such diaries, the diary of Cabrillo's voyage along the coast of California makes careful note of what happened on each day. Almost 500 years later, modern readers can imagine being along on the journey. The passage below was recorded in 1542 in San Diego Bay.

Vocabulary Support

smoke from large fires

a body of water such as a harbor that is well protected

to toss the anchor overboard to keep a ship in place

league • *n.*, unit of measure, about 3 miles

A Cabrillo plaque

This day great smokes were seen on the land. The country appears to be good and has large valleys, and in the interior there are high mountains.

On the following Thursday [September 28, 1542] they went about six leagues along a coast running north-northwest, and discovered a port, closed and very good, which they named San Miguel. . . . Having cast anchor in it, they went ashore where there were people. Three of them waited but all the rest fled. To these three they gave some presents. . . . They gave signs of great fear. . . . While they were in this port a heavy storm occurred, but since the port is good they did not feel it at all."

– From *Relation of the Voyage of Juan Rodriguez Cabrillo*, 1542–1543

76   Chapter 2 • California's Early History

Close Reading

HSS 4.2.2 **Analysis** RE.1, RE.2 **ELA** RI.4.2, RI.4.8

1. **Identify** the first sign that there were people living on the California coast. What happened when they went ashore?

_____

_____

_____

2. **Describe** the features of the land recorded in the diary.

_____

_____

_____

Wrap It Up

1. **Summarize** why you think the writer thought it was important to record information about the land, the people, and the port. Support your answer with information from the chapter. Use examples from the diary shown here.

_____

_____

_____

_____

_____

Primary Source • Journal of Juan Cabrillo's Expedition   77

The source

This question helps you connect the source to the rest of the chapter.

2. Find another Primary Source in your book. What is the source about?

Celebrating California and the Nation

California Plants and Animals

California's plants and animals are symbols of our state. How many of these have you seen where you live or have visited?

State Insect
Look for the outline of a dog's head on the wings of a male California dogface butterfly. This kind of butterfly can only be found in our state!

State Fossil
11 thousand years ago, saber-tooth cats roamed what is now California. You can find out more about them by visiting the La Brea Tar Pits Museum in Los Angeles.

State Marine Mammal
Look closely and you might spot a 50-foot long California gray whale along the coast, making its way south to Baja California.

State Flower
The California poppy was a useful plant to California Indians who used it as a medicine and food source. They also extracted and used its oil.

State Tree
The tallest tree in the world, the California redwood, can live to be more than 2,000 years old.

1. ☑ **Reading Check** Did you know that California has many other state symbols, including a state animal, state gold rush ghost town, and state marine reptile? Research and **identify** other state symbols, and choose one. Create a poster. Write four facts about the symbol, and draw a picture of it.

Political Symbols of California

California's State Flag

California's flag comes from an event known as the Bear Flag Revolt. This happened in 1846, when California was part of Mexico. The leaders of the revolt made a flag with a bear on it. Our state flag today is based on that flag.

The flag shows a five-pointed star, a red bar, and the words "California Republic." It also shows a grizzly bear, a symbol of strength.

2. ✓ **Reading Check**
On a separate sheet of paper, create your own state seal. Include images and words that symbolize California. **Explain** your design to a partner.

California's State Seal

California also has a state **seal**. A seal is an official symbol of a place, group, or political office.

California became the thirty-first state in 1850. The 31 stars shown in a semicircle on the seal stand for each state at that time.

Watching over California is the Roman goddess of wisdom, Minerva.

The grapes and the grizzly bear symbolize farming and wildlife.

The state motto, *Eureka*, is shown here. It means "I have found it." It likely refers to gold being discovered at Sutter's Mill in 1848.

The Sierra Nevada mountain range is shown in the background. The Sacramento River is also featured, with a gold miner working nearby.

Our Holidays

seal

Californians mark many holidays. Some are set aside by the federal or state governments. Offices and schools may be closed on these days. Some are days of celebration, like New Years Day or Independence Day.

Other federal holidays honor people who have contributed to our country. Martin Luther King, Jr. Day takes place every year in January. Martin Luther King, Jr. was a leader in the struggle for equal rights for African Americans. This holiday honors him and his life's work.

Some holidays are celebrated in California but not in every state. One of these is César Chávez Day. It takes place every year on March 31. César Chávez worked to improve life for California farm workers.

On César Chávez Day, many Californians work to help their community in some way. Students around the state learn about César Chávez.

These holidays are a way to learn more about American life and history. They also give attention to the ideals of truth, justice, and morality. Morality is the basic goodness of someone or something. For many Americans, both Martin Luther King, Jr. and César Chávez stand for these ideals.

The birthday of Martin Luther King, Jr. is celebrated on the third Monday in January.

Every year on March 31, Californians celebrate César Chávez Day.

3. **☑ Reading Check** Work with a partner to research César Chávez. Together, **describe** how you might celebrate César Chávez Day.

A Redwood Timeline

A redwood can live to be 2,000 years old! Its rings tell us how old it is. You can see redwood 'timelines' at museums, as in the photograph here. They use a cross section of the tree to show events in the past.

Analyze this illustration of a cross section of a redwood tree. Then answer the questions.

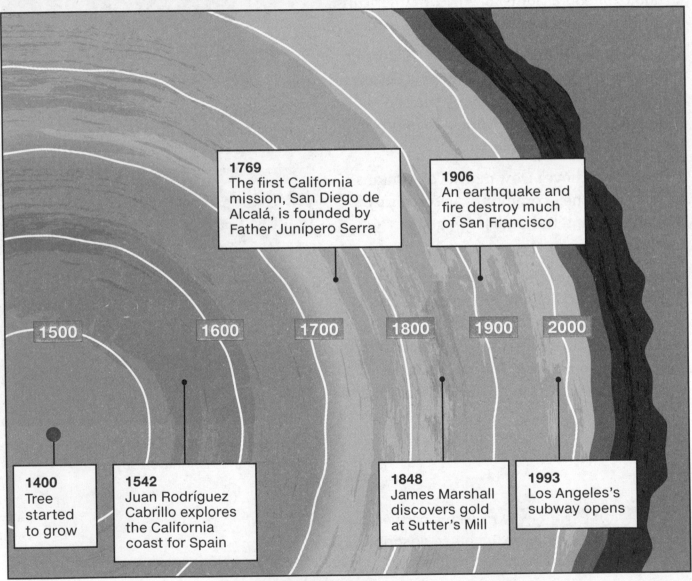

1769
The first California mission, San Diego de Alcalá, is founded by Father Junípero Serra

1906
An earthquake and fire destroy much of San Francisco

1500   1600   1700   1800   1900   2000

1400
Tree started to grow

1542
Juan Rodríguez Cabrillo explores the California coast for Spain

1848
James Marshall discovers gold at Sutter's Mill

1993
Los Angeles's subway opens

4. ☑ **Reading Check** Research and **identify** another important event in California's history. Add it to the timeline.

California State Song

In 1913, Francis Silverwood, a Canadian immigrant, wrote the lyrics to "I Love You, California." Abraham Frankenstein, an orchestra conductor, composed the music. An opera singer named Mary Garden began singing the song, and it soon became popular. Many years later, in 1988, a law was passed making "I Love You, California" the official state song.

I Love You, California

I love you, California, you're the greatest state of all.

I love you in the winter, summer, spring and in the fall.

I love your fertile valleys; your dear mountains I adore.

I love your grand old ocean and I love her rugged shore.

This is the original sheet music for "I Love You, California."

5. ☑ **Reading Check** The words here are only the first verse of the song. Research the other verses of the song. As a class, sing or speak the verses out loud. Then write a new verse to add to the song. You can **describe** an event in California or a favorite place in your state. Afterward, sing or speak your new verse.

_____

_____

_____

_____

California's People and Culture

There are more than 39 million people living in California. We speak many different languages.

A majority, or more than half, of all Californians speak English at home. But people also speak other languages from all over the world. The table shows some of the languages spoken by Californians. It also shows how many people speak each language at home.

Languages Spoken at Home	
Language	**Number of Speakers**
English	19,782,598
Spanish	10,105,385
Chinese	1,058,231
Tagalog	764,743
Vietnamese	521,534
Korean	372,742
Armenian	191,928
Persian	191,138
Arabic	153,635
Hindi	149,301
Japanese	140,575

Source: U.S. Census

6. **☑ Reading Check** Study the table. Circle how many Californians speak English at home. Underline how many speak Spanish at home. Then follow your teacher's instructions to research one of the other languages in the table. **Identify** where else in the world it is spoken.

_____

_____

Vocabulary

culture

Music and dance are part of culture. These Korean dancers are performing at a parade in Pasadena.

More than one quarter of the people living in California are immigrants. That is about 10 million people. About half of the children living in our state have a parent that comes from another country. Immigrants have come here from dozens of countries, such as China, Mexico, and the Philippines.

Immigrants have brought their cultures with them. **Culture** is the beliefs and ways of living shared by a group of people, including its language, customs, traditions, religion, values, holidays, and celebrations.

As immigrant families settle into big cities and small towns, they share their culture with their neighbors. They open restaurants, markets, and clothing stores. They play their music at community celebrations.

7. **☑ Reading Check** Create a brochure that **describes** cultural activities in your city, town, or community. Draw pictures to illustrate it. Write a caption for each picture. Share your work with the class.

These girls are participating in a Sikh cultural festival in Sacramento.

Geography Skills Handbook

Vocabulary

climate

region

Where can places be found?

California is located north of Mexico, south of Oregon, east of the Pacific Ocean, and west of Nevada and Arizona.

Five Themes of Geography

Geography is the study of Earth. That study is divided into five themes: Location, Place, Human/Environment Interaction, Movement, and Region. Each theme reveals something different about an area. You can use these themes to learn about the geography of California.

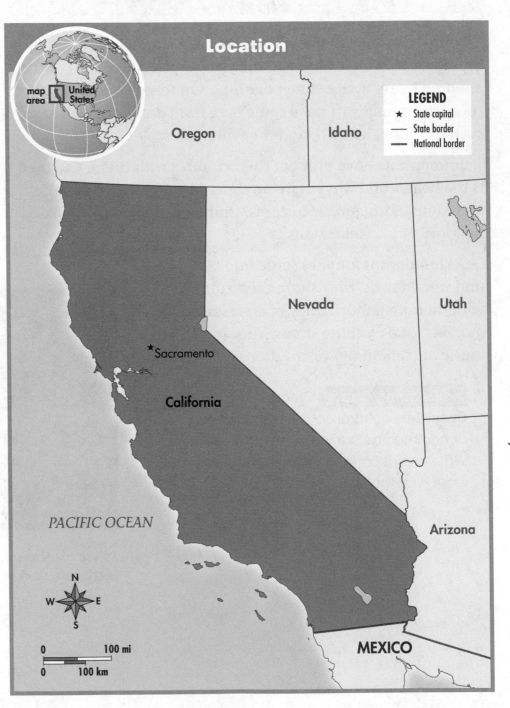

Location

map area — United States

Oregon

Idaho

LEGEND
★ State capital
— State border
— National border

Nevada

Utah

★ Sacramento

California

Arizona

PACIFIC OCEAN

N W E S

0   100 mi
0   100 km

MEXICO

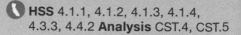

Place

Human/Environment Interaction

How is this place different from others?

Los Angeles is California's largest city. It is on the Pacific Ocean in southern California. It has a warm, dry climate. **Climate** is a place's average weather over time.

How have people changed a place?

Some parts of California are dry. The Shasta Dam, on the Sacramento River in California, was built to store water and provide electricity to California's Central Valley.

Movement

Region

How has movement changed the region?

The Pacific Coast Highway runs for about 150 miles along the California coast. Highways, railroads, harbors, and airports help move people and goods across California.

What is special about California's regions?

A **region** is a large area of land that has similar features. California has four regions. Each region is unique. The Central Valley region, for example, is where many of the fruits and vegetables we eat are grown.

1. ☑ **Reading Check** **Describe** what is special about where you live. Include one sentence about each of the themes of geography.

_____

_____

_____

Geography Skills Handbook   **CA9**

Latitude and Longitude

Look at the world map. You can see it is covered with lots of lines. These are imaginary lines that help geographers locate places on Earth.

The lines that run from east to west, or side to side across the map shown here, are called lines of **latitude**. They measure distance north or south of the **equator**, which is the imaginary line that runs around the center of Earth. These lines are numbered in units called degrees. The equator is located at 0 degrees (0°). Two other important lines of latitude are the Tropic of Cancer and the Tropic of Capricorn. The area between these lines is known as the tropics.

Another set of lines runs from north to south, or up and down on the map shown here. These are lines of **longitude**. They measure distances from the prime meridian. The **prime meridian** is the line of longitude marked as 0°. Other lines of longitude are measured in degrees east or west of the prime meridian, up to 180°. Lines of longitude run from the North Pole to the South Pole. The point on Earth that is farthest north is the North Pole. It is 90° North. The point that is farthest south is the South Pole. It is 90° South.

2. ☑ **Reading Check**
Locate and circle the prime meridian and equator on the map.

Locate and draw a star next to the tropic that is north of the equator.

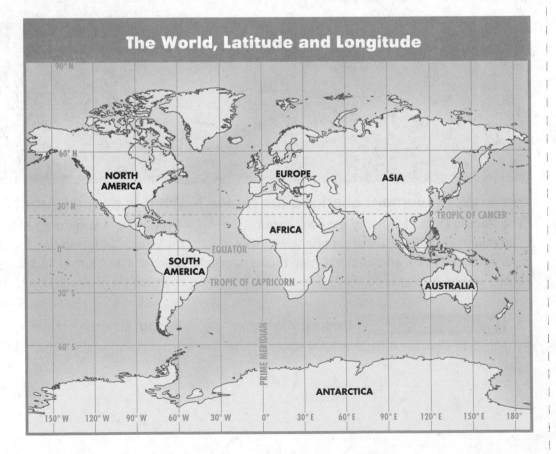

The World, Latitude and Longitude

Together, these lines of latitude and longitude form a coordinate grid around the globe. Coordinates are the numbers that identify a location, like the latitude and longitude of a place. Using a classroom globe may help you see how this works more clearly.

The equator divides Earth into northern and southern hemispheres. The prime meridian and the 180 degree longitude line divide Earth into eastern and western hemispheres. *Hemi* means "half." Each **hemisphere** is half of Earth. California is in both the Northern Hemisphere and the Western Hemisphere.

Vocabulary

latitude
equator
longitude
prime meridian
hemisphere

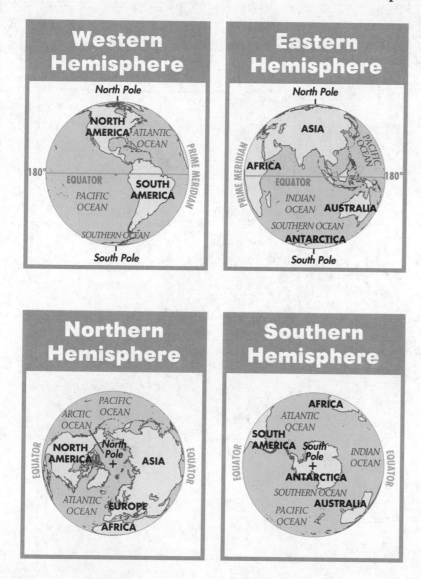

3. ☑ **Reading Check** **Identify** the continent that is in both the Southern and Western hemispheres. **Identify** the line that separates the Northern Hemisphere from the Southern Hemisphere.

Absolute and Relative Location

Absolute location is the exact location of a place on Earth. A place's absolute location does not change. You can find the absolute location of a place on a map or globe by finding its latitude and longitude.

On the map locate the lines of latitude and longitude that are closest to the northeast corner of California. The absolute location of this part of the state is about 42° N and 120° W.

4. ☑ **Reading Check**
Find the coordinates 36° North by 120° West on the map. Mark that location with an X. **Describe** the location to a partner. Is it near where you live?

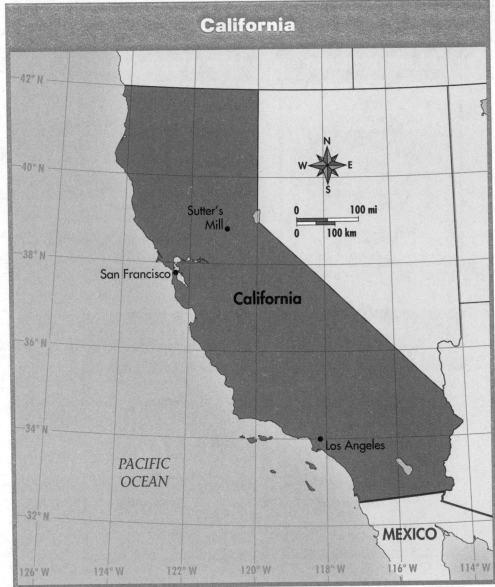

California

5. ☑ **Reading Check** Use the map to **determine** the absolute location of Los Angeles.

Relative location describes where a place is in relation to another place. Look again at the map. You can see that San Francisco is located on the Pacific Ocean. You can use the directions to describe the relative location of a place. For example, you could say that San Francisco is northwest of Los Angeles.

How important a place's relative location is can change over time. San Francisco is a good example. In 1847, it was a small town of less than 1,000 people. Then gold was discovered not too far away at Sutter's Mill. Suddenly, thousands of people came from far away to mine the gold. Many came by boat across the ocean. Where did they first land? San Francisco! The city's population soon grew to 25,000 people. Before gold was discovered, it did not much matter that San Francisco was located near Sutter's Mill. But that changed when the Gold Rush began.

6. ☑ **Reading Check** **Describe** how the importance of San Francisco's relative location changed over time.

_____

_____

_____

The Golden Gate Bridge is in San Francisco.

Using Maps

There are many different types of maps. You can see a physical map here. A **physical map** shows information such as landforms and bodies of water. It may show elevation, or a place's height above sea level.

Some maps also include a locator map. The **locator map** is a simple map that shows the location of an area within a country or in the world.

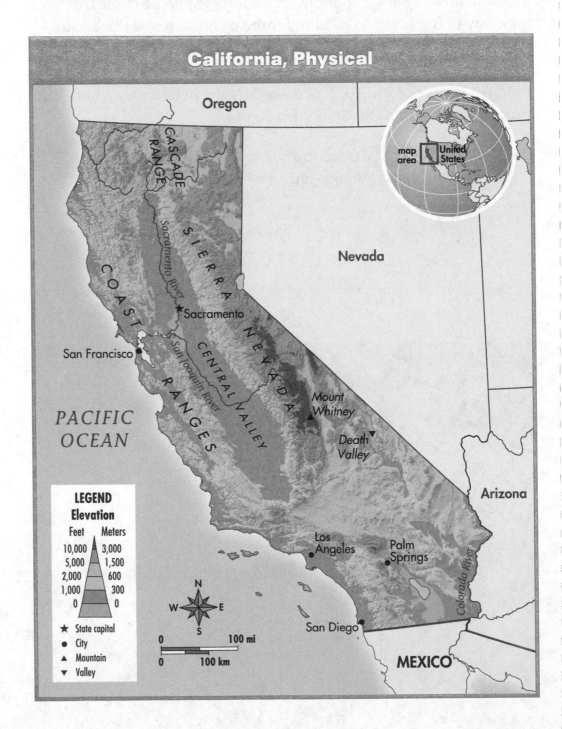

California, Physical

Oregon

CASCADE RANGE

SIERRA NEVADA

Sacramento River

★ Sacramento

San Francisco

San Joaquin River

COAST RANGES

CENTRAL VALLEY

Nevada

Mount Whitney ▲

Death ▼
Valley

PACIFIC
OCEAN

Arizona

Los
Angeles

Palm
Springs

Colorado River

San Diego

MEXICO

map area | United States

LEGEND
Elevation

Feet	Meters
10,000	3,000
5,000	1,500
2,000	600
1,000	300
0	0

★ State capital
● City
▲ Mountain
▼ Valley

N
W — E
S

0   100 mi
0   100 km

Different parts of a map help you learn different things. Look at the physical map of California and find each of these map parts.

- **Title:** On a map, the title is the words that tell its topic.

- **Map legend:** The map legend or key defines the symbols used on the map. Each symbol is a different marking or color that represents something.

- **Scale:** The scale bar shows how distance on the map compares to distance in the real world.

- **Compass rose:** A compass rose shows the cardinal directions of north, south, east, and west. It may also show the intermediate directions of northeast, northwest, southeast, and southwest.

Vocabulary

physical map
locator map
title
map legend
scale
compass rose

7. ☑ **Reading Check** **Identify** the title of this map.

_____

8. **Identify** and draw the symbol for a mountain.

9. **Explain** the purpose of the locator map.

_____

_____

10. **Describe** the location of Sacramento using the nearby landforms.

_____

_____

_____

_____

Types of Maps

Different kinds of maps can show different things about places. You have seen a physical map that shows physical features like mountains.

This is a political map of the United States. A **political map** shows information such as state or national borders. Notice the difference in the thickness of the lines that show the borders between states and between countries. A political map may also show the capital cities of states or countries. You can see this map has the same parts as the physical map you just saw, including a locator map.

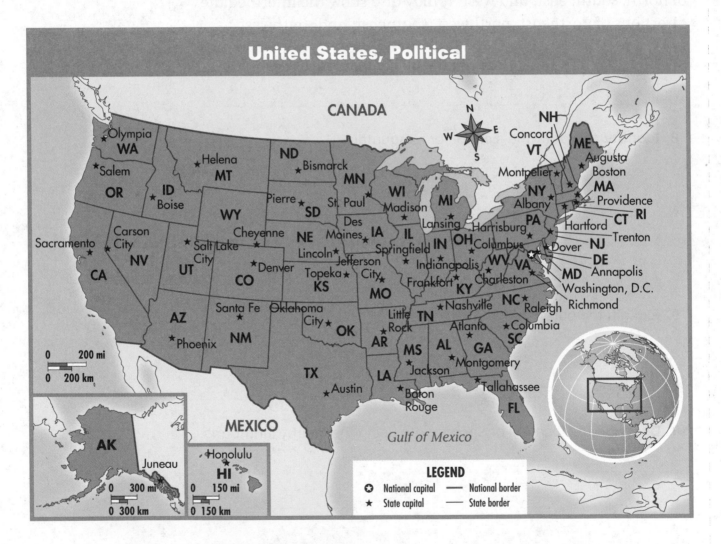

United States, Political

11. ✓ **Reading Check** According to this map, where is the capital of the United States located?

Historical maps are another type of map. A **historical map** shows events from the past. These maps usually include a date in the title. They can be useful for seeing how things have changed over time.

Vocabulary

political map
historical map

Historical maps may show state and national borders from the past that have since changed. For example, California was once a part of Mexico. This map of Mexico in 1821 shows this. Historical maps may also show specific events that happened in the past. They may show battles, for example.

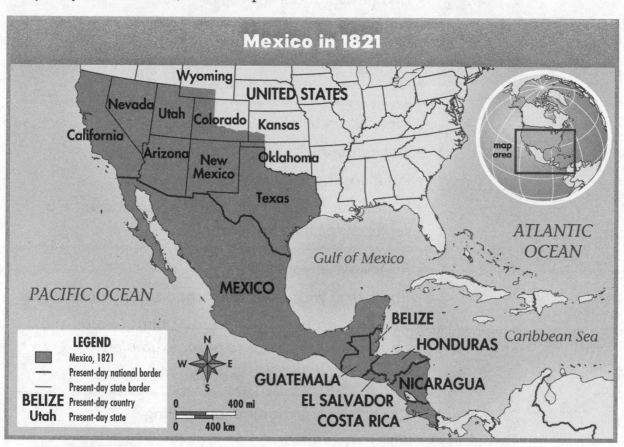

Mexico in 1821

LEGEND
Mexico, 1821
— Present-day national border
— Present-day state border
BELIZE Present-day country
Utah Present-day state

0   400 mi
0   400 km

12. ☑ **Reading Check** **Describe** how you can tell that this is a historical map.

_____

_____

13. **Compare and contrast** this map with a map of North America today. What has changed about California?

_____

_____

Writing Workshop

Keys to Good Writing

Good writers follow five steps when they write.

Plan	• Brainstorm to choose a topic. • Find details about the topic. • Take notes from sources. • Write down your sources. • Plan how to use the details.
Draft	• Write down all of your ideas. • Think about which ideas go together. • Put ideas that go together in groups. • Write a sentence for the introduction and write a sentence for the conclusion.
Revise	• Review what you wrote. • Check that your ideas and organization make sense. • Add time-order words and transitions (words and phrases such as *because* or *for example*). • List any more sources that you used.
Edit	• Check for correct grammar, spelling, and punctuation. • Make a final copy.
Share	• Use technology to print or publish your work. • Make sure that you list all of your sources.

1. ☑ **Reading Check** **Cause and Effect** How might not completing one of these steps affect your writing piece?

_____

_____

_____

There are three main writing genres. They are opinion, informative, and narrative writing. They all have a different purpose.

Opinion Writing

When you write an opinion piece, you share your point of view on a topic. Your goal should be to make your viewpoint clear. You also need to support your point of view with evidence. Read the steps and sample sentences below to see how to write effective opinion pieces.

Many people came to California to find gold.

1	**Introduce the topic.** *People came to California for different reasons, but many came to find gold during the Gold Rush.*
2	**State your opinion.** *It was not worth it for many people to come to California during the gold rush because most did not find gold.*
3	**Support it with reasons, including facts and details.** *Panning for gold was hard work. Many people came to California, but few people found gold. In addition, people had to buy a lot of supplies to look for gold.*
4	**Make sure that your ideas are clear and organized to support your purpose.**
5	**Support your opinion statement with a conclusion.** *Many people came to California in 1849 because they hoped to find gold, but few people were successful.*

2. ☑ **Reading Check** **Explain** How do you support your point of view?

Informative Writing

Building the First Transcontinental Railroad

Informative writing is also called explanatory writing, because you are writing to inform, or teach, and explain a topic to your reader. Credible, or reliable, sources are very important to use in this kind of writing. Make sure to avoid plagiarism. This means using someone else's words without giving that person credit. Take notes on your sources, including what they say and where you found them. Keep in mind that a reader may know nothing about your topic. You must be the expert and be clear in what you write. Read the steps and sample sentences below.

1	**Introduce the topic.** *Many Chinese workers came to California to help build the First Transcontinental Railroad in the late 1800s.*
2	**Develop the topic with facts, definitions, and concrete details.** *There were not enough workers to build the railroad, so Chinese workers immigrated to the United States for this job. To immigrate means to move from one country into another country to live. It was slow, dangerous, and dirty work, but the Chinese were hard workers.*
3	**Link an example with words, phrases, or clauses.** *For example, they had to blast through rock to make tunnels through mountains.*
4	**Use precise language and content words.** *The workers lit the fuse to the dynamite and then ran to take cover before it exploded.*
5	**Write a conclusion that supports your introduction.** *Many Chinese people immigrated to the United States and came to California to find jobs and help build the transcontinental railroad.*

3. ☑ **Reading Check**

Explain Discuss with a partner why it is important to use concrete details and precise language in your writing.

Narrative Writing

When you write a narrative piece, you are telling a story. The story can be about a real or made-up event or experience. Use sensory words to show, rather than tell, the reader what happened. Sensory words describe what a person sees, hears, touches, tastes, or smells. You want the reader to be able to visualize, or see, what you are describing. The events in your narrative should be clear and connect to each other. Read the steps and sample sentences below.

1	**Introduce the story and characters.** *Javier wanted to warm up before his game, and he needed a catcher. His father had promised to help him warm up, but he was busy at work picking almonds. It was harvest time.*
2	**Use dialogue and descriptive words.** *"Dad, when will you be finished? I have to be at the field in less than an hour!" Javier yelled over the huge pile of almonds. Javier had been practicing his fastball all week because it was the championship, and he was going to pitch.*
3	**Use details to develop your writing.** *Javier's eyes lit up when he saw his father shake the last almond tree in the row and grab his mitt from the ground. They hurried to the championship game and had time for a couple practice pitches.*
4	**Strengthen your writing with sensory words.** *During the last pitch of the big game, Javier rubbed the baseball against his sleeve, noticing the strong scent of the leather from his glove. He could almost taste victory.*
5	**Write a strong conclusion to close the narrative.** *After Javier received the championship trophy, he handed it to his father. He felt he would not have won without his father's help, love, and support.*

4. ☑ **Reading Check** **Evaluate** Answer this question with a partner: Do you think the conclusion wraps up the story and is strong?

Researching on the Internet

There are many Web sites on the Internet, but not all of them can be used for research. Look for Web sites with .org, .edu, or .gov, which have reliable content. Content from sites that end in .com cannot necessarily be trusted. If you do use them, check one or two other sources from reliable sites. Also check to see who published the information and how old it is. Is there an author's name listed? Is there a date?

Using a Library Media Center to Write a Research Paper

When you are writing a research paper, it is helpful to use the resources available in your Library Media Center. To use them effectively, make sure that you:

- use different kinds of print and digital sources and make sure they are reliable.
- compare the information you find in sources.
- take notes by paraphrasing or categorizing content from your sources.
- ask a librarian for help if you are unsure what sources to use for your topic.

Follow these steps to write a research paper:

1. Write down two or three questions to guide your research.
2. Use reliable sources to do your research and answer the questions. Revise the questions if needed.
3. Based on the answers to your questions, organize your topic so that details for each part of your topic are together.
4. Write a statement about your topic based on your research and evidence. This will become your introduction.
5. Use evidence in the form of details, examples, and quotes to support your statement.
6. Use transitions and clauses to connect your ideas.
7. Write a strong conclusion that goes back to what you stated in the introduction.
8. Make a list of your sources.

5. ☑ **Reading Check** **Draw Conclusions** Why is it important to check more than one source when you are researching a topic?

_____

_____

_____

Using Primary and Secondary Sources

HSS 4.1.1, 4.5.2 Analysis RE.1, RE.2

Primary and Secondary Sources

A **primary source** is one made or written by a person who witnessed an event firsthand. Primary sources can include diaries, letters, historical documents, photographs, videos, newspaper articles, and interviews. Artifacts, or objects made or used by people, are also a primary source. So are buildings and their architecture, or design. Sources can be written down, like a letter. They can also be **oral**, or spoken, like a recording of a speech or an interview.

A **secondary source** is a source written or created by someone who did not witness an event. The writer of a secondary source did not experience events he or she writes about firsthand. Most books about history are secondary sources even though their writers do much of their research using primary sources. This textbook, for example, is a secondary source. Reference books like atlases and encyclopedias are secondary sources. **Biographies**, or books about people's lives, are also secondary sources.

1. ☑ **Reading Check Identify** two examples of primary sources.

_____

_____

2. **Underline** in the text examples of secondary sources.

Vocabulary

primary source
oral
secondary source
biography

This photo of a Gabrielino California Indian is an example of a primary source since the photographer was at the event when the picture was taken.

Comparing Primary and Secondary Sources

Read these two sources of information about the San Francisco Earthquake of 1906. Then answer the question below.

Primary Source

Zellerbach: I don't think I've told you about the earthquake and fire.

Nathan: No. I'd like to hear about that.

Zellerbach: . . . I was asleep when it started to shake. I buried my head in the pillow; it felt like this was the end of the world. . . . When it finally settled down the side of the house had gone out, right alongside of my room. It opened up the side of the house, and here I was, looking up in the sky. . . . The fire was moving up . . . So our house burned down.

–Interview with Harold Zellerbach, 1971

Secondary Source

On the morning of April 18, 1906, a massive earthquake shook San Francisco, California. Though the quake lasted less than a minute, its immediate impact was disastrous. The earthquake also ignited several fires around the city that burned for three days and destroyed nearly 500 city blocks.

–National Archives, "San Francisco Earthquake, 1906"

3. ☑ Reading Check **Compare** the primary source and secondary source. How are they similar? How are they different?

_____

_____

_____

_____

How to Interpret an Artifact

Archaeologists in Carlsbad, California, found a piece of volcanic rock in 1985 that looked a lot like a bear. California Indians made it about 7,000 to 8,000 years ago. Chipped Stone Bear is an artifact. One way to interpret or understand an artifact is to study the object and then ask questions. Asking questions helps you understand what type of source you are looking at and what it can teach you.

Study the artifact. Then answer the questions to help you interpret it.

Chipped Stone Bear is the official California State Prehistoric Artifact.

4. ☑ **Reading Check** **Interpret** the artifact. What do you think this is? **Describe** what you see. **Write** two questions you have about the artifact.

_____

_____

_____

_____

5. What can you learn about California Indians from Chipped Stone Bear? **Explain** why Chipped Stone Bear is a primary source and not a secondary source.

_____

_____

_____

_____

How to Interpret a Historical Document

Just like artifacts, you can interpret historical documents by studying them and asking and answering questions. The California Constitution is a historical document and a primary source. The constitution provides a plan for the state's government and outlines the basic rights of California citizens. Study Article I of the California Constitution, the Declaration of Rights, and use it to answer the questions.

Primary Source

CALIFORNIA CONSTITUTION

ARTICLE I DECLARATION OF RIGHTS

SECTION 1. All people are by nature free and independent and have inalienable rights. Among these are enjoying and defending life and liberty, acquiring, possessing, and protecting property, and pursuing and obtaining safety, happiness, and privacy.

6. ☑ **Reading Check** **Write** one question that you have about this document.

_____

_____

_____

7. **Synthesize** What would be a secondary source connected to the California Constitution?

_____

_____

_____

How to Interpret Secondary Sources

This textbook will teach you about the building of the transcontinental railroad. But it was not written by someone who was there at the time. The authors did not see or live through the events that are described. They learned by reading other people's writing and looking at primary sources, like photographs, diaries, and letters. We can ask and answer questions to interpret secondary sources just like primary sources. Read the passage below from your textbook and answer the question that follows.

Secondary Source

During the 1850s, people wanted a faster way to travel across the country. Traveling by wagon took too much time. The country needed a transcontinental railroad that connected the eastern part of the United States to the western part.

In 1862, the U.S. government hired two companies to build new tracks. The Central Pacific Railroad company started building tracks in Sacramento, California. The Union Pacific Railroad company began building in Omaha, Nebraska. On May 10, 1869, the two companies joined both of the tracks in Promontory, Utah.

8. ☑ **Reading Check** **Identify** why the United States built a new railroad.

_____

_____

_____

_____

9. Turn to a partner and **identify** one benefit to reading secondary sources about unfamiliar topics.

A ceremony to celebrate the building of the transcontinental railroad

GO ONLINE FOR
DIGITAL RESOURCES

▶ VIDEO

👆 INTERACTIVITY

🔊 AUDIO

🎮 GAMES

☑ ASSESSMENT

📖 ETEXT

The BIG Question **How does geography affect our lives?**

▶ VIDEO

The Golden Gate Bridge
in San Francisco

JumpStart Activity 👆 INTERACTIVITY

Each area in your classroom has been named after a different region in California. Walk around to each area and choose the one that you think would be best to live in. Sit down once you have made your choice. Write why you picked it here.

_____

_____

_____

_____

_____

HSS 4.1.3, 4.1.4, 4.1.5, 4.4.9 **Analysis** CST.1, CST.3, CST.4, HI.2, **ELA** L.4.1, L.4.2, L.4.3, RI.4.1, RI.4.2, RI.4.4, RI.4.7, RF.4.3, RF.4.4, W.4.1, W.4.2, W.4.3

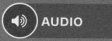

Geography and You

Preview the chapter **vocabulary** as you sing the rap:

Let's define **geography** and California's regions

The outdoor features of the world that we're seeing

The outside weather that makes our flowers grow

Precipitation we should know as either rain or snow

There's four major regions in the state of Cali

The Mountains, Coast, Desert, and Central Valley

Its many mountain ranges in the state that you can visit

But the Sierra Nevada range is the biggest

The type of weather we receive depends on where
we settle

Remember **elevation** is a place's height above sea level

Are you in a high rise or a rural space?

Know the **population** or number of people who live in
a place

1

Where is Sacramento, the capital of California, located?

It is located where the Sacramento River and the American River meet. Find Sacramento on the map. Is it located in the northern or southern part of the state?

Sacramento River

Sacramento ★

American River

PACIFIC OCEAN

Sacramento: The City of Trees

What happened and When?

Read and interpret the timeline to find out about how California's population has changed over time.

TODAY
Nearly 500,000 people live in Sacramento.

1700

1800

1768
Before Spanish missionaries arrive in California, it is home to about 300,000 California Indians.

1848
California's population drops to 157,000, mostly Indians. Then, gold is discovered and many immigrants come to California.

The Regions of California

Mountain Region

Desert Region

Coast Region

Central Valley Region

INTERACTIVITY

Complete the interactive map digital activity.

1900

2000

1860
Because of the Gold Rush, the population grows to about 360,000.

1950
California's population grows during and after World War II. After the war, the population hits 10 million.
TODAY
California has more people than any other state. Follow your teacher's instructions to find our current population.

3

Project-Based Learning

Natural Resources Are My Business!

A natural resource is something that comes from Earth that is helpful to people. Water is a natural resource. So are vegetables and wood.

Businesses use natural resources to make money. A grocery store sells vegetables, for example. A toy store sells toys made from wood.

Quest Kick Off

Your mission is to start a business that uses natural resources found where you live. Write a business proposal that outlines what your business will do and how it uses natural resources.

1 Think About Resources

Think about the area where you live. What natural resources do you and other people use every day? Are any of them found in your area?

....

....

....

....

HSS 4.1.3 ELA L.4.1, L.4.2, L.4.3, W.4.2

2 Think About Businesses

Identify three businesses in your area that use natural resources. Some may sell them directly, like selling an apple. Other businesses make things from resources and sell them, like furniture made from wood.

INTERACTIVITY

Explore natural resources.

....

....

....

....

3 Look for Quest Connections

Throughout the chapter, look for Quest Connections that will help you write your business proposal.

4 Quest Findings
Write Your Business Proposal

Use the Quest Findings page at the end of this chapter to help you write your business proposal.

Where Is California?

Vocabulary

geography
landform
valley
mountain pass
climate
elevation
precipitation

Academic Vocabulary

isolate
resource
unique

Unlock The BIG Question

I will know California's location and be able to describe its climate and physical features.

JumpStart Activity

Look out the window. Are there mountains, or is the land flat? Is it dry or wet out? Discuss what you see with your class. Then draw what you see on a separate piece of paper.

California is a special place. More people live here than in any other state. The world's largest tree lives in California too! Our state has many different natural features, including hot, dry deserts and rainy forests. We can go to the beach or climb a mountain without going too far from home. You are going to study California's **geography**. This means learning about its location, people, places, and natural features.

California's Location

California is located on the western edge of North America in the Northern Hemisphere. It is one of the 50 states that make up the United States of America. The state of Oregon is to the north of California, and Nevada and Arizona are to the east. To the west is the Pacific Ocean, and the country of Mexico is to the south.

California is **isolated** from other parts of North America by its location. It is surrounded by deserts and mountain ranges. These are groups of mountains that are close together. The deserts and mountains separate California from other areas where many people live. This means that if you wanted to travel to a big city outside of California, you would need to cross mountains or deserts to get there.

Academic Vocabulary

isolate • v., to separate or set apart from other things

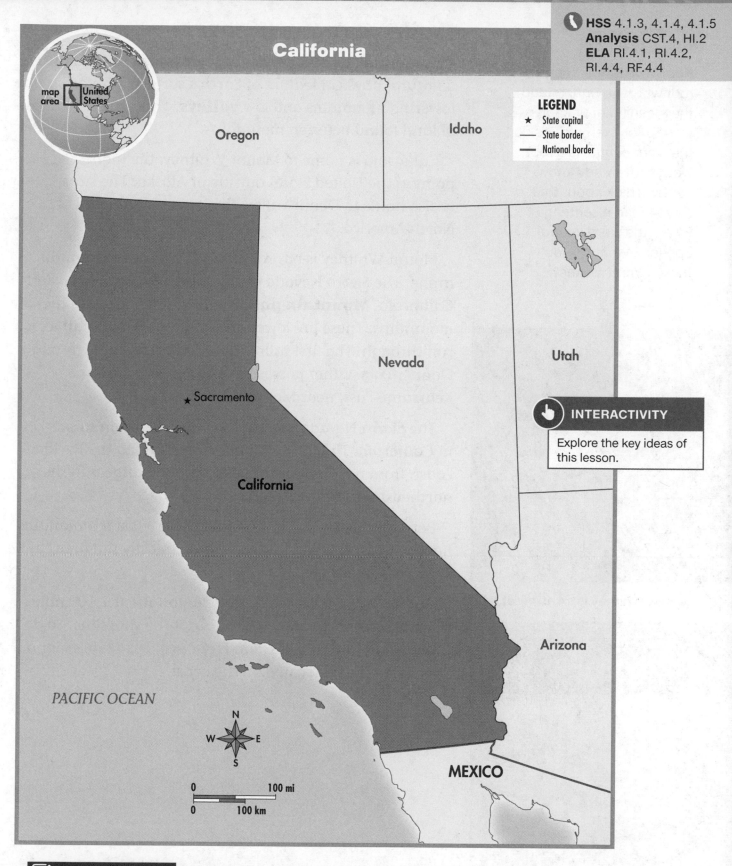

California

map area / United States

Oregon

Idaho

LEGEND
★ State capital
— State border
— National border

Nevada

Utah

★ Sacramento

California

INTERACTIVITY
Explore the key ideas of this lesson.

Arizona

PACIFIC OCEAN

N
W   E
S

0   100 mi
0   100 km

MEXICO

1. ☑ **Reading Check** **Interpret** the map's legend and then **identify** California's capital by circling it. Underline the names of the states, the country, and the ocean that border California. **Describe** California's location to a partner.

California's Landforms

California has many kinds of **landforms**. A landform is a natural physical feature of Earth's surface. California has towering mountains and low **valleys**. These are low areas of land found between mountains.

California is home to Mount Whitney, the highest point in the United States outside of Alaska. The state is also home to Death Valley, the lowest point in all of North America.

Mount Whitney is part of the Sierra Nevada mountain range. The Sierra Nevada extend north to south in eastern California. **Mountain passes** allow travel through the mountains. These are lower areas that a road or path can run through. The first railroad to California came through Donner Pass. Other passes include Forester Pass and Kearsarge Pass, near Mount Whitney.

The Sierra Nevada are not the only mountain range in California. The Coast Ranges extend along the Pacific coast, from north to south. The Cascade Range is in the northeast part of the state.

Between the Sierra Nevada and these coastal mountains lies the Central Valley. This is a large, mostly flat area that is very useful for farming.

California's Pacific coast stretches for about 1,100 miles. Coastal bays and natural harbors dot the shoreline. So do California's largest cities. San Francisco, Los Angeles, and San Diego are all located on the coast.

Mount Whitney is 14,494 feet tall.

Death Valley's Badwater Basin is 282 feet below sea level.

The port of Los Angeles is on the coast of southern California. It is one of the busiest harbors in the world. Many people work at ports. They may work at a warehouse, for example, or help ships dock safely.

California's rivers provide water to our state. The Colorado River forms the border between California and Arizona. It also cuts through the land to create a wide river valley called the Lower Colorado River Valley. The Sacramento and San Joaquin rivers flow through the Central Valley and empty into the California Delta. A delta is an area of flat land where a river fans out and empties into a larger body of water.

The California Delta empties into Suisun Bay, which flows into San Francisco Bay. Most of the delta area has been used for growing crops. The delta also provides water to southern California.

The southeastern corner of the state is largely desert. Deserts are very dry areas with extreme temperatures.

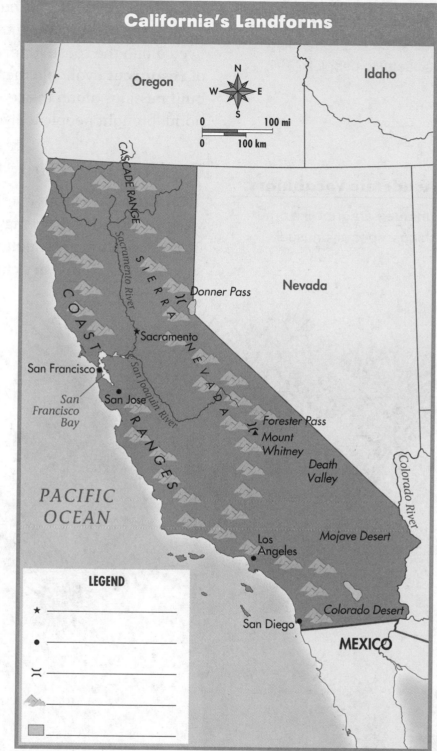

California's Landforms

2. ☑ **Reading Check** **Interpret** the symbols in the map legend. **Identify** what each symbol stands for by writing its name on the lines. Circle two mountain passes. Mark an X on a valley. Underline three important rivers and one bay.

Academic Vocabulary

unique • *adj.*, not like other things; special, unusual

California's landforms have always played a role in where people settle. Long ago, many California Indian groups lived along the coast, for example. They took advantage of **resources** available there. Spanish missionaries also built missions along the coast. Good farmland, on the other hand, brought people to live in the Central Valley.

California's Climate

Climate is a place's average weather over time. Today the weather where you live may be cold and rainy, for example. But if the weather is usually hot and dry, geographers would say you live in a hot, dry climate.

California's climate patterns are **unique**. Inside California, the climate varies widely. Like much of the western United States, a large part of California has an arid, or dry climate for most of the year.

Joshua trees can survive in the dry Mojave desert.

Elevation, or a place's height above sea level, affects the climate. So does how far north or south a place is. Higher areas are usually cooler than lower areas. In the Northern Hemisphere, areas to the north are usually cooler than areas to the south.

The Pacific Ocean also affects climate in California. Areas closer to the ocean have a milder climate. They are warmer in the winter and cooler in the summer.

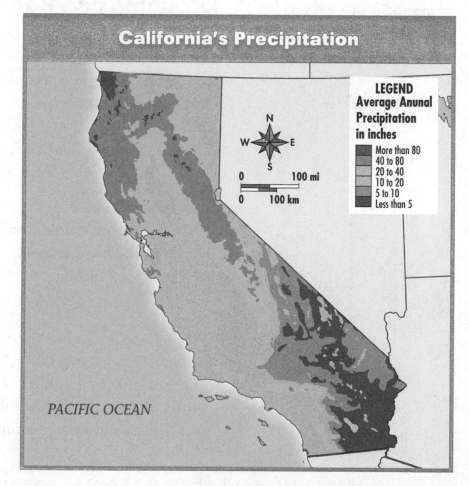

Redwood trees grow in wet northern forests.

Desert areas like Death Valley are extremely dry. They get very little **precipitation**, or rain and snow. On the other hand, parts of northern California are very wet. Forests near the coast can receive many inches of precipitation in a single year. Rain and snow are more common in areas of higher elevation.

3. ☑ **Reading Check**
Interpret the colors in the legend. **Identify** the areas with the highest rainfall by circling them. Draw lines across the areas with the lowest rainfall.

The climate affects the kinds of plant and animal life an area can support. For example, some desert plants have leaves that are coated in wax, which keeps moisture inside. Small desert animals like cactus mice eat these juicy plants. Larger animals, like foxes, feed on the smaller animals.

Forests along the rainy northern coast have rich, wet soil. It is ideal for tall redwood trees. The desert supports different plants and animals. Joshua trees, found only in the Mojave Desert, survive the desert heat by storing water. The desert is home to many types of snakes, lizards, and birds that need little water to live.

California's Precipitation

N
W   E
S

0   100 mi
0   100 km

LEGEND
Average Anunal Precipitation in inches

More than 80
40 to 80
20 to 40
10 to 20
5 to 10
Less than 5

PACIFIC OCEAN

During a drought, plants like orange trees may dry up and die.

Droughts and Floods

California's climate is sometimes drier than usual, which means that the state has a drought. Less rain than normal falls during a drought. People need water to drink, to wash, and to water crops. California's state government understands that drought is a serious issue for the state. The governor said this about a drought in 2015:

Primary Source

Today we are standing on dry grass where there should be five feet of snow. This historic drought demands ... action.

–Governor Edmund G. Brown, April 1, 2015

Sometimes more precipitation falls than usual. This can lead to floods as water overflows from rivers onto land that is normally dry. Flooding can destroy buildings and lead to deaths. In fact, the state capital was once briefly moved to San Francisco because Sacramento was under water!

4. ☑ **Reading Check** **Identify** one reason why droughts are a serious issue.

_____

_____

☑ **Lesson 1 Check**   ⓘ **HSS** 4.1.3, 4.1.4 **Analysis** HI.2
ELA RI.4.1, RI.4.2, RI.4.4, RF.4.4

5. Compare and Contrast Analyze how California's deserts are different from the forests along the northern coast.

_____

_____

_____

_____

6. Identify a landform in California and write a description of it.

_____

_____

7. Identify the physical characteristics of California and **describe** one that makes the state's geography unique.

_____

_____

_____

Watch a video about interpreting physical maps.

Interpret Physical Maps

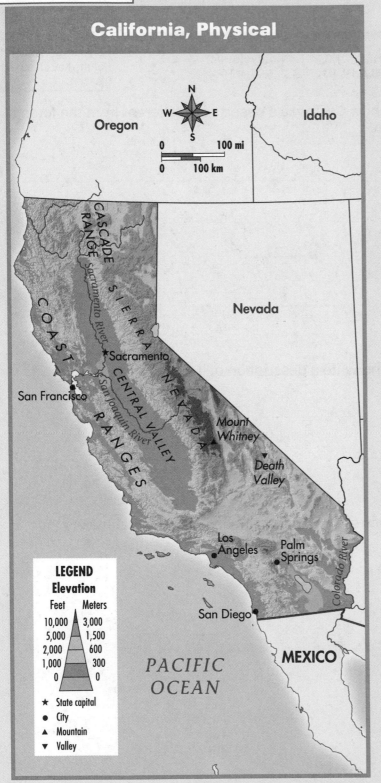

California, Physical

N W E S

0   100 mi
0   100 km

Oregon

Idaho

CASCADE RANGE

Sacramento River

SIERRA NEVADA

COAST RANGES

★ Sacramento

San Francisco

San Joaquin River

CENTRAL VALLEY

Nevada

Mount Whitney

Death Valley

Los Angeles

Palm Springs

Colorado River

San Diego

MEXICO

PACIFIC OCEAN

LEGEND
Elevation

Feet	Meters
10,000	3,000
5,000	1,500
2,000	600
1,000	300
0	0

★ State capital
● City
▲ Mountain
▼ Valley

Every map shows special information. For example, you can use a political map to learn the absolute location of a place. A physical map shows the physical features of a place. It often shows an area's elevation. It may show mountainous regions with shadows so you can see the slopes of the mountain ranges. It may also show major bodies of water, including oceans, lakes, and rivers.

To interpret a physical map, first look at its title to learn the topic of the map. Read the map legend. It gives you information about the symbols or colors on the map. The map here shows California's physical features. On this map, the lowest elevations are colored green and the highest elevations are brown.

The map scale lets you measure distance in miles or kilometers between places on the map. The compass rose shows the directions north, south, east, and west. Use the information you gain from looking at the map to interpret the map.

1. Suppose you are taking a trip from San Diego to Sacramento. **Identify** these cities on the map by interpreting the symbols in the legend. Then, draw a straight line between them. Finally, use the chart to identify three landforms or bodies of water you will pass on your trip.

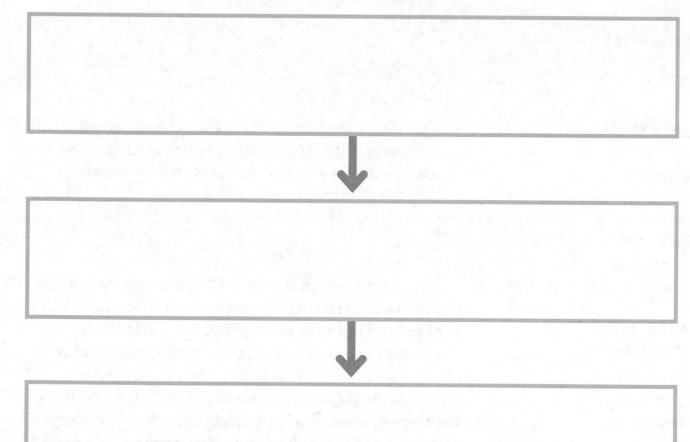

2. Use the map scale and compass rose to describe your trip. How many miles have you traveled? What direction did you travel in?

_____

_____

2 California's Regions

INTERACTIVITY

Participate in a class discussion to preview the content of this lesson.

Unlock
The **BIG**
Question

I will know and describe California's regions.

Vocabulary

region
population
humid
wildlife
agriculture
tourism
irrigation

Academic Vocabulary

economy
environment
develop

JumPstart Activity

Follow your teacher's instructions and move to one of four areas in the room, each representing a region in California. With your group, act out an outdoor activity you can do in that region.

Do you know which region of California you live in? Do you live near the coast? Are you in a valley or a desert? A **region** is a large area of land that has similar features. California has four major natural regions: the mountains, coast, desert, and Central Valley. Each of California's regions is unique and has its own physical characteristics. Each region also has its own landforms, climates, plants, and animals. These differences affect each region's people.

The Mountains

Mountains cover more than half of the state of California! You have already read about several mountain ranges. The Sierra Nevada is the tallest range in the state. This range runs 400 miles from north to south in eastern California. One of the most famous national parks in the country, Yosemite National Park, is located in the Sierra Nevada mountain range.

The climate of the mountain region is cool, and that affects the types of plants and animals that live there. Douglas pine trees grow well in cool mountain forests. Black bears, with their thick fur, live there as well.

Snow falls in the Sierra Nevada, and when it melts, it provides water to farms and cities in the Central Valley and across the state. In this way, the mountains support the state's people and **economy**.

As you have read, mountains lie along California's coast, too. These are called the Coast Ranges. In the northern part of the Coast Ranges, summers are cool and dry, and winters are mild and rainy. In the southern part of the Coast Ranges, both seasons are warmer and drier.

Most of the people who live in the mountain region live on farms, ranches, or in small towns. The **population** of the mountain region is low. A population is the number of people living in a place. However, many people visit the mountains for their natural beauty, and they also come to ski or snowboard.

Some mountains in the Cascade Range in northeastern California were formed when volcanoes erupted. Mount Shasta is a volcano, though it has not erupted in many years. Lassen Peak is also a volcano, and it last erupted in 1915.

In addition to volcanic eruptions, earthquakes and erosion can affect the mountains. Erosion is the wearing away of land by rain, snow, water, and wind.

1. ☑ **Reading Check**
Use Evidence From Text
Highlight a sentence that describes how the mountains provide a resource for people.

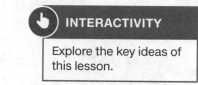

🖊 **HSS** 4.1.3, 4.1.4, 4.1.5 **Analysis** HI.2
ELA RI.4.1, RI.4.2, RI.4.4, RF.4.3, RF.4.4, W.4.3

Academic Vocabulary

economy • *n.*, the way a region produces resources, goods, and services in order to meet its people's needs and wants

👆 **INTERACTIVITY**

Explore the key ideas of this lesson.

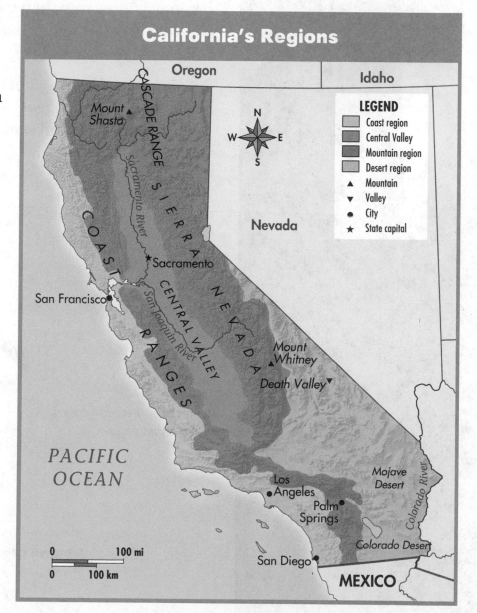

California's Regions

Oregon

Idaho

Mount Shasta

CASCADE RANGE

Sacramento River

SIERRA

LEGEND
- Coast region
- Central Valley
- Mountain region
- Desert region
- ▲ Mountain
- ▼ Valley
- ● City
- ★ State capital

Nevada

COAST

★ Sacramento

San Francisco ●

CENTRAL VALLEY

San Joaquin River

NEVADA

RANGES

Mount Whitney ▲

Death Valley ▼

PACIFIC OCEAN

Los Angeles ●

Mojave Desert

Palm Springs ●

Colorado River

San Diego ●

Colorado Desert

MEXICO

0 ___ 100 mi
0 ___ 100 km

The Coast

California has a long coastline on the Pacific Ocean. In northern California, mountains extend all the way down to the coast, which is made of steep, rocky cliffs. In southern California, beaches and wide plains lie between the mountains and the ocean. People come to visit this part of southern California because of the beaches and the mild climate.

As you have learned, California's three largest cities lie along the coast. San Diego and Los Angeles are in the south. San Francisco is farther north, at about the middle of the state.

In most of the coast region, the climate has dry summers and slightly rainy winters. The northern part of the coast gets much more rain than the southern part. In fact, it gets so much that some areas in northern California are considered rain forests!

California's famous giant redwood trees live in this part of the state. They can reach over 350 feet tall. They need the **humid**, or wet and warm, climate to survive.

Tall redwood trees grow in the coast region.

A brown pelican

People come to California's coast to see the **wildlife**, or animals living in nature. Animals along the coast include sea lions, green sea turtles, brown pelicans, elephant seals, and many shorebirds. Humpback whales also migrate, or move, along the coast twice a year.

Agriculture, or farming, and **tourism** are important industries in the coast region. Tourism is traveling to a place for fun. Tourists come to see the region's cities, swim and surf, go whale watching, or enjoy fresh seafood. Tourism provides jobs and helps the region's economy.

A surfer rides a wave off the California coast.

2. ✅ **Reading Check** Imagine you are on a trip somewhere in the coast region. Write a postcard to a friend. In the space, draw a picture of California's coast. On the lines, **describe** the weather and what you have seen and done.

Quest Connections

Underline details on this page that show how natural resources can be used for fun.

👆 INTERACTIVITY

Think about fun activities that involve California's natural resources.

The Desert

The two main areas of desert in California are the Mojave, which is known as the High Desert, and the Colorado, or Low Desert. High deserts have a higher elevation than low deserts. Death Valley is located in the Mojave Desert.

The climate in the desert can be extreme. Summer temperatures reach 100° or higher. The region gets very little precipitation.

Despite the extreme climate, the desert is home to a variety of vegetation, or plants, as well as animals. Desert plants include the Joshua tree, desert paintbrush, prickly pear cactus, and yucca. Many plants have special leaves that hold water.

Birds called roadrunners survive in the desert by eating lizards and insects. Desert bighorn sheep can go for a long time without drinking water. Other animals, like the desert tortoise, store water in their bodies.

Like plants and other animals, we also need water to live. In the desert, water is pumped from deep wells. This is where people in the desert get most of their drinking water. They also get water from nearby mountain streams.

To bring water to desert farmers, people have built canals, ditches, and pipes. This is called **irrigation**. It is one important way that people interact with, or affect, their environment. For example, water from the Colorado River and other sources irrigates crops in the Colorado Desert. This water lets farmers grow many kinds of fruits and vegetables.

Irrigation is an important service for desert communities. This ditch carries water from the Colorado River.

People live in California's deserts. The Colorado Desert is home to cities like Palm Springs, Indio, and Blythe. The cities of Lancaster and Victorville are located in the Mojave Desert. Lancaster is in the Antelope Valley, and Victorville is in the Victor Valley. The Mojave's population outside of these valleys is small. The summer heat and limited water make it a challenge to live in the desert region.

A desert roadrunner eating a lizard

3. ✅ Reading Check Fill in the ovals to **describe** the desert region. Then, choose one plant or one animal and **explain** to a partner how it survives in the desert.

California's Desert Region

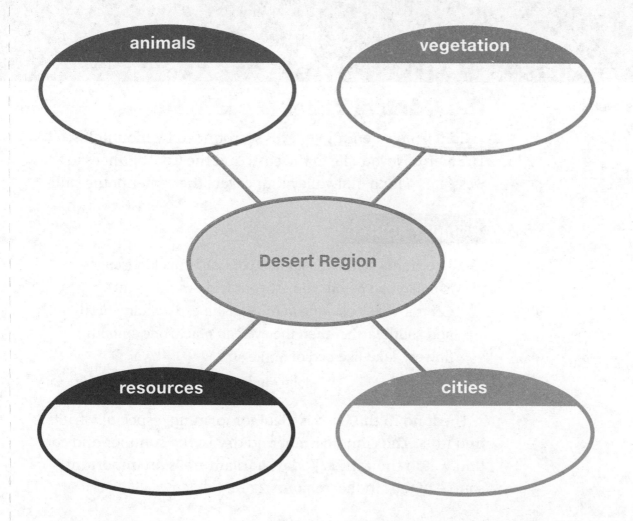

animals

vegetation

Desert Region

resources

cities

The sun rises over the Central Valley.

The Central Valley

California's Central Valley is surrounded by mountains. The Sierra Nevada lie to the east, and the Coast Ranges to the west. It is a long, flat valley that covers the center of the state.

Primary Source

The grandest and most telling of California landscapes is outspread before you. At your feet lies the great Central Valley glowing in the sunshine, extending north and south farther than the eye can reach, one smooth, flowery, lake-like bed of fertile soil.

—John Muir, *The Mountains of California*

The land in this area is ideal for farming, especially fruits and nuts. The climate is hot and dry in the summer and cool and wet in the winter. Today, agriculture is an important source of jobs in this region.

The Central Valley's landscape and climate also support ranching, or raising animals like cows in large areas. Ranching has been a part of California's economy since the 1700s.

Long ago, before Europeans came in the 1700s, the **environment** of the Central Valley was very different from what it is today. It was grassland, with many marshes, rivers, and lakes. Today, people have **developed** the valley into an area covered by farmers' fields and ranches instead of grasslands. They have drained many of the marshes, lakes, and smaller rivers.

People in the Central Valley need water to support farms and cities. The valley gets water from melted mountain snow and wells dug in the ground. Rivers also supply water.

More than 6 million people live in the Central Valley. It is the fastest-growing region in California. Several major cities are located in the valley, including Sacramento, the state capital. Other big cities include Bakersfield, Fresno, and Redding.

Academic Vocabulary

environment • *n.*, natural surroundings in an area, or the natural world in general
develop • *v.*, to grow or expand

4. ☑ **Reading Check**
Ask a partner a question that asks them to **explain** how the Central Valley's physical features affect people. Then answer your partner's question.

👆 **INTERACTIVITY**
Check your understanding of the key ideas of this lesson.

☑ **Lesson 2 Check**   ◆ **HSS** 4.1.3 **Analysis** HI.2
ELA RI.4.1, RI.4.2, RF.4.4

5. **Identify Main Idea and Details Describe** the physical characteristics of the coast region.

_____

_____

_____

6. **Explain** how the climate affects people and provides resources in a region in California.

_____

_____

7. **Understand** the **Quest** Connections Name two types of businesses that you might find in the coast region.

_____

A photograph of Yosemite's Half Dome by Ansel Adams

Ansel Adams, *The Portfolios of Ansel Adams*

You have read about Yosemite National Park, one of the best-known national parks in the country. Yosemite is located in the Sierra Nevada. In the park, you can visit thick pine forests, giant rock cliffs, waterfalls, and streams. It attracts tourists from all over the world.

One person who visited Yosemite in the 1900s was the photographer Ansel Adams. He loved Yosemite and took famous photographs of it. He also wrote about the natural wonders he found in the Yosemite Valley.

Vocabulary Support

that can match the power

the huge size may be all you notice at first

we see and appreciate the details

edifice, *n.*, building, structure
patina, *n.*, thin layer
colossal, *adj.*, huge
dominate, *v.*, control

"Yosemite Valley, to me, is always a sunrise, a glitter of green and golden wonder in a vast edifice of stone and space. I know of no sculpture, painting, or music that exceeds the compelling spiritual command of the soaring shape of the granite cliff and dome, of patina of light on rock and forest, and of the thunder and whispering of the falling, flowing waters. At first the colossal aspect may dominate; then we perceive and respond to the delicate and persuasive complex of nature."

– Ansel Adams, *The Portfolios of Ansel Adams*

Close Reading

HSS 4.1.5, 4.4.9
ELA RI.4.1, W.4.1

1. **Identify** and draw a square around a place where Adams refers to large rock structures like Half Dome. Circle a place where he refers to waterfalls.

2. **Identify** three things Adams compares to the natural wonders in Yosemite.

_____

_____

_____

Wrap It Up

Ansel Adams worked to preserve the Yosemite Valley. Do you agree that it is important to preserve beautiful natural places? Why or why not?

_____

_____

_____

_____

_____

_____

_____

_____

California's Human Geography

INTERACTIVITY

Participate in a class discussion to preview the content of this lesson.

Unlock
The **BIG**
Question

I will understand how California's physical features and climate affect its people and how people affect the environment.

Vocabulary

mineral
population density
rural
industry
urban
transportation system
architecture
solar plant

Academic Vocabulary

community
service

JumPstart Activity

With a small group, talk about how cold and hot weather can change the choices you make in daily life. Then vote with the class to say if cold or hot weather affects people the most.

You have studied California's physical features. Now you will learn about its human geography. This means studying where people live and how they make a living in different places. You will see that California's landforms and climate strongly affect its people.

This road in a rural community (left) is different from the highway in an urban community (right). You can see how they are different in their population density, land use, and transportation.

Living and Working in the Mountains

HSS 4.1.3, 4.1.4, 4.1.5
Analysis CST.3, HI.2 **ELA** RI.4.1, RI.4.2, RI.4.4, RI.4.7, RF.4.3, RF.4.4

The mountains can be a challenging region to live in, but they have many resources. Mountain forests provide wood. Streams flow down from mountains to lower lands and bring water to farms and cities. Ranchers bring their sheep and cows to the mountains when there is grass for them to eat in the summer.

People mine gold, quartz, and other **minerals** in the Sierra Nevada. Minerals are nonliving, natural things that do not come from plants or animals. The discovery of gold in the Sierra Nevada and the Central Valley in the 1800s brought many thousands of immigrants to California.

Think about a busy street. Then think about an empty field. Which is more crowded? **Population density** is a way geographers measure how crowded an area is. They compare how many people live in one square mile of a city, for example, to how many people live in one square mile in the country. The city will have many more people in the same amount of land. This means it has a higher population density.

The mountain region has a low population density. It is less dense than the coast or the Central Valley. Physical features such as steep, rocky cliffs make many areas difficult to reach. Snow and ice also make mountain passes hard to drive through in the winter.

INTERACTIVITY

Explore the key ideas of this lesson.

1. **☑ Reading Check**
On the map, **locate** the area around Los Angeles. Work with a partner to **describe** its population density.

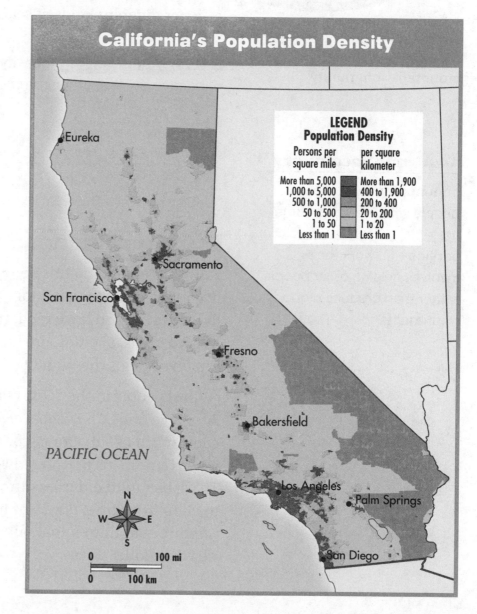

California's Population Density

LEGEND
Population Density

Persons per square mile	per square kilometer
More than 5,000	More than 1,900
1,000 to 5,000	400 to 1,900
500 to 1,000	200 to 400
50 to 500	20 to 200
1 to 50	1 to 20
Less than 1	Less than 1

Eureka
Sacramento
San Francisco
Fresno
Bakersfield
PACIFIC OCEAN
Los Angeles
Palm Springs
San Diego

N W E S

0   100 mi
0   100 km

People enjoy visiting the mountains to ski, snowboard, or hike. Most of the **communities** in the mountain regions are **rural**, which means they are made up of small towns and open areas rather than cities or large towns. Houses in this region may have steep roofs that are shaped like the letter A, so snow can easily slide off the roof.

Skiing helps make tourism an important industry in the mountains. **Industry** refers to the businesses that make one kind of product or offer one kind of **service**. Different communities offer different kinds of services.

These skiers are enjoying a service provided by a mountain community.

2. ☑ **Reading Check** **Identify** a service provided in your community that other communities might not have.

My community provides us with a lot of Shops, and

Academic Vocabulary

community • *n.*, a group of people who live in the same area

service • *n.*, work that involves helping other people, rather than producing goods or products

Living and Working on the Coast

If you are reading this book, there is a good chance you live in the coast region. More than half of all Californians live there. As you have read, many of California's largest **urban** areas, or cities, are located along the coast. This region also has the highest population density.

Most people in the coast region live between San Francisco and San Diego. Fewer people live along the coast north of San Francisco. This part of California is where enormous fir and redwood trees can be found. These beautiful old trees attract tourists. People used to chop these trees down for lumber. Logging is still important in this region, but people mostly cut down newer, smaller trees.

Urban communities on the coast need strong **transportation systems**. These include highways, railroads, and subways. People need these to move from place to place. Traffic can be a serious problem.

Tall skyscrapers are a popular type of **architecture**, or building design, in big cities. In these buildings, apartments or offices are stacked high on top of one another. Skyscrapers can hold many more people than smaller buildings. Rural communities do not need skyscrapers.

Many people in this region live in suburbs. These are communities that are near cities. They have fewer people than cities and are more spread out.

Many different industries in the coast region provide jobs. People move to the region for jobs. This makes towns and cities grow. Some industries are based on natural resources. The region has oil and natural gas, as well as fish in the Pacific Ocean. As you have read, the coast also has busy ports. Ships come and go from these ports. They bring goods to California. They take goods from California to other places around the world.

Other industries are very important in this region, too. Many of the world's largest technology and entertainment companies are based there. Tourists spend millions of dollars along the coast every year.

3. ☑ **Reading Check** With a partner, ask and answer questions about the coast region. **Explain** how the region's geography and landforms affect settlement patterns, or where people live.

Los Angeles skyscrapers at sunrise

Living and Working in the Desert

The desert region has a low population density. The lack of water makes living there a challenge. So do the extreme temperatures. Because water is scarce in the desert, people have to be careful about how much water they use.

Millions of acres of the desert are protected by the California Desert Protection Act. This means that the government works to keep these as natural places. Death Valley and Joshua Tree National Parks and the Mojave National Preserve are protected. They attract many tourists.

People who live in the desert build houses that have insulation, or layers built into the walls. This helps the houses stay cool in the summer and warm in the winter. These houses are often made of adobe, or clay and rocks. This makes them similar to the homes of southwestern American Indians in the past.

Although desert life is challenging, the desert region has its own resources. People have built **solar plants** in the Mojave Desert. These power plants use solar panels to take energy from the sun and turn it into electricity. Flat land and good soil are also resources in this region. They make agriculture possible when the land is irrigated.

4. ☑ **Reading Check** On the map, circle the Central Valley region. With a partner, **identify** three things that are grown there.

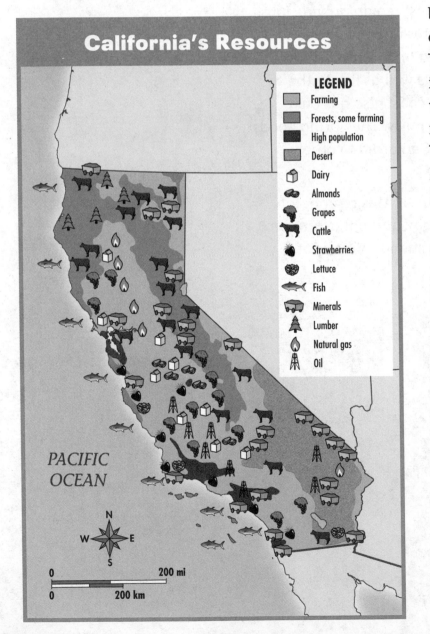

California's Resources

LEGEND
- Farming
- Forests, some farming
- High population
- Desert
- Dairy
- Almonds
- Grapes
- Cattle
- Strawberries
- Lettuce
- Fish
- Minerals
- Lumber
- Natural gas
- Oil

PACIFIC OCEAN

N W E S

| 0 | 200 mi |
| 0 | 200 km |

Miners first came to the desert region in the 1800s. Today they mine boron, a mineral used to make soap, detergent, fertilizer, and glass. They also mine silver, gold, and iron. They use the desert to provide stone and gravel. Salt is taken from the desert's salt flats.

Living and Working in the Central Valley

If you saw the Central Valley from an airplane, you would see green fields stretching from one end of the valley to the other. The Central Valley became famous for farming in the early 1900s. Today, it grows more fruits, vegetables, and nuts than any other region in the country. In fact, about one-fourth of all the food eaten in the United States is grown there!

More than 300 different crops are grown in the Central Valley. Most of California's agricultural land is in this region. Because frost is rare, farmers can grow crops for much of the year. Agriculture is the biggest industry in the Central Valley. Ranchers also raise cattle there.

Hot and dry summers mean that the Central Valley depends on irrigation for water. Melting snow from the Sierra Nevada flows into the Sacramento and San Joaquin rivers. These two rivers provide water to the Central Valley. They are among the most important water resources in California.

Looking at the Central Valley from an airplane, you would also see towns and cities. Sacramento, our state's capital, is located there. Bakersfield, Fresno, and Redding are also important cities in the region.

Quest Connections

On a separate sheet of paper, draw a picture that shows how people use a resource found in the desert or Central Valley.

INTERACTIVITY

Learn about how a natural resource is used to provide a service.

California's Top Five Crops

Crop	Value in 2014 (in billions)
Almonds	$5.89
Grapes	$5.24
Strawberries	$2.48
Lettuce	$2.03
Walnuts	$1.84

Source: *California Agricultural Statistics Review, 2014–2015*

Features of California's Regions

Mountains	Coast	Desert	Central Valley

5. **☑ Reading Check** **Summarize** what you learned about California's regions and communities by filling in the chart with details about each region.

Earthquakes

Earthquakes occur frequently in California. Most are too small to be felt, but you may remember one that happened in your town. They affect California because of its location. Earth's surface is made up of giant blocks of rock called plates. The North American and Northern Pacific plates meet in California. The line where they meet is called the San Andreas Fault. Other fault lines are also located in California. When plates move against each other at fault lines, an earthquake occurs.

As you know, earthquakes can cause serious problems for people. They can destroy buildings, bridges, and roads. They can also cause flooding. People are sometimes injured or killed in earthquakes. You will read later about an earthquake that destroyed the city of San Francisco in 1906.

Earthquakes can cause serious damage to buildings.

People can prepare for earthquakes through careful planning. They can build buildings that will not fall down when the ground shakes. Schools and families can make earthquake plans together. They can hold earthquake drills to practice what to do in an emergency. They can also store important supplies such as water and first aid kits.

6. ✓ **Reading Check** **Cause and Effect Identify** the cause of earthquakes in the first box. In the second box, **explain** how earthquakes affect people.

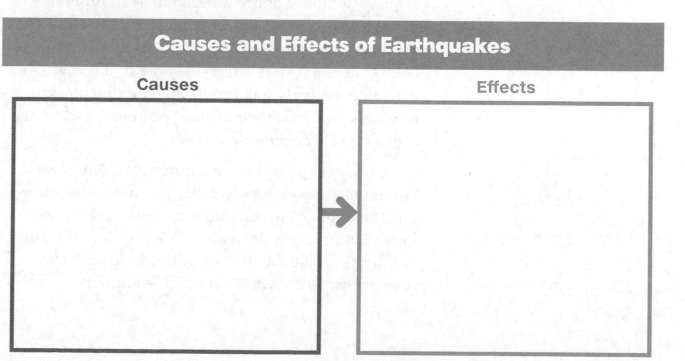

Causes and Effects of Earthquakes

Causes	Effects

Planting trees is a way to care for our resources.

Caring for California's Resources

We have to be smart about how we use resources. People need natural resources to live. Not all resources can be replaced. However, resources can be conserved, or saved.

Many Californians are working to help conserve resources and protect the environment. Many farmers are doing their part, for example. They are growing crops that require less water. They are trying new irrigation methods, too. People are planting grass that needs less water for their lawns. The grass on some golf courses is also being watered less.

We can help protect our environment in other ways. We can plant trees, for example. This makes the air we breathe cleaner. We can also recycle or reuse things instead of throwing them away. We can conserve water, too. Turning off the faucet while brushing your teeth saves water. So does making sure the faucet is all the way off.

7. ✓ **Reading Check Identify** a way you can conserve resources. In the space, draw a picture of it.

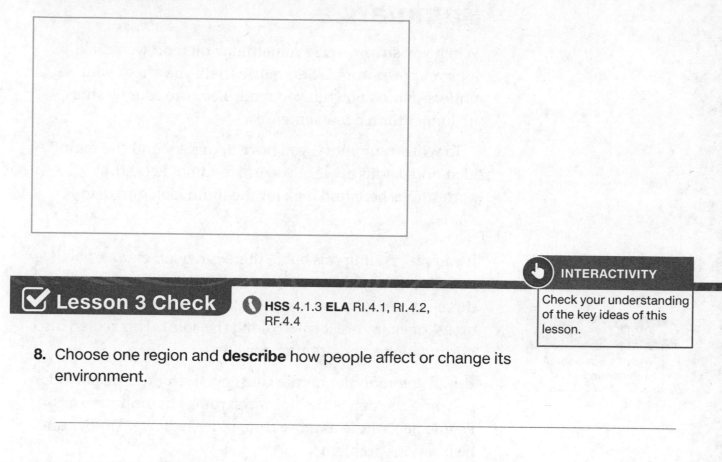

✓ **Lesson 3 Check** 🜂 **HSS** 4.1.3 **ELA** RI.4.1, RI.4.2, RF.4.4

👆 **INTERACTIVITY**

Check your understanding of the key ideas of this lesson.

8. Choose one region and **describe** how people affect or change its environment.

_____

_____

_____

9. Describe how geography affects the kinds of jobs people have. Give an example to support your answer.

_____

_____

_____

10. Understand the *Quest* **Connections Identify** three natural resources found or grown in California. Explain how you use one of them in your own life.

_____

_____

_____

Summarize

When you **summarize** something you read, you retell it in your own words. Summaries help you check your understanding of what you read. They are usually short, no longer than a few sentences.

To write a summary, you have to understand the main idea and details of what you are reading. Read the paragraphs here and look for the main idea and details.

> ▶ VIDEO
>
> Watch a video about summarizing.

If you are reading this book, there is a good chance you live in the coast region. More than half of all Californians live there. As you have read, many of California's largest urban areas, or cities, are located along the coast. This region also has the highest population density.

Urban communities on the coast need strong transportation systems. These include highways, railroads, and subways. People need these to move from place to place. Traffic can be a serious problem.

Tall skyscrapers are a popular type of architecture, or building design, in big cities. In these buildings, apartments or offices are stacked high on top of one another. Skyscrapers can hold many more people than smaller buildings. Rural communities do not need skyscrapers.

Your Turn!

HSS 4.1.3, 4.1.5 ELA RI.4.1, RI.4.2

1. Fill in the graphic organizer showing the main idea and details of the selection. Then use the summary box to write one or two sentences that summarize the paragraphs.

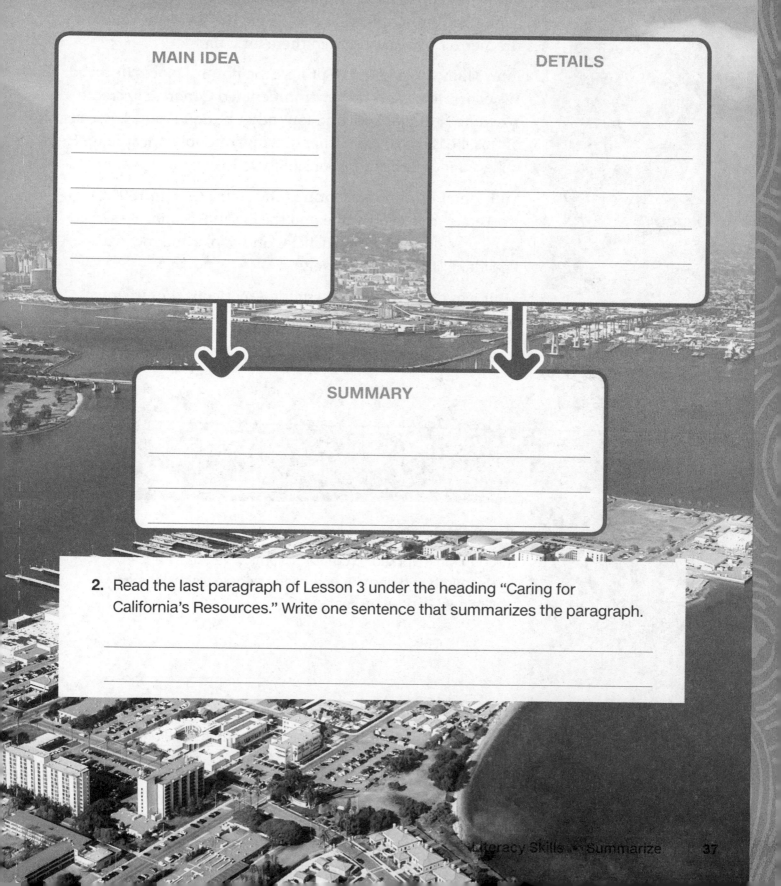

MAIN IDEA

_____
_____
_____
_____
_____

DETAILS

_____
_____
_____
_____
_____

SUMMARY

_____
_____

2. Read the last paragraph of Lesson 3 under the heading "Caring for California's Resources." Write one sentence that summarizes the paragraph.

_____
_____

★ Citizenship

Quality:
Determination

John Muir 1838–1914
Standing up for Nature

John Muir was an interesting man. He was an inventor, a writer, and an activist. He enjoyed nature. He spent many years exploring natural places. He explored the Yosemite Valley and the Sierra Nevada, and lived there for a time.

John Muir worked hard to protect the natural places he loved. His efforts to protect the environment led Congress to create Yosemite National Park and four other national parks. Because of this, he is called the Father of Our National Park System. He believed in America's responsibility to take care of nature.

Muir and his supporters formed the Sierra Club in 1892. It worked to protect Yosemite and the Sierra Nevada. He served as its president. He wrote articles and books and met with President Theodore Roosevelt.

Muir was determined to persuade Americans that we must protect our environment. The Sierra Club has carried on his cause. Today, it still works to preserve the environment.

Find Out More

1. John Muir worked to create Yosemite National Park. Research and find out how many people visit Yosemite National Park every year.

_____

_____

2. Today, people still work hard to preserve the environment. Work with a partner to find a local group that helps preserve the environment. What do they do?

Visual Review

Use these graphics to review some of the vocabulary, people, and ideas from this chapter.

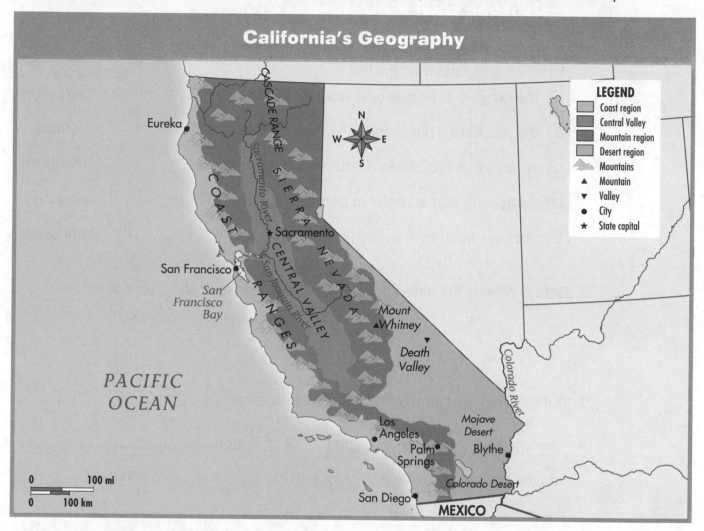

California's Geography

LEGEND

- Coast region
- Central Valley
- Mountain region
- Desert region
- Mountains
- ▲ Mountain
- ▼ Valley
- ● City
- ★ State capital

Eureka

CASCADE RANGE

SIERRA NEVADA

COAST RANGES

CENTRAL VALLEY

Sacramento River

San Joaquin River

★ Sacramento

San Francisco

San Francisco Bay

PACIFIC OCEAN

▲ Mount Whitney

▼ Death Valley

Colorado River

Los Angeles

Palm Springs

Mojave Desert

Blythe

San Diego

Colorado Desert

MEXICO

0   100 mi

0   100 km

California's Resources

Region	Resources
coast	wood, oil, natural gas, fish
mountains	minerals, grass for cows and sheep
Central Valley	fruits, vegetables, nuts, cattle
desert	solar power, minerals, stone, gravel, salt

☑ Assessment

🎮 GAMES

Play the vocabulary game.

Vocabulary and Key Ideas   🕐 HSS 4.1.3, 4.1.5

1. Use the word bank to **identify** the word that matches each definition and write it on the line.

   Word Bank

   - elevation
   - climate
   - resource
   - region
   - population

   (A) the number of people who live in a place _____

   (B) the height of a place above sea level _____

   (C) an area that has similar features _____

   (D) something that is useful to people _____

   (E) average weather in a place over time _____

2. **Define** What is the difference between an urban area and a rural area?

   _____

   _____

3. **Define** What are two different kinds of precipitation? _____

4. **Identify** Fill in the blanks to complete the sentence. The _____ region

   has the highest population density, and the _____ region has

   the lowest.

5. **Analyze** Fill in the circle next to the best answer. California is having a drought. How can you help?

   (A) I can pick up trash.

   (B) I can write to the mayor.

   (C) I can brush my teeth.

   (D) I can conserve water.

Critical Thinking and Writing

HSS 4.1.3, 4.1.5 Analysis HI.2
ELA W.4.2

6. **Infer** What region is most likely shown in the picture? How do you know? Think about how the land is being used.

_____

_____

_____

7. **Explain** Why does California have many earthquakes?

_____

_____

8. **Infer** What are some of the reasons people choose to live in a certain region?

_____

_____

_____

9. **Analyze** How can we protect natural resources that we need to use? Give an example to support your answer.

_____

_____

_____

10. **Revisit the Big Question** How does the geography of where you live affect your daily life? Support with examples.

_____

_____

_____

11. **Writer's Workshop: Compare and Contrast** On a separate sheet of paper, write two short paragraphs comparing the human and physical features of the coast and desert regions. Explain how these features help make these regions unique.

Analyze Primary Sources   🔹 **ELA** RI.4.1

Let us leave a splendid legacy for our children. Let us turn to them and say, this you inherit: guard it well, for it is far more precious than money, and once destroyed, nature's beauty cannot be repurchased at any price.   —Ansel Adams, on the environment

12. What do you think Adams meant by the phrase "and once destroyed, nature's beauty cannot be repurchased at any price"?

_____

_____

_____

_____

Summarize   🔹 **HSS** 4.1.5 **ELA** W.4.2

13. Go back and review all the maps, charts, and pictures in the chapter. Pick a region other than the one you live in. Write a summary of what it would be like to live in a community in that region. Consider the following: the region's land use, vegetation, wildlife, climate, population density, architecture, services, and transportation systems. Consider how these things would be different there than in your community. Refer to images to support your answer.

_____

_____

_____

_____

_____

_____

_____

Quest Findings

INTERACTIVITY

Use this activity to help you prepare to write your business proposal.

Write Your Business Proposal

You've read the lessons in this chapter and now you're ready to write your business proposal. Remember that the goal of your proposal is to explain what your business will do and how it will use natural resources in your area.

1 Prepare to Write

Write down the name of your business. List the resources it needs. Then write a sentence explaining why the business is important. These notes will help you write your proposal.

2 Write a Draft

Use your outline and the answers from your Quest Connections to write the best business proposal you can. Make sure your proposal answers these questions:

- What is the name of your business?
- What does your business do?
- How does it use natural resources?
- Why is it important or needed?

3 Share With a Partner

Exchange your draft proposal with a partner. Invite your partner to ask questions about your proposal and to make suggestions. When it is your turn, politely do the same.

4 Revise

Make changes to your business proposal after meeting with your partner. Correct any grammatical or spelling errors, or make changes to content if you need to.

GO ONLINE FOR
DIGITAL RESOURCES

▶ VIDEO

👆 INTERACTIVITY

🔊 AUDIO

🎮 GAMES

☑ ASSESSMENT

📖 ETEXT

The BIG Question How do people adapt to where they live?

▶ VIDEO

California Indians in the Yosemite Valley

Jumpstart Activity 👆 INTERACTIVITY

What's the weather like today? Work with a partner to identify three things you are wearing because of today's weather. Did you wear a raincoat? Are you wearing a sweater?

Write down the clothing you and your partner described. Count six months from today. Do you think you will be wearing the same kinds of clothes then? Put a checkmark next to anything that would be the same and explain why.

_____

_____

_____

_____

♪ **Rap** About **It!** ♪

 AUDIO

Land and People

Preview the chapter **vocabulary** as you sing the rap:

North America, in the lands to the west,

As the California Indians' name would suggest,

This land was where they lived
and they had called it home first.

Their ways of life were very different,
meaning they were **diverse**.

The California Indians, home we call a **village**,
or small community.

Though some had a thousand **inhabitants**,
they were all family.

Their cultures were unique
when each group was compared.

Culture is the beliefs and ways of life that are shared.

Shasta

Hupa

Yokuts

Chumash

Gabrielino

Santa Monica Mountains

• Los Angeles

Mojave

Where do different groups of California Indians come from?

California Indians have long lived throughout the state. This map shows where several California Indian groups come from.

What modern city is located where the Gabrielino people live?

Satwiwa Native American Indian Culture Center

TODAY
You can visit the Satwiwa Native American Indian Culture Center. This photo shows a Gabrielino ceremony.

What happened and When?

Read the timeline to find out about California Indians and European explorers.

9000 B.C.

2000 B.C.

1480

9000 B.C.
First inhabitants had settled in California.

2000 B.C.
Large coastal villages established.

TODAY
More American Indians live in California than in any other state.

Who will you meet?

Gabrielino People
California Indians who live along the southern California Coast

Hupa People
California Indian group who live in northern California

Juan Rodriguez Cabrillo
Leader of the first European voyage to explore California

Sir Francis Drake
English pirate and explorer who landed in California on his trip around the world

INTERACTIVITY

Complete the interactive timeline digital activity.

1520

1560

1600

1492
Columbus reaches the Americas.

1519
Spanish begin conquest of Mexico.

1542
Cabrillo explores California coast.

1579
Drake lands on Point Reyes peninsula.

Quest
Project-Based Learning

My California Life—
Then and Now

My name is Marie Pole, and I am a member of the Hupa people. We are California Indians. My ancestors have lived in northern California for about a thousand years!

I am proud of our history and want everyone to know about my people. One way to share information with others is to create a wiki.

Quest Kick Off

Your job is to create a wiki about California Indians. Work with a group to research California Indians in one region. Learn about Indians groups in this region in the past and today.

1 Ask Questions

INTERACTIVITY

Explore a map to see what California was like long ago and what it is like today.

HSS 4.2.1
Analysis CST.2, CST.3

How did California Indians in the region you are studying make a living in the past? What might their lives have been like? How did they change over time? Write down two questions of your own.

....

....

....

....

....

3 Look for *Quest* Connections

Turn to the next page to begin looking for Quest Connections that will help you create your wiki.

2 Research

Follow your teacher's instructions to find examples of wikis on the Internet. What is a wiki?

....

....

....

....

....

....

4 *Quest* Findings
Create Your Wiki

Use the Quest Findings page at the end of the chapter to help you create your wiki.

Lesson 1
California Indians and Their Environment

👆 **INTERACTIVITY**

Participate in a class discussion to preview the content of this lesson.

Vocabulary

glacier
adapt
diverse
hunter-gatherer
cultivate

Academic Vocabulary

speculate

Fishing was an important source of food for many California Indians.

Unlock The BIG Question

I will know how California Indians used and changed their environment.

JumpStart Activity

Imagine that you and your family are moving somewhere that has a different climate from the place where you live now. Work with a partner to decide what new things you might need. What activities might be different? Write two of your answers on the board to share with the class.

People have lived in California since at least 9000 B.C. At that time **glaciers**, or large sheets of ice, covered much of what is now northern California. Historians have long debated when and how people arrived. Archaelogists **speculated** for years that they crossed into North America from Asia. That theory has now been widely accepted.

W Langdon Kihn 46

At that time, the sea level was lower. Land connected Asia and North America in the far north. People walked from Asia into North America, or went by boat along the coast. Over time, they moved south. They settled in what is now California. They were the ancestors of today's California Indians. Eventually the earth warmed and the environment changed. So the people had to **adapt**, or change, to survive. Because the land and climate in California were so varied, so too were the **diverse**, or different, ways of life that developed.

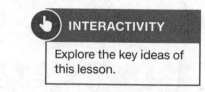

HSS 4.2.1 **Analysis** CST.3, CST.4, CST.5, RE.2, HI.2, HI.3 **ELA** RI.4.3, RI.4.4

Academic Vocabulary

speculate • v., to think about an idea and make guesses about it

INTERACTIVITY

Explore the key ideas of this lesson.

Diverse Lands, Diverse Lives

Over thousands of years, the first Californians learned to live in very diverse environments. They lived in the mountains and in deserts, along the coast, in forests, and in valley grasslands. They developed ways of life that depended on the environments in which they lived. They used the natural resources around them to meet their needs. They also traded with their neighbors.

The first Californians were hunter-gatherers. A **hunter-gatherer** is a person who collects plants and hunts wild animals for food. Men followed animals and hunted using spears, bows and arrows, or traps. They fished in the ocean, lakes, and rivers. Women gathered nuts, seeds, roots, and fruit. They gathered acorns, which they turned into flour to make bread. Some tribes also recognized two-spirit people, whose roles could come from either men's or women's tasks or a mix of both. California Indians also ate birds, clams, antelope, deer, chia, yucca, and berries.

1. ☑ Reading Check **Identify** and circle the place on the map that allowed people to cross from Asia to North America. How do you know by looking at the map?

_____

_____

Routes of First Americans

ASIA

Bering Strait

Beringia Land Bridge

NORTH AMERICA

PACIFIC OCEAN

ATLANTIC OCEAN

SOUTH AMERICA

0   2,000 mi
0   2,000 km

LEGEND
☐ Dry land in the past
☐ Glacier in the past
→ Route of first people

N W E S

2. ☑ **Reading Check**

Put a star on the map where the Shasta lived. With a partner, **compare** to a map of California today. Discuss what you find about their location.

Making a Living

By the late 1700s, about 300,000 people lived in California. They were not one single nation. They spoke more than 90 different languages and lived in many different culture groups. The people of each group spoke the same or similar languages. They shared customs and beliefs. You will learn more details about several of these diverse California Indian groups. One reason there were so many different groups was because of California's geography. The mountains and deserts made it hard for people to travel far. This separated groups.

California Indian Groups

Tolowa
Yurok
Karuk
Shasta
Modoc
Achumawi
Wiyot
Mattole
Sinkyone
Wintu
Yana
Nomlaki
Yuki
Konkow
Atsugewi
Maidu
Northern Paiute
Washoe
Pomo
Patwin
Nisenan
Coast Miwok
Miwok
Mono Paiute
Owens Valley Paiute
Western Mono
Shoshone
Costanoan
Yokuts
Esselen
Salinan
Tubatulabal
Kawaiisu
Southern Paiute
Kitanemuk
Chumash
Tataviam
Serrano
Chemehuevi
Mojave
Gabrielino
Halchidhoma
Juaneño
Luiseño 11
Cahuilla
Gabrielino
Kumeyaay
Quechan

1. Chilula
2. Whilkut
3. Hupa
4. Chimariko
5. Nongatt
6. Lassik
7. Wailaki
8. Cahto
9. Lake Miwok
10. Wappo
11. Cupeño

LEGEND
Yokuts   California Indian group
——   State border

California Indians worked together to supply the food, clothing, and shelter they needed. California Indians adapted to their locations. Their economic activities and how they made a living depended on where they lived. In far northern California, the Shasta men fished for salmon and hunted bear, deer, and small animals. Women and children gathered mussels by diving into the Klamath River. They also gathered acorns. Their neighbors, the Hupa, fished for salmon and ground acorns into flour. Hupa men hunted deer and elk with dogs they had trained.

About 40 or 50 Yokuts groups who spoke similar languages lived in central California. They fished in lakes and rivers for trout, salmon, and other fish. A later traveler wrote:

Quest Connections

On the map, circle the region of California that you are studying. What culture groups come from that region?

INTERACTIVITY

Learn more about how different groups of people had different ways of life.

Primary Source

The abundance of fish of all kinds in these waters is absolutely astonishing. The waters seem alive with them, and the variety is as great as the quality of most of them is good.

–Traveler through California, 1851

Along the southern California coast, the Chumash ate a wide variety of food from the sea, such as sharks, mussels, and whales. They also relied on acorns. Their neighbors, the Gabrielino, gathered food inland, as well as along the coast. Gabrielino people who lived on the coastal islands ate mostly seafood, as there were few plants on the islands.

Most California Indians did not farm. They were able to modify the environment in order to have enough food without farming. But the Mojave people, who lived in the desert, did farm. The annual flooding of the Colorado River provided rich soil. Men cleared the land, and women planted seeds to grow corn, beans, and melons. Women also gathered cactus. Men also hunted rabbits and fished in the Colorado River.

Fish like these salmon were an important source of food for many California Indians.

Modern wildfires are dangerous disasters. They can destroy homes and property. But for California Indians, setting controlled fires was a useful way to manage the environment.

Changing the Environment

California Indians took advantage of what their environment offered them. But they also changed their environment, just as people do today. For example, some **cultivated** the land, or prepared and used it for growing plants. They also pruned, cut, and replanted wild plants. Another way they changed the land was through the use of fire.

At certain times of the year, many California Indians set controlled fires in large areas to manage the environment. They saw what happened to the land after a wildfire. Fires reduced the undergrowth, or shrubs and plants under trees. This created more land for food plants, such as berries. Hunting was easier without so many small bushes and trees. Setting controlled fires also burned away dead grasses and plants. This protected California Indians against more dangerous wildfires.

3. ☑ **Reading Check** **Identify** one way California Indians changed their environment.

_____

_____

☑ Lesson 1 Check

🖐 HSS 4.2.1 **Analysis** HI.2, HI.3
ELA RI.4.2, RI.4.3

4. **Cause and Effect** How did the environment affect the California Indians?

_____

_____

5. **Compare** How did the Mojave differ from other California Indian groups?

_____

_____

6. **Quest** Connections Based on what you have learned, how did people make a living in the region you are studying?

_____

_____

Compare and Contrast

VIDEO

Watch a video about comparing and contrasting.

Which do you like better—apples or oranges? Summer or winter? When you need to make a choice, it can be helpful to **compare** and **contrast**.

To compare two things means to find the ways in which they are the same. Both apples and oranges are fruit, both are round, and both grow on trees. But to help you choose one over the other, you contrast them. You think of the ways in which they are different. Apples are crunchy and oranges are squishy, for example.

Comparing and contrasting information is an important way to analyze what you are reading. You can better understand California Indians, for example, by understanding how their ways of life were similar and different. Read the description in the paragraph below. Compare and contrast the information.

Fish was an important source of food for many California Indians. Different groups used different methods of fishing, however. Living along the coast, the Gabrielino built canoes from wood planks, logs, or reeds. They used canoes to travel and fish in the ocean. On the other hand, the Mojave people were not coastal people. They lived inland. They fished from the banks of the Colorado River. They also farmed land along the river.

Use the organizer on the facing page to compare and contrast details from this paragraph.

1. How were the Gabrielino and the Mojave similar? How were they different? Complete the Venn diagram. List similarities in the center. Under each group, list differences.

Gabrielino

Mojave

2. Read the first paragraph under the head "Diverse Lands, Diverse Lives" in the previous lesson. What does it say in common with the paragraph on the previous page?

_____

_____

Lesson 2 California Indian Cultures

I will know about California Indians' different cultures.

INTERACTIVITY

Participate in a class discussion to preview the content of this lesson.

Vocabulary

culture
village
inhabitant
spiritual
shaman

Academic Vocabulary

typically

A Chumash village

JumpStart Activity

What is one of your chores? Follow your teacher's instructions to conduct a class poll. Create a bar graph with the results to see your classmates' similarities and differences. Then compare those chores to those of California Indian children.

You have read about California's many environments. California has a rugged coast and redwood forests, mountains and desert. These environments supported many different California Indian cultures. A **culture** is the way of life shared by a group of people, including their beliefs and customs. Each California Indian group had its own unique culture.

Communities and Homes

Since California Indians were able to modify their environments to supply enough food, they usually lived in one location. Unlike American Indians in some other parts of North America, California Indians did not have to travel far in search of food.

California Indians lived in **villages**, or small communities. A few hundred people lived in most villages, although the Chumash, who lived along the Santa Barbara coast, had villages with about a thousand inhabitants. An **inhabitant** is a person who lives in a certain place. Today, California's cities are sometimes located on the sites of Indian settlements, especially in places where rivers meet the coast. For example, Los Angeles is located where the Gabrielino-Tongva lived.

HSS 4.2.1 **Analysis** HI.2
ELA RI.4.1, RI.4.3

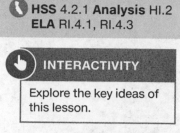

INTERACTIVITY

Explore the key ideas of this lesson.

A Chumash house made of tule

1. ☑ **Reading Check**
Cause and Effect
Underline the reason why California Indians did not have to travel far in search of food.

California Indian sweathouse

Quest Connections

Remember the names of different groups in the region you are studying. Underline text in this lesson that describes their cultures.

👆 INTERACTIVITY

Learn how shelter is different then and now.

Across California, Indians built their homes using the materials around them. A common house in the warmer southern areas was made from poles covered with brush, reeds, or mats made of a kind of grass called tule (bulrush), as shown on the previous page. These types of homes were open-air and cooler. In the cooler northern areas, people like the Hupa built houses of redwood, designed to keep them warm. Some were large enough to hold up to 50 people. Groups near the mountains built their homes from redwood bark and pine.

A Spanish explorer described the houses in a Chumash village when he visited in 1792. He wrote:

Primary Source

They arrange their houses in groups. The houses are well constructed, round like an oven, spacious and fairly comfortable; light enters from a hole in the roof. Their beds are made on frames and they cover themselves with skins and shawls . . . in the middle of the floor they make a fire for cooking seeds, fish, and other foods.

– José Longinos Martinez, Spanish explorer

In many culture groups, social life centered on a temescal, or sweathouse. This was a structure built partly underground that often looked like a grassy hill since it was covered with brush or reeds. It was used mostly by men. They would gather there in the evenings for several hours, sometimes to perform rituals before hunts or ceremonies.

Clothing and Art

Like their homes, the clothing of California Indians used local natural resources and was suited to the local climate. Clothing varied from region to region. In the north, Shasta men and women wore long shirts or two-piece aprons. Men wore deerskin leggings and caps. In winter, they wore fur capes. Farther south, Chumash women wore deerskin aprons. Yokuts women wore skirts made of rabbit skins, reeds, or grasses, while men wore a deerskin tied around their waists. Mojave women wore aprons made of pounded willow bark.

While ancient California Indians had many diverse cultures, they left no written records. We can learn about their lives from the things they left behind, such as paintings found in caves like the one shown here. Other examples include baskets and other tools and crafts.

Word Wise

Multiple-Meaning Words
When you see the word *records*, what is the first thing you think of? Records are written accounts of events or actions. Records are also a kind of disc that plays music. If you say *record* a little differently, it can be a verb, or action word, as in the sentence "Please record the score of the game." It means to keep an account of something.

Chumash petroglyphs in a cave in Santa Barbara

Families

Family was the most important relationship in California Indian groups. As a man from a northern California group, the Pomo, said:

Primary Source

A man is nothing. Without family he is of less importance than that bug crossing the trail, of less importance than spit . . .

–Tom Jimerson, Pomo elder

Family is still important to California Indians today.

Families cared for and protected their members. Parents were generally responsible for providing food for the group. Grandparents, aunts, and uncles **typically** raised the children of the group. There were no schools, so adult family members taught children what they needed to know. Girls learned how to take care of the home, gather food, cook, and make crafts such as baskets. Boys learned how to build houses and how to hunt and fish.

Marriage was almost always arranged by families. In many communities, the wife would live with or near the husband's family. This is known as patrilocal lineage. The mother-in-law would teach the new wife the ways of the group.

Academic Vocabulary

typically • *adv*., ordinarily, usually

2. ☑ **Reading Check** **Identify** What does patrilocal lineage mean?

_____

_____

_____

Religion

Spiritual, or religious, practices were important to California Indians, as they are important to many people today. In California Indian cultures, some men and women were believed to have special religious powers. Historians call these people **shamans**.

Shamans had an important role. Together, chiefs, or village leaders, and shamans performed ceremonies. Shamans were responsible for dealing with the world of spirits. Their jobs included tending to the sick, predicting the future, and giving advice. Some, called Snake Doctors, focused on healing snakebites. Others were known as Bear Doctors. These shamans dressed in bearskins and claimed to transform into grizzly bears. Both men and women could be shamans.

This woman, a Hupa shaman, was photographed in the 1900s.

Each culture group had its own particular ceremonies. Each fall, for example, the Gabrielino honored birth and death. Every child born that year was given his or her name. And all in the group who had died were remembered. The Mojave, too, came together once a year to mourn the dead.

Culture groups also had their own myths or legends. Legends are traditional stories that are passed down verbally from one generation to another. The Yokuts had a legend about the creation of land. According to the legend, Eagle, Crow, and Duck worked together to build land out of mud after a great flood. But Crow took more mud than Eagle. Because of this, Eagle's half became the mighty Sierra Nevada, while Crow's became the smaller Coast Ranges.

3. ☑ **Reading Check** **Identify** some of the roles of a shaman.

_____

_____

Economics and Government

For the most part, California Indians lived peacefully, although there was some warfare. Each group was able to modify and use land and sea in order to meet its needs. There was little history of fighting over resources. Most California groups traded goods with other groups. Shells, medicines, and baskets were common items to trade.

For California Indians, family and village relationships were the most important structure of people's lives. Most California Indian groups did not have a central government. Some, like the Chumash, were led by chiefs. All groups had their own rules and laws. The Yurok, for example had rules about who could use resources like acorns or redwood trees. Did they belong to everyone or only certain people or families? In some groups, chiefs made decisions and rules.

Chiefs also guided people in how to live. A chief of the Nomlaki people was known for waking his people every morning by advising: "Do right; don't get into trouble; help your neighbor!"

4. ☑ **Reading Check** Complete this chart. In the first column, **identify** a rule you follow. In the second column, write either *Family, School,* or *Government* to explain who makes the rule. An example has been provided for you.

Rule	Who Makes It?
I raise my hand to talk.	School

California Indians Today

The traditional lives of California Indians changed when Europeans arrived. Over time, the population of California Indians decreased. You will read much more about how and why this happened in later chapters.

Today, however, California has the largest population of American Indians in the United States. American Indians from many different groups have come to California or were sent there by the government. Members of more than 100 groups of California Indians still live in the state. Some live in special areas called reservations or rancherias, but many live in California communities large and small. They have built museums and cultural centers where they proudly preserve their traditions.

A modern California Indian girl making bread

INTERACTIVITY

Check your understanding of the key ideas of this lesson.

✓ Lesson 2 Check

HSS 4.2.1 **Analysis** HI.1 **ELA** RI.4.2

5. **Compare and contrast** the way climate affected California Indians who lived in the north and the south.

_____

_____

_____

6. **Summarize** three ways that California Indian cultures were different from one another.

_____

_____

_____

7. **Quest** Connections Based on what you have read, list three facts about life for California Indians in the region you are studying.

_____

_____

▶ VIDEO

Watch a video about how to analyze images.

Analyze Images

A member of the Pomo California Indian group weaves a basket.

Images can be used as primary sources. An image can tell you something in a way that writing cannot. When you analyze an image, you look at it closely and in a new way. You can look at the people, objects, details, and activities in the image to learn what is happening.

California Indians are famous for the beautiful baskets they wove. Using reeds and grasses, they made baskets for all occasions and many uses. They carried babies in baskets. They gathered food in baskets, cooked in baskets, and sometimes ate from baskets. They also used them to help carry heavy items.

Study the image here. What can you learn about basket making from the image? Look carefully at what the woman is doing, what she is using, and what the basket looks like.

1. Look at the image on the opposite page. What can you tell about the basket and the basket maker by studying this image? Describe what you see next to each topic.

   Size _____

   _____

   Materials _____

   _____

   Design _____

2. Look at the picture of the Chumash village in Lesson 2. What is one detail that can you learn from that image?

   _____

3. Imagine you were looking at a photo of your classroom today. **Identify** three clues that would show it is a classroom and not another kind of room.

   _____

   _____

Lesson 3 — Early European Exploration

INTERACTIVITY

Participate in a class discussion to preview the content of this lesson.

Unlock The BIG Question

I will know which Europeans first explored California and why.

Vocabulary

viceroy
expedition
encounter
galleon
circumnavigate

Academic Vocabulary

describe
current

JumpStart Activity

Divide into teams and imagine you are planning a trip to Mars. You know it is in space, but you don't know anything about its environment. Figure out what you would take with you and why. Discuss how you feel about going to an unknown place so far away.

In 1492, Christopher Columbus landed on an island in the Caribbean Sea, and European nations such as Spain found out that there was a "new world." To the people of the Americas, including California Indians, it was an old world. The coming of Europeans would change their world forever.

🕐 **HSS** 4.2.2
Analysis CST.4, CST.5, RE.2, HI.1, HI.3
ELA RI.4.1, RI.4.3

Spain and the New World

In 1504, 12 years after Columbus's arrival, another Spanish explorer came to the Americas. His name was Hernán Cortés. He landed in Mexico. Like other explorers of the time, Cortés wanted to take control of land for Spain. He expected to find gold. And like Columbus and others, he believed he could find a new route from Europe to Asia that would make trade easier.

Cortés conquered Mexico. It became New Spain, part of the Spanish empire. Other areas later became part of New Spain. Then in the 1530s, Cortés began to send explorers to what the Spanish soon called California. He and others were sure that great riches lay to the north. In their travels they reached Baja, or lower, California. Today the peninsula of Baja California is a part of the country of Mexico. Cortés himself tried to establish a settlement there, but the dry, rocky land was not welcoming. The Spanish refused to give up their dream, however. Instead, they chose another route—by sea.

Word Wise

Suffixes The suffix *–er* can mean someone who does something: *make, maker; write, writer*. Circle a word on this page that ends with *–er* and means someone who does something.

Hernán Cortés arriving in Mexico by ship

1. ☑ **Reading Check**
What drew early explorers like Hernán Cortés to Baja California?

_____

Juan Cabrillo Heads North

In 1542, the Spanish **viceroy**, or governor, of New Spain sent explorer Juan Rodriguez Cabrillo north with three ships. His assignment was to explore the coast north of Baja California, towards Alta, or upper California. More importantly, he was to search for a route linking the Atlantic and Pacific Oceans.

Cabrillo's **expedition**, or organized journey, sailed with three ships and a crew of about 200 men. He traveled with sailors, soldiers, and a priest. Among them were American Indians from Mexico, and likely Africans as well.

A little more than 100 days after they left Mexico, the ships reached what is now San Diego Bay. Cabrillo claimed the land for Spain. He **described** the bay as "a closed and very good port." He meant that it was protected from the strong winds and currents of the Pacific. This was an important feature, because it meant that other Spanish ships could find a safe harbor there.

The ships continued north to Monterey Bay and may have reached as far north as Point Reyes. Along the way, strong winds and storms forced them out to sea. They stopped at islands where the explorers met many California Indians, such as the Chumash people. By February, however, the ships faced winter storms. As the journal of the voyage describes:

Primary Source

... the wind shifted to the southwest with great fury, the seas coming from many different directions, causing them great fatigue and breaking over the ships ... they concluded they were about to be lost.

-From *Relation of the Voyage of Juan Rodriguez Cabrillo, 1542–1543*

Juan Rodriguez Cabrillo

Academic Vocabulary

describe • *v.*, to explain something

By the end of the journey, Juan Rodriguez Cabrillo had died. He was the first European to explore the coast of Alta California. He was also the first to visit California from the sea. Cabrillo made the first reports of California Indians whom he **encountered**, or met, along the coast.

2. ☑ **Reading Check** **Understand Cause and Effect** Write how natural forces affected Cabrillo's expedition.

_____

_____

Word Origins

The word *circumnavigate* contains a verb you know, *navigate*. By adding *circum*, the word takes on a special meaning. *Circum* comes from a Latin word meaning "around." What clue does that give you to the meaning of *circumnavigate*?

Sir Francis Drake in California

For the next few decades, Spain did not send any more explorers to Alta California. But then Spain took control of the Philippine Islands, on the other side of the Pacific. There, the Spanish could trade for Asia's spices and other valuable goods. Soon Spanish **galleons**, large sailing ships, were carrying treasure from the Philippines to Mexico.

Sir Francis Drake

The English pirate Francis Drake decided to attack these treasure ships. He planned to **circumnavigate**, or travel completely around, the world. Only one explorer had done this before. Along the way, Drake planned to steal Spanish treasure. He would also look for a faster route between Europe and Asia.

Drake set sail from England in 1577. He had a fleet of five ships. By June 1579, only one ship remained, the *Golden Hinde*. It was bursting with treasure and needed repair. So Drake pulled into a quiet bay on what is now Point Reyes peninsula in northern California. Drake claimed the land for Elizabeth, the queen of England. He called it *Nova Albion,* which means New England. Drake went on to travel around the world.

Additional Explorers

Academic Vocabulary

current • *n.*, a continuous movement of water in the same direction

The Spanish realized that the best way to sail from the Philippines to the Americas was to follow ocean **currents**. These are strong flows of water in one direction. They helped sailing ships move. Currents carried treasure ships west from the Philippines to the coast of Alta California. They could then sail south to Mexico. The ships that traveled this route were called the Manila Galleons. Manila is a city in the Philippines. The first Filipinos to visit California came as soldiers and explorers on one of these ships.

The trip from the Philippines to Mexico took six to nine months. The viceroy of New Spain wanted to find ports in Alta California where the ships could stop along the way. That way they could get more food and water.

In 1595, explorer Sebastián Cermeño sailed from the Philippines to California to find good ports. In November 1595, Cermeño sailed into what is now called Drake's Bay, near what is now San Francisco Bay.

3. ☑ **Reading Check** **Discuss** with a partner why the Philippine Islands were important to the Spanish.

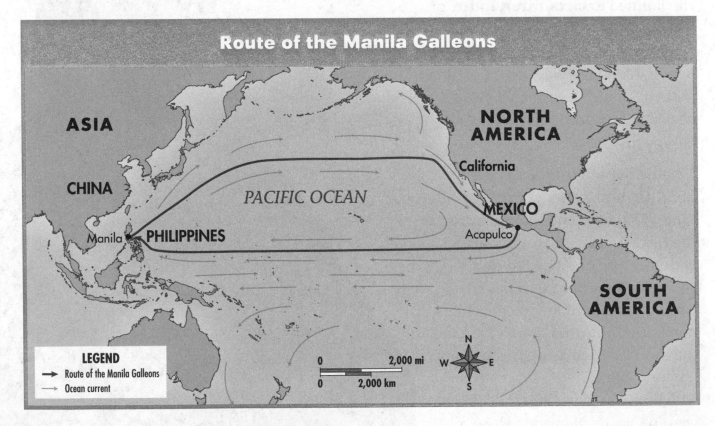

Route of the Manila Galleons

ASIA

CHINA

PACIFIC OCEAN

Manila · **PHILIPPINES**

NORTH AMERICA

California

MEXICO

Acapulco

SOUTH AMERICA

LEGEND
→ Route of the Manila Galleons
⇢ Ocean current

0   2,000 mi
0   2,000 km

N W E S

Before Cermeño could leave the California coast, his ship was wrecked. But Spanish officials in Mexico wanted to try once more to find a safe port. So, in May 1602, several ships left Mexico for Alta California under the command of Sebastián Vizcaíno.

By wintertime, Vizcaíno had explored the California coast as far north as Mendocino. He had visited and named the Bay of San Diego and the bay at Monterey.

4. ☑ **Reading Check** **Compare** the two maps shown here. How was the route of the Manila Galleons different from the route of the three explorers?

_____

_____

_____

_____

_____

_____

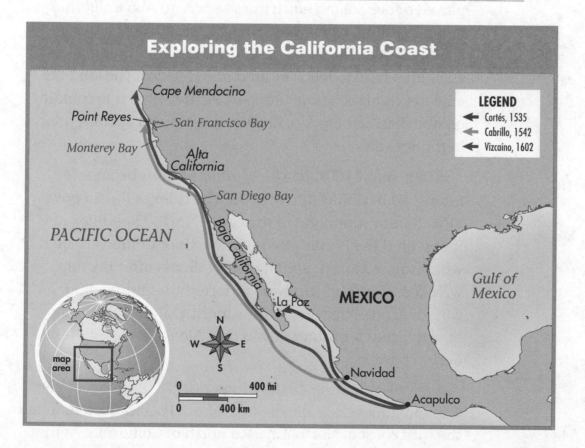

Exploring the California Coast

Cape Mendocino
Point Reyes — San Francisco Bay
Monterey Bay
Alta California
San Diego Bay

PACIFIC OCEAN

Baja California

La Paz

MEXICO

Gulf of Mexico

Navidad

Acapulco

map area

N W E S

0   400 mi
0   400 km

LEGEND
← Cortés, 1535
← Cabrillo, 1542
← Vizcaíno, 1602

The ship led by Vitus Bering wrecked in 1741 due to storms.

Exploring the Pacific

In spite of Sebastián Vizcaíno's reports, Spain did nothing to settle Alta California for almost 170 years. Why? Geography played a role. Sailing north from Mexico to Alta California meant battling strong winds and currents. Later, Spanish explorers would find that deserts and mountains made California hard to reach by land from Mexico. The land the explorers had seen from the coast did not appear to contain great riches. Settling Alta California was not a Spanish priority in those years.

By the mid-1700s, however, other nations became interested in California. In 1732, the ruler of Russia gave Vitus Bering command of the Great North Expedition. It explored the Pacific Ocean far north of California, near what is now Alaska. Bering died of illness after his ship wrecked. However, survivors reported that fur trading would be possible with North America. Today, the body of water that separates Russia and Alaska is called the Bering Strait.

A few decades later, in the winter of 1778, British explorer Captain James Cook explored the North Pacific. Cook mapped the west coast of North America north of California. At that time, Cook was already a busy and successful explorer.

Cook had explored the waters around New Zealand. He had made the dangerous journey to circumnavigate Antarctica. And in 1776, like other explorers before him, he set off to see whether there was an easier route between the Atlantic and the Pacific Oceans. It was his third and final voyage. Although he reached the Bering Strait, he failed to find an easy route between the oceans.

In time, the Spanish realized that other nations were interested in California. If Spain did not take control of Alta California, someone else might. That would threaten Spain's rule of Mexico. You will read much more about this in the next chapter.

5. ☑ Reading Check **Summarize** the importance of Bering and Cook to California's history.

_____

_____

_____

INTERACTIVITY

Check your understanding of the key ideas of this lesson.

☑ Lesson 3 Check   ⓘ HSS 4.2.2 Analysis HI.1 ELA RI.4.1, RI.4.3

6. **Sequence** Number the following explorers in the order that they explored California:

Vizcaíno _____

Cabrillo _____

Drake _____

7. **Identify** one reason why Cortés did not settle in Baja California.

_____

8. **Summarize** the role that the Pacific Ocean played in European exploration of California.

_____

_____

_____

Journal of Juan Cabrillo's Expedition

Explorers like Christopher Columbus and Juan Rodriguez Cabrillo made sure that their voyages were carefully recorded in diaries or journals. Usually it was one of the ship's officers who kept the records. Like other such diaries, the diary of Cabrillo's voyage along the coast of California makes careful note of what happened on each day. Almost 500 years later, modern readers can imagine being along on the journey. The passage below was recorded in 1542 in San Diego Bay.

Vocabulary Support

smoke from large fires

a body of water such as a harbor that is well protected

to toss the anchor overboard to keep a ship in place

league • *n.*, unit of measure, about 3 miles

A Cabrillo plaque

"This day great smokes were seen on the land. The country appears to be good and has large valleys, and in the interior there are high mountains.

On the following Thursday [September 28, 1542] they went about six leagues along a coast running north-northwest, and discovered a port, closed and very good, which they named San Miguel. . . . Having cast anchor in it, they went ashore where there were people. Three of them waited but all the rest fled. To these three they gave some presents. . . . They gave signs of great fear. . . . While they were in this port a heavy storm occurred, but since the port is good they did not feel it at all."

- From *Relation of the Voyage of Juan Rodriguez Cabrillo*, 1542–1543

Close Reading

HSS 4.2.2 **Analysis** RE.1, RE.2 **ELA** RI.4.2, RI.4.8

1. Identify the first sign that there were people living on the California coast. What happened when they went ashore?

_____

_____

_____

2. Describe the features of the land recorded in the diary.

_____

_____

 Wrap It Up

1. Summarize why you think the writer thought it was important to record information about the land, the people, and the port. Support your answer with information from the chapter. Use examples from the diary shown here.

_____

_____

_____

_____

★ Citizenship

Quality:
Individual responsibility

Elsie Allen (1899–1990)
Keeping Traditions Alive

Elsie Allen was born in 1899 near Santa Rosa, California. Raised by her grandmother, Elsie learned the traditions of her Pomo Indian people. For centuries, Pomo women have been highly skilled in making baskets from the plants that grow around them. In the past, the skill was passed down within a family. Outsiders were not taught how to make the complex and beautiful Pomo baskets.

In Elsie's time, some California Indian traditions were being forgotten. But Elsie did not want the art of basket weaving to be lost. She took responsibility for keeping the tradition alive. She taught others how to make beautiful baskets.

"Basket weaving needs dedication and interest and increasing skill and knowledge," Elsie Allen said to her students. "It needs feeling and love and honor for the great weavers of the past who showed us the way. . . . You also can create matchless beauty and help me renew something that should never be lost."

Find Out More

1. Why do you think Elsie Allen believed that it was so important to preserve the art of basket weaving? How did she take responsibility for what she believed?

_____

_____

_____

_____

_____

2. Today, we pass down many traditions just like Elsie Allen passed down basket weaving. Talk with a partner about different traditions you learned from your family or community.

Visual Review

Use these graphics to review some of the vocabulary, people, and ideas from this chapter.

How Most California Indians Were Alike	How California Indians Varied
• Hunter-gatherers • Lived in settled villages • Used land and water resources to meet their needs • Managed the environment	**Culture** • More than 90 languages • Many different culture groups **Homes** • In cool climates: enclosed houses made of wood • In warm climates: often open-air, made of reeds, brush, or tule (bulrush) **Food** • Most hunted, gathered, and fished. • Some farmed.

Early Explorers of California and the Pacific

1542: Cabrillo reaches San Diego Bay and Monterey. Claimed land for Spain.

1579: Drake arrives at Point Reyes and encounters California Indians. Claims land for England.

1595: Cermeño sails to California and reaches Bay of San Francisco. Claims land for Spain.

1602: Vizcaíno reaches Monterey and Mendocino.

1741: Bering expedition reaches North America.

1778: Cook explores the North Pacific and maps the northern Pacific coast.

☑ Assessment

🎮 GAMES
Play the vocabulary game.

Vocabulary and Key Ideas 🦶 HSS 4.2.1, 4.2.2 **Analysis** RE.2

1. **Define** Write a sentence using the vocabulary word **hunter-gatherers**.

   _____

   _____

2. **Define** What does someone do when they **cultivate** the land?

   _____

   _____

   _____

3. **Identify** Fill in the blank to complete the sentence. High winds and

   _____ made California hard to reach by sea from Mexico.

4. **Draw** a line to match the definitions with the correct terms.

   to change or adjust   **expedition**

   a small community   **circumnavigate**

   an organized journey   **village**

   to meet   **adapt**

   to travel around the world   **encounter**

5. **Analyzing an Image**
   Analyze this photograph. What materials do you think California Indians used to build this house?

   _____

   What does this tell you about the location of the people who lived in it?

   _____

   _____

6. **Identifying Main Idea and Details** Fill in the circle next to the best answer. What was a major goal of the early California explorers?

   (A) to sail to the Philippines on large ships

   (B) to find a passage to link the Atlantic and Pacific Oceans

   (C) to build settlements in Mexico

   (D) to buy spices to trade with the rest of the world

7. **Summarize** What was an important way in which California Indians managed their environment?

   _____

   _____

8. **Analyze** How did Spain's control of the Philippines affect the exploration of California?

   _____

   _____

   _____

9. **Revisit the Big Question** Using the California Indians as an example, summarize how people can adapt to where they live.

   _____

   _____

   _____

10. **Writers Workshop: Write a Narrative** On a separate sheet of paper, write two short paragraphs that might have appeared in your journal if you were a sailor with Juan Cabrillo's expedition. Describe the events of a day when you first arrived in California.

Analyze Primary Sources ❖ HSS 4.2.2 **Analysis** RE.2, HI.1 **ELA** RI.4.3

"The Spaniards never had any dealing, or so much as
set a foot in this country [California]."

–Sir Francis Drake, from *The World Encompassed*, 1579

11. Based on what you have read about the voyages of Cabrillo and Drake, is this
true? Explain your answer. Why do you think this was included in the journal?

_____

_____

_____

_____

_____

_____

Summarize ❖ HSS 4.2.1 **Analysis** HI.1 **ELA** RI.4.2

12. Why did explorers come to California? What challenges did they face?

_____

_____

_____

_____

Quest Findings

INTERACTIVITY

Use this activity to help you prepare to create your wiki.

Create Your Wiki

You've read the lessons in this chapter, and now you're ready to create your wiki. Remember that the goal of your wiki is to tell people about California Indians in one region of the state. You want people to understand how California Indians lived long ago and to understand how their lives have changed.

1 Prepare to Write

Your group is focusing on California Indians from a particular region. Identify culture groups from that region and research them. Read about the foods they ate and homes they built. Find out where they live today.

2 Write a Draft

Using index cards, write a paragraph about each topic you researched. Be sure to note the sources of your information.

3 Build the Wiki

Follow your teacher's instructions to turn your index cards into a class wiki.

4 Revise

Make changes to your wiki after discussing with your group. Correct any grammatical or spelling errors.

3 Missions and Mexican Rule

GO ONLINE FOR DIGITAL RESOURCES

- ▶ VIDEO
- 👆 INTERACTIVITY
- 🔊 AUDIO
- 🎮 GAMES
- ☑ ASSESSMENT
- 📖 ETEXT

The BIG Question
▶ VIDEO

How does the past shape our present and future?

Lesson 1

Explorers and Missionaries

Lesson 2

California Indians and the Missions

Lesson 3

Mexico's Independence

Jumpstart Activity
👆 INTERACTIVITY

Walk around your classroom and talk with classmates about skills and school rules you learned while in kindergarten or first grade. Imagine what fourth grade would be like if you had never learned those things. How does what you learned in the past help you in the present?

_____

_____

_____

_____

_____

HSS 4.2.2, 4.2.3, 4.2.4, 4.2.5, 4.2.6, 4.2.7, 4.2.8 **Analysis** CST.1, CST.3, CST.4, HI.3 **ELA** L.4.4, RI.4.1, RI.4.2, RI.4.3, RI.4.4, RI.4.7, RI.4.9, W.4.1

Rap About It!

 AUDIO

Missions and Ranchos

Preview the chapter **vocabulary** as you sing the rap:

Missionaries came from Mexico and Spain

And when they arrived they decided to remain

In what is now California, next to the sea

They built twenty-one **missions** that we can still see.

But it's hard to walk in and make friends too

If you take away freedom and don't treat people cool

To make California Indians farm instead of hunt and gather

A **pastoral economy** is what Spain would rather

Mexico won its freedom and **land grants** were given

These official papers gave land to make a living

On large property in California they could own and keep

These were called **ranchos**—home for horses, cattle and sheep

Missions and Mexican Rule

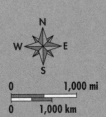

Alta California

NORTH AMERICA

SOUTH AMERICA

N
W   E
S

0   1,000 mi
0   1,000 km

Where was Alta California located?

The area known as Alta California included the modern state of California and other lands to the east. It was part of the Spanish empire, shown in yellow on this map.

Interpret the map and locate Alta California. Where was it within the Spanish empire?

Mission San Carlos Borromeo

TODAY
Today, you can visit Spanish missions like this one in Carmel near Monterey.

What happened and When?

Interpret the timeline to find out about important events related to Spanish and Mexican rule in California.

1500

1600

1542
Juan Cabrillo explores the coast of present-day California.

Who will you meet?

Charles III
The king of Spain from 1759–1788 who expanded Spanish colonies in the Americas

Gaspar de Portolá
A Spanish soldier, explorer, and first governor of Alta California

Junípero Serra
A Spanish missionary who founded many of California's 21 missions

Nicolás José
A San Gabriel Indian leader who fought to protect his people

👆 **INTERACTIVITY**

Complete the interactive timeline digital activity.

1775
Juan Bautista de Anza leads an expedition by land to Alta California.

1821
Mexico becomes independent.

1700

1800

1769
Junípero Serra founds Mission San Diego de Alcalá.

TODAY
You can travel the Juan Bautista de Anza National Historic Trail, which runs through California and Arizona.

3 Quest
Document-Based Writing

Mission: Museum!

In the late 1700s, Spain took control of California. The Spanish built missions and worked to spread their religion to California Indians. These missions changed the lives and cultures of many California Indian groups.

Quest Kick Off

Your job is to write an essay to persuade the state government to build a new Mission Museum. It would honor the people whose lives were affected by Spanish missions. Use documents you find in this chapter to help you make your case.

1 Ask Questions

How do you think Spanish missions affected California Indians? Write down two questions you have about missions and the role they played in California's history.

Junípero Serra

2 Plan

INTERACTIVITY

View an image gallery of California museums.

How can you learn about Spanish missions? What kinds of sources do you think might help you write your essay? Write down some ideas here.

....

....

3 Look for *Quest* Connections

Turn to the next page to begin looking for Quest connections that will help you write your essay.

4 *Quest* Findings
Write Your Essay

Use the Quest Findings page at the end of the chapter to help you write your essay.

Lesson 1 Explorers and Missionaries

INTERACTIVITY

Participate in a class discussion to preview the content of this lesson.

Vocabulary

colony
settler
convert
mission
Franciscan
pueblo
presidio

Academic Vocabulary

secure
objective

Spanish explorers once visited areas of California's coast like this one.

Unlock The BIG Question

I will know how Spanish explorers and missionaries affected California and California Indians.

Jumpstart Activity

Imagine you are visiting a new place. You meet people who do not speak your language and who have a very different culture. How do you approach this new group? How will you work with them? Stand up and act out a meeting between the two groups.

If you looked at a map of California, you would see many Spanish place names, including San Diego, Los Angeles, and San Francisco. How did this happen? In this lesson, you will learn how Spain sent missionaries, soldiers, and other people to California in the 1700s. They changed California in many ways that you can still see today.

Spanish Explorers

HSS 4.2.2, 4.2.3, 4.2.4, 4.2.5, 4.2.6
Analysis CST.4, HI.3 ELA RI.4.1,
RI.4.3, RI.4.4, RI.4.7

As you know, Spain controlled much of the Americas in the 1700s. Spain had ruled Mexico since the 1500s. It was part of a larger **colony** called New Spain. A colony is land controlled by another nation. New Spain was run by Spanish officials and soldiers. Spanish settlers lived there, alongside native people. A **settler** is someone who moves to a new place to live.

INTERACTIVITY

Explore the key ideas of this lesson.

Alta California was not yet a colony at this time. As you read, the Spanish did not settle in California in the 1500s or 1600s. They did not think it was valuable. Ocean currents, mountains, and deserts also made it hard to reach from Mexico. In fact, for more than 200 years after Juan Cabrillo first visited California, Spain had little interest in it at all.

However, in the late 1700s, King Charles III of Spain began to worry that Russia or Britain might take control of California. The Spanish did not want a foreign country in charge of California. They thought this might threaten Mexico. Britain had already taken control of the Spanish colony of Florida.

Academic Vocabulary

secure • *v.*, to get hold of or take possession of

In 1769, Spanish explorer Gaspar de Portolá led an expedition to Alta California. Then, in the 1770s, Juan Bautista de Anza, led another exploration of the area. The King wanted to found settlements in Alta California. This would help to **secure** the region for Spain. Indians from northern Mexico came on these early expeditions, along with Spanish soldiers and sailors.

1. **✓ Reading Check**
Turn to a partner and **describe** the reasons why Spain sent explorers to California in the late 1700s.

Juan Crespí

Academic Vocabulary

objective • *n.*, a goal or purpose

Word Wise

Root Words

When you see an unfamiliar word, try using root words to figure out the meaning. For example, you have already learned the word *mission* in this lesson. What do you think the word *missionary* means? Use what you now know about missions to help you understand the meaning of this new word.

In 1769, Portolá set up the first Spanish settlements in California. He traveled by land and sea up the California coast and sailed as far north as the San Francisco Bay area. The journey north was long and difficult.

In 1775, de Anza and a group of 200 settlers set out from Sonora, Mexico, and journeyed to Alta California by land. They had to cross a desert and the Colorado River to reach San Francisco. Indian guides helped the settlers find a route. They helped build Spain's California settlements. Later groups could not use the de Anza route to travel to California, however. The Quechan Indians fought with the Spanish and blocked the route.

Spanish Missionaries

Spain sent the Portolá expedition to take control of Alta California. But the Spanish had a second **objective**. They wanted to **convert** California Indians to their religion, Roman Catholic Christianity. To convert is to change from one religion to another. To do this, they planned to build **missions**. A mission is a kind of settlement with the goal of spreading a religion.

At these missions, the Spanish would teach California Indians about Catholicism and their way of life. Spain had already built missions in other parts of their empire, including in Florida and Texas. Missions spread Spanish influence and Catholicism.

The first California missions were built during the time when American colonists fought for independence from Britain. Spain supported the colonists. Spain wanted to be the most powerful empire in North America instead of Britain.

Junípero Serra was a Catholic priest and a missionary. He belonged to an order, or religious group, called the **Franciscans**. Serra was a teacher in Spain. He wanted to spread Catholicism around the world. So in 1749, he traveled to Mexico City. That was the capital of New Spain.

Serra lived for many years in Mexico where he managed missions. In 1769, he traveled to Alta California. His assignment was to found new missions there. Today, Serra is considered a saint by the Roman Catholic Church.

Mission San Diego de Alcalá, founded in 1769

Primary Source

California is my life and there I hope to die.

-Junípero Serra, *Writings of Junípero Serra*

A missionary named Juan Crespí went with Serra. Like Serra, Crespí was a priest in the Franciscan order. During the expedition, he kept a diary of their journey. He described the group's travels and recorded their experiences. Crespí traveled with Portolá as far north as the San Francisco Bay area.

Over time, the missions Serra built grew into small villages. Typically, a mission included a church and homes. It also had workshops, storage areas, and guardhouses. California Indians lived and worked there. Missions controlled large areas of land for farming and raising animals.

The Spanish also built small towns called **pueblos** at this time. Unlike missions, pueblos were not founded to teach religion. Instead, they were farming communities that grew food for Spanish soldiers. Spanish soldiers protected pueblos from attack. Over time, many pueblos grew into large towns and cities that still exist today. These include Los Angeles and San Jose.

2. ☑ **Reading Check**
Use Evidence From Text Identify and underline in the text Spain's reasons for building missions in California.

California's Missions

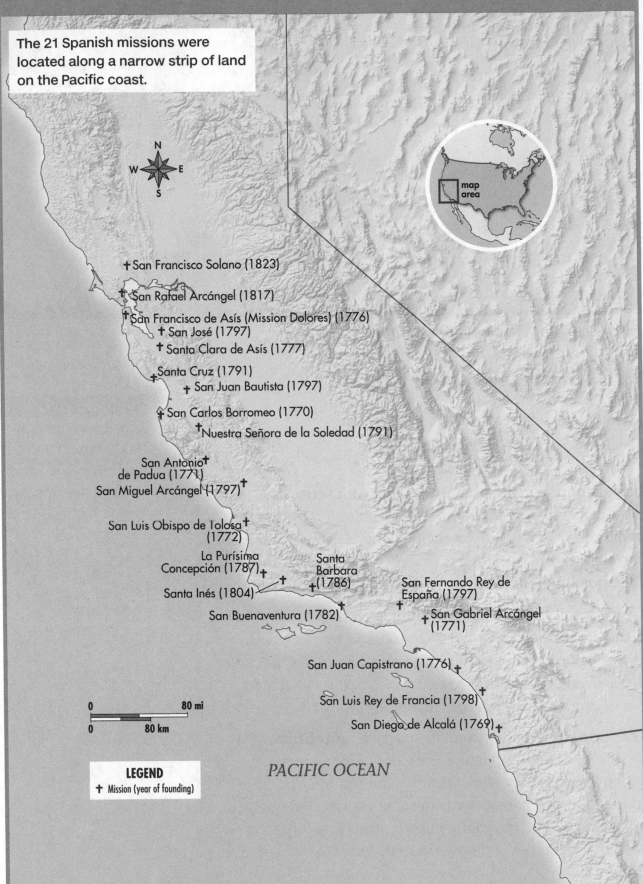

The 21 Spanish missions were located along a narrow strip of land on the Pacific coast.

map area

✝ San Francisco Solano (1823)

✝ San Rafael Arcángel (1817)

✝ San Francisco de Asís (Mission Dolores) (1776)
  ✝ San José (1797)
    ✝ Santa Clara de Asís (1777)

  ✝ Santa Cruz (1791)
    ✝ San Juan Bautista (1797)

  ✝ San Carlos Borromeo (1770)
    ✝ Nuestra Señora de la Soledad (1791)

San Antonio ✝
de Padua (1771)
San Miguel Arcángel (1797) ✝

San Luis Obispo de Tolosa ✝
(1772)

La Purísima
Concepción (1787) ✝   Santa
                           Barbara
      ✝   ✝ (1786)   San Fernando Rey de
Santa Inés (1804)   España (1797)
                                              ✝
        San Buenaventura (1782) ✝   ✝ San Gabriel Arcángel
                                                 (1771)

                    San Juan Capistrano (1776) ✝

                      San Luis Rey de Francia (1798) ✝

                        San Diego de Alcalá (1769) ✝

0   80 mi
0   80 km

PACIFIC OCEAN

LEGEND
✝ Mission (year of founding)

California Missions

Over several years, Serra and Crespí traveled up the California coast building missions. Under Serra's leadership, the Spanish founded nine missions. They included Mission San Diego de Alcalá, Mission San Juan Capistrano, and Mission San Buenaventura. Over time, the Spanish built 21 missions.

Mission Locations

The locations of missions were mapped out carefully. They were founded in places that had fresh water and good soil for farming. These areas had resources, like trees that could be used for building. Most importantly, missions were near Indian settlements.

3. ☑ **Reading Check** Use the map to **identify** the mission closest to your community. When was it founded?

_____

_____

Mission San Juan Bautista

A room at Mission San Juan Bautista used for baptism ceremonies

Spain's missions stretched from San Diego in the south to the San Francisco Bay area in the north. If you look at a map of California today, you will see that this is only part of the state. Spanish control did not reach northern California. The missions also did not extend very far inland.

Missionaries and California Indians

Missionaries worked to baptize California Indians. Baptism is a ceremony that, according to Catholic beliefs, makes a person a Catholic.

California Indians did most of the work at the missions. The missions depended on them. Indians worked large areas of land, farming and ranching. Some only worked a few weeks a year. Others worked year-round.

The church at Mission San Juan Bautista as it appears today

California Indians came to the missions for many reasons. In the next lesson, you will learn how the Spanish changed California's landscape. These changes made it harder for Indians to meet their needs in the ways they had before. Over time, the missionaries built a steady supply of food. They also held interesting ceremonies.

Some Indians came willingly because missions provided food. However, some were kept at the missions against their will and made to work. You will read more about this in the next lesson.

4. ☑ **Reading Check** Turn to a partner and **identify** the reasons why Indians came to missions.

Mission Saint Luis Rey

Missionaries perform a religious service with soldiers and California Indians.

This illustration shows a presidio. It was built in 1776 in what is now San Francisco.

Spanish Soldiers

Remember that spreading their religion was not Spain's main goal. Spain wanted to take control of California and keep other European countries out. So they sent soldiers along with the missionaries.

The Spanish founded a total of four **presidios**, or military forts. The first were built in San Diego and Monterey. Presidios protected missions and pueblos from attacks by foreigners and California Indians who resisted. Some presidio soldiers and pueblo settlers had African origins.

Missions, pueblos, and presidios were designed to support one another and keep control over Alta California. But sometimes, Spanish missionaries, soldiers, and officials clashed. Junípero Serra argued with a military leader named Pedro Fages about the unfair treatment of soldiers and workers in Monterey. The problem became so bad that Serra went to Mexico City and had the government remove Fages from his post.

Together, Spanish explorers, soldiers, and missionaries made part of what is now California into Spanish territory. They made a lasting impact on California's people and environment.

5. ☑ **Reading Check** **Explain** the difference between a mission and a presidio.

_____

_____

_____

_____

_____

☑ **Lesson 1 Check** ① **HSS** 4.2.3, 4.2.4, 4.2.5 **Analysis** HI.3
ELA RI.4.1, RI.4.2, RI.4.3

👆 **INTERACTIVITY**

Check your understanding of the key ideas of this lesson.

6. Compare and Contrast Analyze the similarities and differences between missions and pueblos. **Identify** why each one was founded.

_____

_____

_____

7. Explain why King Charles III decided to establish a Spanish colony in Alta California.

_____

_____

_____

8. Review and **analyze** the primary source quote by Junípero Serra. What does it suggest about how he felt about being a missionary?

_____

_____

_____

_____

Junípero Serra, on Founding a New Mission

As you have read, Junípero Serra founded the first nine missions in California. Finding the right location for each new mission was very important. Missions had to be close to water, and they needed good soil for growing crops. They also needed to be near Indian villages. When they found the right spot, the missionaries celebrated with a ceremony. In this letter Junípero Serra describes the ceremony held before the founding of Mission San Carlos Borromeo.

Vocabulary Support

prepared, ready ·······

with a lot of emotion ·

venerate, v., honor with great respect

a cross, the symbol of Christianity ·······

cannon fire ·

Quest Connections

What do you learn about life at the missions from this primary source?

Then we all made our way to a gigantic cross which was <u>all in readiness</u> and lying on the ground. With everyone lending a hand we set it in an upright position. I sang the prayers for its blessing. We set it in the ground and then, with <u>all the tenderness of our hearts</u>, we venerated it. I sprinkled with holy water all the fields around. And thus, after raising aloft the <u>standard of the King of Heaven</u>, we unfurled the flag of our Catholic Monarch likewise. As we raised each one of them, we shouted at the top of our voices: "Long live the Faith! Long live the King!" All the time the bells were ringing, and our rifles were being fired, and from the boat came the <u>thunder of the big guns</u>. . . . A few days later the expedition moved to a pretty plain about a rifle shot from the beach, and there established the presidio and the mission to it.

- letter from Junípero Serra to Juan Andres, June 12, 1770

Close Reading

HSS 4.2.3, 4.2.4, 4.2.5
ELA RI.4.1, RI.4.3

1. **Identify** and highlight three things that show Serra is describing an important ceremony.
2. **Describe** what you think the missionaries felt about the new mission. What evidence supports your conclusion?

_____

_____

_____

_____

_____

_____

_____

Wrap It Up

Based on this primary source and what you read in Lesson 1, **explain** how missions helped Spain control Alta California.

_____

_____

_____

_____

_____

_____

_____

Lesson 2 California Indians and the Missions

INTERACTIVITY

Participate in a class discussion to preview the content of this lesson.

Vocabulary

pastoral economy
subject
indigenous
kinship
revolt

Academic Vocabulary

traditional
heritage

Unlock The BIG Question

I will know how the lives of California Indians changed during the Mission Period.

JumpStart Activity

Study the illustration of a mission on the next page. Work with a partner and find the church and the Indian homes. Point them out. Talk about what you think the different buldings were used for.

When the Spanish came, the lives of many California Indians changed forever. Their cultures, languages, and religions changed. So did the kinds of work they did. Even California's landscape itself was changed by the arrival of the Spanish.

Daily Life in the Mission Period

No two missions were exactly alike. However, they all had certain things in common. Since the missionaries worked to spread Catholicism, the church was the most important building. It was usually the first building to be built. In the early days, it looked much like other mission buildings. Later, larger churches were built.

Daily life was busy. Missionaries, soldiers, and California Indians had separate roles and tasks. Missionaries were responsible for religious activities. They performed services and ceremonies. They also directed the mission and community.

If you were to visit a mission today, you would see a church and other nearby buildings. But remember that missions also controlled large areas of land around these buildings. California Indians worked on this land. They tended the crops and animals.

California Indian men were also made to build mission buildings. Women wove fabric in workshops. Even children took part in the work of the mission. California Indians also worked at crafts like carpentry.

California Indians helped build presidio forts, too. Soldiers lived there and worked to protect missions. Life was difficult, and supplies often ran low. The soldiers depended on the missions to survive. Sometimes, presidios did not have enough food, money, or weapons on hand.

Pueblos were farming communities. To encourage people to settle there, the Spanish government gave settlers land, farm animals, and money for clothes and supplies. If settlers successfully farmed their land for five years, they could keep it. California Indians also did much of the work in pueblos.

HSS 4.2.3, 4.2.4, 4.2.5, 4.2.6
Analysis HI.3 ELA RI.4.1, RI.4.3, RI.4.4, RI.4.7

INTERACTIVITY

Explore the key ideas of this lesson.

1. ☑ **Reading Check**
Turn to a partner and **describe** a typical day at a mission for both a missionary and an Indian worker. How were they similar? How were they different?

A typical mission had different areas and kinds of buildings. Each one served a special purpose in daily life.

Homes for Indians

Livestock

Homes for Indians

Central Courtyard

Cemetery

Church

Priests' Living Area

This illustration shows California Indians at work making baskets and rope at a mission.

Land and Cultures Change

The coming of the Spanish changed California Indians' way of life and California's landscape. Remember that in the past, Indians had hunted, gathered, and fished for food.

But now, Spanish missionaries and settlers brought European farming to the area. They brought crops like wheat and animals like cows that were not found in California before. They introduced a **pastoral economy**, which is an economy based on raising animals. Over time, farming and ranching changed the environment. So did new plants and animals.

This damaged the **traditional** sources of California Indian's food. They could no longer rely on meeting all of their own needs. To survive, many Indians had to depend in part on the missions. As a result, more and more had to live there. They came for the supply of food available at the missions.

Spanish officials wanted to turn Indians into loyal Spanish **subjects**. A subject is a person who is ruled by a king or queen. Spain believed this would help them stay in control of the colony. To do this, they not only baptized California Indians, but also introduced them to Spanish culture and language. Some Spanish settlers married Indians, too. California Indians began to wear Spanish clothes and speak the Spanish language.

Academic Vocabulary

traditional • *adj.*, based on long-standing customs, beliefs, and ways of doing things

However, Indians did bring their own cultures with them when they came to the missions. As a result, Spanish culture combined with the **indigenous**, or native, culture. California Indians combined Catholicism with their own beliefs. The mixing of Spanish and Indian ways shaped a new culture and society in California. Many traditional practices, such as two-spirit traditions, however, were not continued or adapted because colonizers forced such Native Americans to conform to European gender roles.

Living at a mission was not easy for California's Indians. Days were long and full of hard work. Indians may have missed the freedom of living in their own villages. But Indians who had been baptized were not allowed to leave without permission from the missionaries. If they tried to return to their villages, presidio soldiers forced them to come back.

Junípero Serra, founder of nine missions, died in 1784. At the time of his death, nearly 5,000 Indians at his missions had been baptized. Thousands more were baptized in the decades after. All together, the California mission system baptized about 54,000 Indians.

2. ☑ **Reading Check**
Use the chart to **identify** some of the effects of the mission system on the California Indians.

Effects of Missions on California Indians

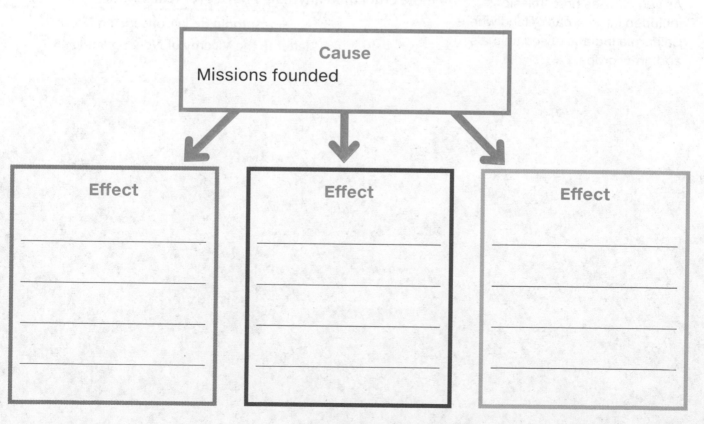

Cause
Missions founded

Effect

Effect

Effect

California Indians Face Challenges

Quest Connection

The primary source quote says that California Indians were treated cruelly. Highlight places in the text that show how Indians faced challenges on missions.

INTERACTIVITY

Answer a question about the cruel treatment of Indians during the Mission Period.

As the mission system grew, California's Indian population decreased. Spanish settlers carried diseases from Europe that California Indians had never had before. Their bodies could not fight them off. Many died as a result. Being forced to live and work on the missions took a toll on Indian families as well. California Indians had fewer children. During the Mission period, the population of Indians living near the missions fell from about 72,000 to about 18,000.

The new communities created at missions were tightly controlled. California Indians who lived there had very little freedom. As you read, soldiers kept baptized California Indians from returning to their villages. Missionaries also worked to replace the Indians' cultures with Spanish culture. Indians were not allowed to wear their traditional clothing. They had to dress like the Spanish did. The missionaries wanted Indians to use Spanish customs, and Indians who broke these rules were punished.

Primary Source

The manner in which the Indians are treated is by far more cruel than anything I have ever read about.

–Antonio de la Concepción Horra, letter to the Viceroy of New Spain, 1798

As you can see here, missions included large areas of land where California Indians raised animals and grew crops.

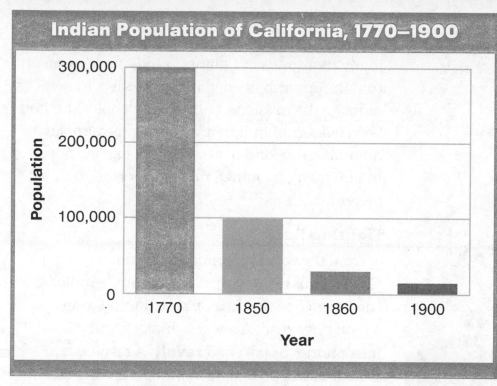

Indian Population of California, 1770–1900

Population

| 300,000 | 200,000 | 100,000 | 0 |

Year: 1770 · 1850 · 1860 · 1900

* Source: *Handbook of North American Indians*

3. ☑ **Reading Check**
The population of California Indians over time is difficult to be sure of. This graph shows historians' estimate, or best guess, of how many Indians lived in California at various times. **Analyze** the graph and circle the year when the population was highest.

California Indians Adapt and Fight Back

Many California Indians living near the missions faced hard times under Spanish rule. However, they lived as well as they could. They did their best to protect their culture and pass it on. They worked to preserve their **heritage**, or customs and history. To do this, they both adapted to the new system and fought back against it.

Academic Vocabulary

heritage • *n.*, something that is handed down from the past

Adapting

At the missions, some Indians became farmers and learned to live that way of life. For instance, at Mission San Luis Rey, they grew crops, such as wheat, grapes, and oranges. They also raised cattle, sheep, and other animals. As at other missions, Indians did most of the work. They tended their crops and made clothing. Children helped in these tasks.

California Indian cultures changed in other ways. The Indians may have used a Catholic form of **kinship**, or relationship. Known as *compadrazgo*, it is the tie formed between someone who is baptized and his or her godparent. A godparent has a role in the baptism ceremony. California Indians served as godparents. This may have helped Indians living at missions strengthen their ties to one another.

California Indians continue to keep their traditions alive and perform rituals at missions throughout the state.

Remember that there were only a tiny number of Spanish missionaries and soldiers, compared to many thousands of California Indians. This meant that the Spanish needed Indian leaders to help manage the missions. Sometimes people who had been leaders of Indian groups became *alcaldes*. An *alcalde* is a kind of government official. Some Indian men also joined mission choirs and orchestras.

Fighting Back

From the very beginning, many native Californians resisted the Spanish. Some Indians tried to escape the missions by running away, as you have read. A few fought back and killed missionaries as part of a **revolt**. A revolt is a violent attack on people in power. As early as 1769, there are reports of Indian attacks on Spanish soldiers. Several missions also experienced organized rebellions. In 1775, the Kumeyaay people attacked the Mission of San Diego. They burned buildings and killed a priest. Spanish troops later captured the leaders of the revolt.

In 1785, a California Indian woman named Toypurina became angry with Spanish settlers. She was a leader in her community. Along with several other leaders, including Nicolás José, she organized an Indian revolt at the San Gabriel mission. However, Spanish soldiers defeated the rebellion. Toypurina and José were sent far from their homeland as punishment.

Over time, California Indians adapted to Spanish rule. They also fought back. But they did not disappear. They continued to practice their traditions and preserve their cultures.

Today, we can visit mission buildings to learn about this period of California's history. They can help us find out about the struggles of the California Indians who lived and worked there.

4. ✓ **Reading Check** **Summarize** how California Indians resisted Spanish rule.

_____

_____

_____

_____

_____

Today, visitors can tour California's missions to learn about their history.

✓ **Lesson 2 Check**   ⏱ **HSS** 4.2.3, 4.2.5, 4.2.6 **ELA** RI.4.1, RI.4.3

👆 **INTERACTIVITY**

Check your understanding of the key ideas of this lesson.

5. What is a pastoral economy? **Explain** how it was a change for California Indians.

_____

_____

6. **Describe** the different ways California Indians adapted to life on the missions.

_____

_____

_____

7. **Quest** Connections Do you think Toypurina and Nicolás José would agree with the primary source quotation? Why or why not?

_____

_____

_____

Critical Thinking Skills

Compare Viewpoints

VIDEO

Watch a video about comparing viewpoints.

Authors write for different reasons. Every author has a different point of view. Even two people who agree about something might feel that way for different reasons.

It is important to identify an author's point of view when you read. This will help you understand why the author has written the text and what he or she wants you to learn. When you read two or more texts by different authors on the same topic, it helps to compare and contrast their points of view. Look for the main ideas. Also look for words or examples the author uses to influence readers.

Not everyone agrees about the mission system's place in history. Some believe missionaries like Junípero Serra deserve praise for spreading their culture. Others believe that they were responsible for the mistreatment of California Indians. Some believe a little of both. Read the two viewpoints about missions and missionaries shown here. Valentin Lopez is a modern-day California Indian leader. Rubén G. Mendoza is a historian. Then use the organizer on the next page to describe the writers' points of view.

Viewpoint 1

"They [the missionaries] totally destroyed our culture. They destroyed our people. They destroyed our environment. And they stole our land. ... They brought diseases. Thousands of our people died."

-Valentin Lopez, chairman of the Amah Mutsun Tribal Band, 2015

Viewpoint 2

"Serra endured great hardships to evangelize [teach Catholicism to] Native Californians. In the process, he orchestrated [started] the development of a chain of missions that helped give birth to modern California .... dig a little deeper and you'll find evidence of a new diverse society flourishing, one that makes California and its Latino culture unique."

-Rubén G. Mendoza, *Los Angeles Times*, March 17, 2015

1. Complete this organizer to list each writer's main viewpoint on the mission system.

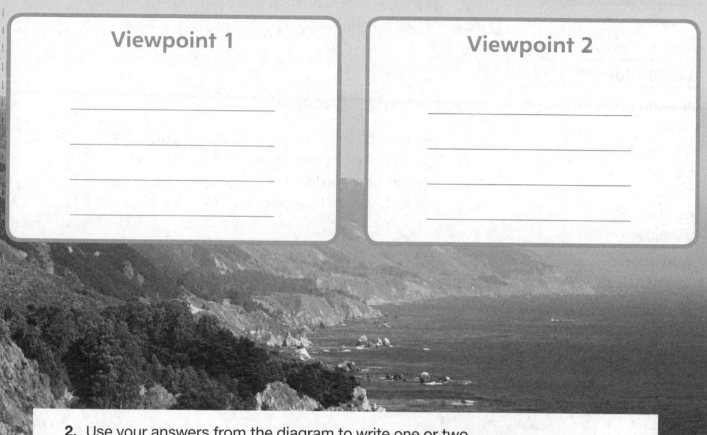

Viewpoint 1

_____

_____

_____

Viewpoint 2

_____

_____

_____

2. Use your answers from the diagram to write one or two sentences that explain the authors' different points of view.

_____

_____

_____

3. Which opinion do you agree with, and why? Include details from the viewpoint to support your answer.

_____

_____

_____

_____

Mexico's Independence

INTERACTIVITY

Participate in a class discussion to preview the content of this lesson.

Vocabulary

independence
republic
secularize
land grant
Californio
rancho
commerce

Academic Vocabulary

transfer

Unlock
The **BIG**
Question

I will know how Mexico gained its independence and what that meant for Alta California.

JumpStart Activity

Imagine you live in a colony ruled by people from a distant country. The government in that country decides how you live. How might you react? Gather in a small group to have a roundtable talk.

In 1821, Mexico was much bigger than it is today. In fact, parts of ten U.S. states and eight present-day countries were once part of Mexico.

Mexico in 1821

LEGEND

Mexico, 1821
Present-day national border
Present-day state border
BELIZE Present-day country
Utah Present-day state

As you have read, Mexico, California, and other lands were once part of New Spain, ruled by the Spanish empire. However, many of the people who lived there did not like being ruled by another country. They wanted to decide how they would be governed. So they decided to fight for their freedom. In the early 1800s, their struggle began.

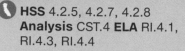
HSS 4.2.5, 4.2.7, 4.2.8
Analysis CST.4 **ELA** RI.4.1, RI.4.3, RI.4.4

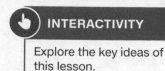
INTERACTIVITY

Explore the key ideas of this lesson.

Mexican War for Independence

The Mexican War for Independence started in 1810. A Catholic priest named Miguel Hidalgo y Costilla demanded **independence**, or freedom, for Mexico. He called for an end to 300 years of Spanish rule and gained the support of thousands of Mexicans.

The fight lasted for years. Finally, in 1821, Mexico won its independence by Spain. It was free from European rule.

New Spain eventually became the Mexican Republic. A **republic** is a different form of government. While the Spanish empire had a king and queen, a republic is run by elected leaders. The Mexican Republic included California and its missions. It also included many areas that are not part of Mexico now. Today, some of these places are independent countries like Costa Rica. Others, like Alta California, are now part of the United States.

Miguel Hidalgo y Costilla led the fight for Mexico's independence from Spain.

1. ☑ **Reading Check** **Analyze** the map and **interpret** the map legend. Which parts of Mexico in 1821 are part of the United States today? Which parts are independent countries?

_____

_____

_____

_____

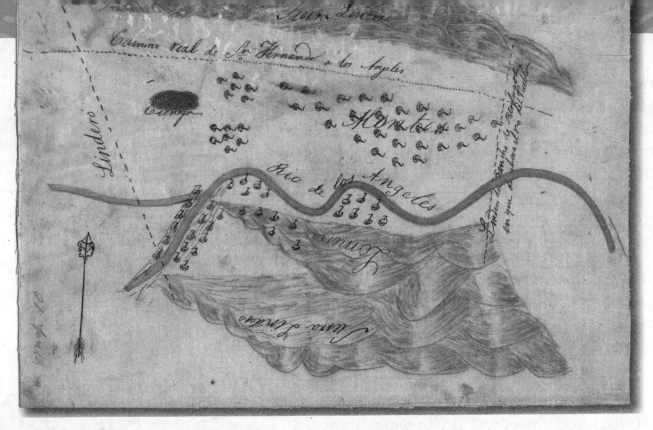

This image shows a hand-drawn *diseño*. What do you think the different map symbols mean?

Academic Vocabulary

transfer • *v.*, to change hands, or to move from one place to another

Word Wise

Root words Find the word *apply*. Do you know what the word means? Now find the word *applicant*. Its root word is *apply*. What do you think an *applicant* is?

The End of the Missions

As early as the late 1700s, there was a campaign to **secularize** the missions, which means to take them away from religious control. Some officials believed missions were old fashioned and did not benefit Indians. They also wanted to own the land controlled by missions.

In 1834, Mexico finally brought an end to the mission system in California. The law that did this was put into place by the governor of Alta California, José Figueroa, who had a mixed Spanish and Indian background. All mission lands were **transferred** from the control of Catholic Church to other people.

To get land, people had to apply for a **land grant**. That was an official document that gave a person the right to own land. Applicants had to be Mexican citizens, members of the Catholic Church, and provide a *diseño*. This was a hand-drawn map of the area that showed how big the area was and what was on the land. Having a map helped officials decide where land grants would be located. But having a *diseño* was only part of a longer process. People had to prove the land was not being used.

Early plans called for California Indians to receive half the land. Some did get land they were promised. But **Californios** received most of the land. These were people descended from Spanish settlers. Usually, these Californios had been loyal to the local authorities. Some were friends or relatives of government officials.

Many Indians stayed and worked for the new landowners. Others moved to towns like Los Angeles to find work.

2. ☑ **Reading Check** **Draw a conclusion** Why do you think California Indians never received the mission lands they were promised?

_____

_____

_____

The Rancho Period

The period between the years 1833 and 1846 is sometimes called the rancho period. **Ranchos** were large areas of land used for raising cattle, sheep, and horses. Ranchos were owned by Californios. After secularization, Indians were free to leave missions, and many moved to ranchos, looking for work. Some rancho owners hired dozens of Indians workers. Others hired hundreds! They looked after the animals. Many Indian workers had previously lived at missions. Bear hunting, bull fights, and horse races were popular activities for people who lived on the ranchos.

A California rancho during the era of Mexican rule

After the Mexican government took control, 800 land grants were given out. This compared to about 20 land concessions that were given out when Spain ruled the area.

John A. Sutter

3. ☑ **Reading Check**
Turn and **analyze** the image with a partner. What details show that San Francisco was a place for commerce?

Early San Francisco

New settlers came to California during the rancho period. Some received land grants. One new settler was a businessman named John A. Sutter. He was an immigrant who came to America from Switzerland in 1834. Sutter settled in Alta California. After living there for a time, he was given a land grant. He built a settlement and a ranch. He also built a fort, Sutter's Fort, in an area that later became Sacramento. You will read more about John Sutter in the next chapter.

After independence, Mexico opened up California to international **commerce**, or business. The government encouraged trade with other nations. As a result, merchants, traders, and sailors began arriving from the United States and England.

People living on ranchos traded hides and tallow. Hides are the skins of cattle. Hides were sent to the eastern United States to be made into shoes. Tallow was animal fat that had been melted down. Tallow was used to make candles and soap. Ships from the eastern United States brought things like clothing, pots and pans, and coffee to be traded for hides and tallow.

As new settlers came to California, the population became more diverse. This meant there were people of different backgrounds living there. California had greatly changed from the days when it was ruled by Spain.

INTERACTIVITY

Check your understanding
of the key ideas of this
lesson.

Lesson 3 Check

HSS 4.2.7, 4.2.8 **Analysis** HI.3 **ELA** RI.4.1, RI.4.3

4. **Identify** multiple reasons why the Mexican government issued land grants in the early 1800s.

_____

_____

_____

5. **Explain** how Mexican independence led to the growth of California.

_____

_____

6. Complete this diagram to **compare and contrast** California under Spanish rule and under Mexican rule. In the outer areas, list how it was different. In the inner area, list how it was the same.

Spanish Rule   Mexican Rule

Distinguish Fact From Opinion

VIDEO

Watch a video about distinguishing facts from opinions.

How can you tell the difference between a fact and an opinion? A **fact** is a statement of information that you can prove to be true. Facts tell what actually happened. An **opinion** is a statement of feelings that cannot be proven true or false. Opinions usually contain words such as *I believe, I think, favorite,* and *probably.* Another way to think about this is that facts do not change, no matter who says them, where opinions may change from person to person.

When you read, it's important to be able to distinguish— or tell the difference between—facts and opinions. Read the paragraph below and look for statements of fact and opinion.

California under Mexican rule was an interesting place. Mexico gained its independence in 1821. Mexico secularized the missions. It promised land to California Indians, but it did not give it to them. This was very unfair. Many new settlers came to Mexican California. California history during this period is fun to study!

1. What are the facts and opinions included in the paragraph on the facing page? Fill in the organizer with sentences from the paragraph.

FACT	OPINION

2. Read the following sentences. Decide if each one is a fact or an opinion and check the appropriate box. Then explain why you think the statement is an example of a fact or an example of an opinion.

I think Mexico should not have fought a war against Spain.

☐ Fact   ☐ Opinion

_____

_____

Mexico became independent in 1821.

☐ Fact   ☐ Opinion

_____

_____

★ Citizenship

Quality:
Leadership

Nicolás José (1748–?)
California Indian Rebel Leader

Nicolás José was a California Indian leader. He was one of the first to be baptized at the San Gabriel Mission during the 1700s. At the time, José was 26 years old. Although he worked with Spanish settlers and was baptized, he continued to take part in Gabrielino Indian dances and celebrations.

However, the Spanish priests did not allow Indians at the mission to practice their culture. Nicolás José disagreed. He wanted to preserve and protect Gabrielino customs and traditions. So in 1785, he joined other Indians in a plan to rebel against the mission. Nicolás José became a leader of their group.

Nicolás José was a strong leader because he decided to fight for what he believed was right. When faced with a hard choice, he decided to stand with his people. He encouraged many others to join the cause. His efforts brought together Indians from eight different villages in the surrounding area.

Leaders, like Nicolás José, are people who stand up for their beliefs. They inspire others and lead by example. They also look for creative solutions to problems. Nicolás José saw a problem in his community. He did not like how Spanish settlers treated the Indians of California. So he made a choice to try to stop it and inspired many other people to follow.

This is an artist's idea of what Nicolás José might have looked like.

Find Out More

1. How did Nicolás José set himself apart as a leader?

_____

_____

_____

_____

2. Talk to an older family member or friend about important customs or traditions they practice. Talk about why those traditions are important and why it is important to protect them.

3 Visual Review

Use these graphics to review some of the vocabulary, people, and ideas from this chapter.

Key Dates in Spanish and Mexican California

1769–1776
Gaspar de Portolá and Juan Bautista de Anza explore Alta California.

1785
Nicolás José and Toypurina lead the San Gabriel Rebellion.

1823
The Mexican Republic is established.

1765 **1790** **1815** **1840** **1865**

1769–1782
Junípero Serra founds nine missions in Alta California.

1810–1821
Mexico fights for independence from Spain.

1833–1846
Mexico issues land grants to settlers in Alta California.

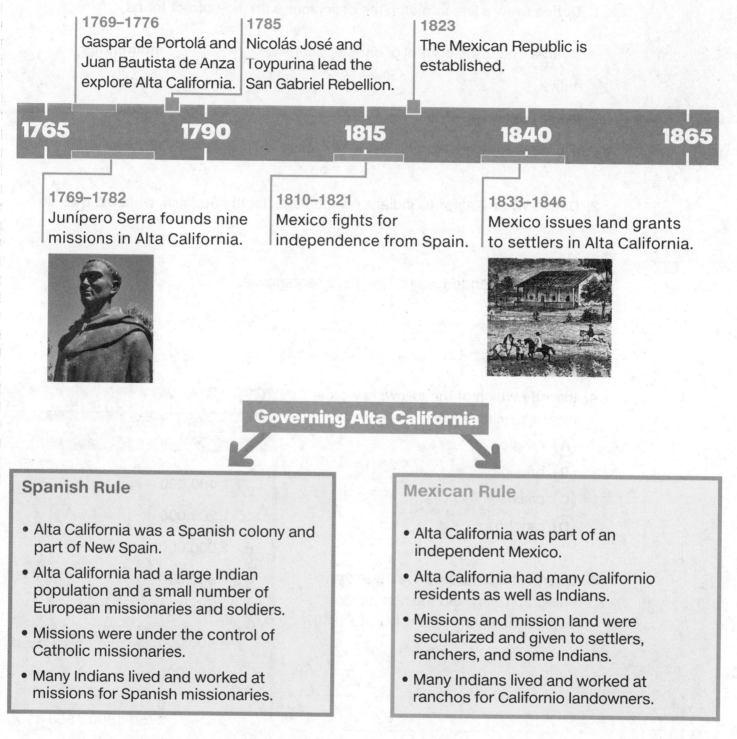

Governing Alta California

Spanish Rule

- Alta California was a Spanish colony and part of New Spain.

- Alta California had a large Indian population and a small number of European missionaries and soldiers.

- Missions were under the control of Catholic missionaries.

- Many Indians lived and worked at missions for Spanish missionaries.

Mexican Rule

- Alta California was part of an independent Mexico.

- Alta California had many Californio residents as well as Indians.

- Missions and mission land were secularized and given to settlers, ranchers, and some Indians.

- Many Indians lived and worked at ranchos for Californio landowners.

☑ **Assessment**

🎮 GAME

Play the vocabulary game.

Vocabulary and Key Ideas 🕐 **HSS** 4.2.3, 4.2.7 **ELA** RI.4.4, L.4.4

1. **Define** Draw a line to match the definitions with the correct terms.

   an area under the control of another country   **indigenous**

   native   **republic**

   family relationship   **colony**

   a form of government with elected officials   **kinship**

2. **Define** When California Indians revolted against the Spanish, what did they do?

   _____

3. **Define** independence and use it in a sentence. _____

   _____

   _____

4. **Identify** Which of the following words means a military fort?

   (A) mission

   (B) presidio

   (C) *diseño*

   (D) rancho

5. **Interpret a Line Graph** Analyze the line graph. How did the non-Indian population change from 1770 to 1849?

   _____

   _____

   _____

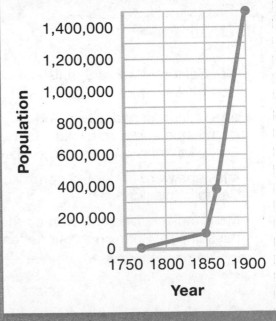

Non-Indian Population of California, 1770–1900

* Source: California State Parks: Office of Historic Preservation

HSS 4.2.3, 4.2.5, 4.2.7 **Analysis**
CST.3 **ELA** RI.4.1, RI.4.3

6. **Determine the Cause** Which of the following led directly to the secularization of Spanish missions in California?

Ⓐ Indian revolts at several missions

Ⓑ Increased immigration from the United States

Ⓒ Mexican independence

Ⓓ A declining number of missionaries

7. **Analyze** How does Spanish settlement in the 1700s still affect your community or state?

_____

_____

_____

_____

8. **Analyze** Who influenced this period of California's history more: Spanish explorers, Spanish missionaries, or California Indian groups? Explain your answer.

_____

_____

_____

9. **Revisit the Big Question** How did the meeting of Spanish missionaries and California Indians shape our state's present and future?

_____

_____

_____

_____

10. **Writer's Workshop: Informative Text** On a separate piece of paper, write two paragraphs that explain how the lives of California Indians both changed and stayed the same during the Mission Period.

At sunrise the bell is rung, then they assemble in the church, recite the 'Doctrina' while they hear Holy Mass which is celebrated at the same time. When functions in the Church are ended, they go forth to their respective tasks. . . . At eleven or a little later, they take their 'pozole' [a kind of soup] and eat and rest until one or until two when they go forth another time, for their work; and before sunset they take another ration of [food]. The repast [meal] finished, the bell is rung once more, and they return to the church to pray, concluding as in the morning.

-a priest, at Mission San Antonio, 1812

11. Based on this missionary's account, which adjectives could be used to describe everyday life at a mission?

_____

_____

_____

Distinguish Fact From Opinion HSS 4.2.3

Exploring Alta California in the late 1700s was a fantastic experience. King Charles III sent explorers to establish settlements for the Spanish crown. They got to see a very beautiful place. They met California Indians. The whole experience probably amazed them.

12. On the lines below, identify one fact and one opinion. Then, explain how you know the difference.

_____

_____

_____

_____

_____

Quest Findings

Write Your Essay

You've read the lessons in this chapter and now you're ready to write your essay. Remember that the goal of your essay is to convince California's government to build a new Mission Museum. It would teach people about how the missions affected California's people. Use documents from this chapter to support your arguments.

1 Prepare to Write

Write your three strongest arguments and add facts to support them. Then write down which documents in the chapter will help you support your argument.

2 Write a Draft

Use your notes and the evidence from your Quest Connections to write the most persuasive essay you can. Make sure your essay answers the following questions:

- How were people's lives affected by the missions?
- Why is it important to understand the role of missions in California's history?

3 Share with a Partner

Exchange your draft essay with a partner. Tell your partner what you like about his or her essay and what could use improvement. Be polite when you provide suggestions.

4 Revise

Make changes to your essay after meeting up with your partner. Correct any grammatical or spelling errors.

GO ONLINE FOR
DIGITAL RESOURCES

▶ VIDEO

👆 INTERACTIVITY

🔊 AUDIO

🎮 GAMES

☑ ASSESSMENT

📖 ETEXT

The BIG Question How can change create opportunities?

▶ VIDEO

Many Americans moved to California during the Gold Rush in hopes of striking it rich. As a result, the state's population grew rapidly.

JumpStart Activity

👆 INTERACTIVITY

Think about a time when you were in a group and felt that change was needed. When it is your turn, explain why a change was needed. If the change happened, walk to the left of the room. If the change did not happen, walk to the right of the room. Talk with your group about the change you thought was needed.

_____

_____

_____

_____

HSS 4.3.1, 4.3.2, 4.3.3, 4.3.4, 4.3.5, 4.4.2 **Analysis** CST.1, CST.3, HI.3, RE.3 **ELA** L.4.2, L.4.3, L.4.4, RI.4.1, RI.4.2, RI.4.3, RI.4.4, RI.4.5, RI.4.7, RF.4.4, W.4.1, W.4.2, W.4.3, W.4.7

♪ Rap About It! ♪

 AUDIO

Gold Rush!

Preview the chapter **vocabulary** as you sing the rap:

Trailblazers from across the land

Packed their belongings and began

Making new routes to get to this location.

Traveling was hard, not like a vacation.

When gold was found, then **miners** came.

They found a good spot and staked out a **claim**.

Using picks and shovels they dug for gold,

Each one of them hoping to find a **lode**.

So many people came in a short time,

Boomtowns were a thing you would find.

Small towns would grow very fast,

Most of them were not built to last.

The Gold Rush and Statehood

Where was gold discovered in California in 1848?

It was found at Sutter's Mill, near modern-day Sacramento.

A nugget of gold discovered in California during the Gold Rush

TODAY
You can visit the site where gold was discovered at Marshall Gold Discovery State Historic Park.

Map labels:
Sutter's Mill
Fort Ross
Sutter's Fort
San Francisco
Monterey
California
Santa Barbara
San Diego

What happened and When?

Read the timeline to find out about the events surrounding the Gold Rush and California's journey to statehood.

1845　　**1846**　　**1847**

April
Mexican-American War breaks out.

Who will you meet?

James Wilson Marshall

a carpenter who discovered gold in 1848 and started the California Gold Rush

John C. Fremont

an American explorer and soldier who fought Mexico for control of California

Mariano Guadalupe Vallejo

a Californio leader who helped write California's first constitution

Biddy Mason

an enslaved woman who won her freedom and became a successful nurse and entrepreneur in Los Angeles

January
Gold discovered at Sutter's Mill.

INTERACTIVITY

Complete the interactive map digital activity.

1848

1849

1850

February
War with Mexico ends; California becomes part of the United States.

September
California becomes a U.S. state.

TODAY
California has more people than any other state.

Quest
Project-Based Learning

From Gold to Golden State
Quest Kick Off

Hi! My name's John. I'm going to California to get rich mining gold! While I'm there, I'm going to collect things to show in a museum exhibit. Will you help me? Your mission is to find things, quotes, or images to display in an exhibit about how California changed during the Gold Rush and when it became a state.

1

Plan Your Exhibit

Think about the kinds of things you can find in a museum. Identify and write three different things here.

....

....

....

....

....

Get Organized

HSS 4.3.3, 4.3.4, 4.3.5, 4.4.2
ELA L.4.2, L.4.3, W.4.2

How might a museum organize an exhibit? What items from your list might go in the same room?

....

....

....

....

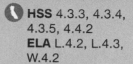

INTERACTIVITY

Preview ideas and images related to the Gold Rush and California's statehood.

3 Look for

Quest Connections

Turn to the next page to begin looking for Quest Connections that will help you create your museum exhibit.

4 **Quest** Findings
Create Your Exhibit

Use the Quest Findings page at the end of this chapter to help you and your group create your museum exhibit.

California Becomes a U.S. Territory

INTERACTIVITY

Participate in a class discussion to preview the content of this lesson.

Vocabulary

immigrate
trailblazer
wagon train
mountain man

Academic Vocabulary

influence
challenge
authority

Unlock The BIG Question

I will know how American and other settlers came to California while it was under Mexican rule and how California became part of the United States.

Jumpstart Activity

With your group, act out what it might look like to travel across a mountain, through the desert, or by ship.

You have learned that California was once a part of Mexico. But you know that today it is part of the United States. How did this happen?

Coming to California

During the years of Mexican rule, a small number of Mexican settlers moved to California. Like the Spanish before them, they settled near the coast. They moved to places like San Diego, Santa Barbara, and San Francisco. These cities all grew due to Mexican settlement.

Americans also moved to California when it was part of Mexico. The early 1800s were a time of growth for the United States. Americans moved to California for economic reasons.

Some new California settlers were farmers hoping to find land. Others were fur trappers. That meant they wanted to trap animals and sell their fur. Still others wanted to make money by trading and selling supplies to other settlers. Some eastern farmers came to California because they could not buy land to farm where they lived.

Some people came to California from places farther away than the United States. These people also immigrated for economic reasons. To **immigrate** means to come to another country to live.

In the 1700s, people from Russia, a country across the Pacific Ocean, came to Alaska and settled there. They caught seals and sea otters and sold their fur. Hoping to find more of these animals, the Russians moved southeast into California. By 1812, they had built a fur-trading post at Fort Ross. Fort Ross is on the Pacific coast about 70 miles north of San Francisco. The Russians also grew crops and raised animals around Fort Ross.

However, by the 1820s, the sea otter population was slowly being used up. Trade became difficult as new settlers arrived. Also, relations with the Mexican government were tense. As a result, the Russians left Fort Ross. Today, people can visit the state park there and learn more about the Russian **influence** on California's early history.

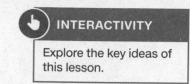
HSS 4.3.1, 4.3.2, 4.3.5
Analysis CST.3, HI.3 **ELA** RI.4.1, RI.4.3, RI.4.5, RF.4.4

INTERACTIVITY

Explore the key ideas of this lesson.

1. ☑ **Reading Check**
Underline a sentence that connects the past to the present. **Interpret** what has changed and what has stayed the same and discuss this with a partner.

Academic Vocabulary

influence • *n.*, effect, impact

Fort Ross was built by Russian settlers in 1812.

Trailblazers

Travelers going from the eastern United States to California had to find new routes across the continent. These explorers were trailblazers. A **trailblazer** is someone who finds or makes a new path between places.

Trailblazers had the difficult task of crossing hot deserts, jagged mountains, and rushing rivers. However, they were often helped by American Indians. In California, trailblazers followed paths used by California Indians. At this time, there more than 100,000 California Indians living in the state.

Jedediah Strong Smith was another trailblazer. Smith was the first American to journey into California over land and then also leave it by land. In 1826, he led a group of trappers across the Mojave Desert. After they received help from a California Indian village and two Indian guides, they safely reached Mission San Gabriel east of Los Angeles. After Smith's expedition, hundreds of American settlers followed.

This photograph from 1845 shows explorer John C. Fremont (left) and the mountain man who guided him, Kit Carson (right).

In 1841, a young teacher named John Bidwell organized a party, or group, to travel to California. They left from Independence, Missouri. Bidwell's group was the first to travel by wagon train to California. A **wagon train** was a group of covered wagons that traveled together over a long distance. Some wagon trains were made up of 100 wagons!

The Bidwell party struggled for six months over the Rocky Mountains and the Sierra Nevada before finally arriving in the Central Valley. Bidwell's route later became known as the California Trail. Bidwell wrote articles describing this expedition.

In 1842, the United States government sent a soldier named John C. Fremont into the Rocky Mountains to map and survey the land. Fremont would make a total of four trips to the American West. During his second trip, which began in 1843, he explored areas north and east of California. Then, he traveled south into present-day Nevada. Finally, he made a dangerous winter crossing over the Sierra Nevada and arrived at Fort Sutter, in what is now Sacramento, in March, 1844. It was Fremont's first trip into California.

Kit Carson, a western trapper and guide, helped Fremont and his group arrive safely. Carson had become famous as a **mountain man**. Mountain men worked as trappers and guided others in the West. Carson later used his guiding skills to help American troops in the Mexican-American War.

James Beckwourth was another skilled mountain man. He led settlers west in the 1850s by traveling through the lowest pass in the Sierra Nevada. Today, that pass is called Beckwourth Pass. The nearby town of Beckwourth is also named for him.

James Beckwourth was an African American mountain man who led settlers through the Sierra Nevada in the 1850s.

2. ☑ Reading Check **Identify** three trailblazers and write them in the order in which they explored the West. Write the year (or years) of their exploration as well.

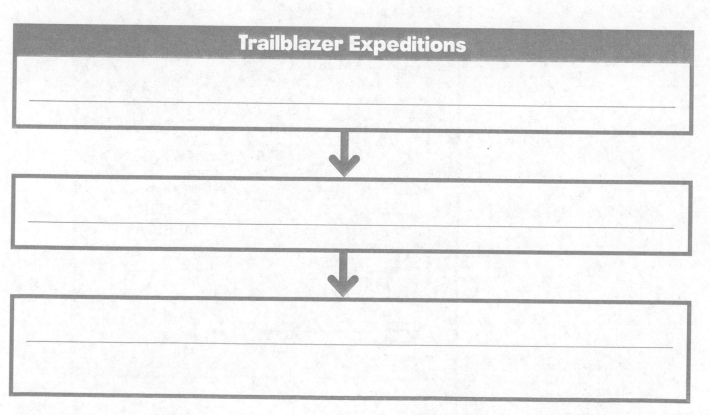

Trailblazer Expeditions

The Journey West

Some Americans from the East traveled to California by ship, though this was expensive. This 17,000-mile journey could take five to eight months. Ships had to travel around Cape Horn, at the tip of South America. Travelers could expect rough storms, freezing temperatures, seasickness, and little fresh food or water.

There was a shortcut, though. Travelers could sail to the Isthmus of Panama. This is a small strip of land in Central America. On one side is the Atlantic Ocean, and on the other is the Pacific Ocean. Travelers could sail to the Atlantic side, cross the isthmus by land, and then catch another boat on the Pacific side. This route was faster than the Cape Horn route. It took about two to three months.

Academic Vocabulary

challenge • *n.*, something that is hard to do

The Panama route cost more money, though. It also meant passing through a dangerous jungle. The jungle brought many **challenges**, such as poisonous snakes, insects, and diseases.

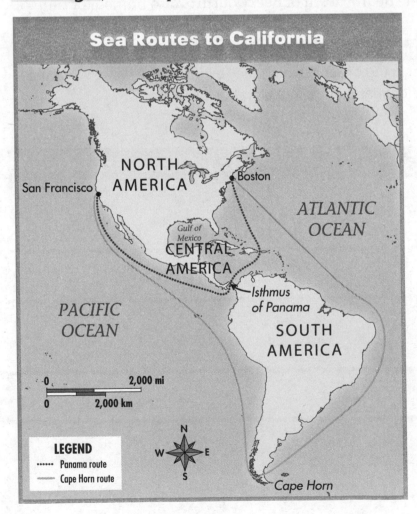

Sea Routes to California

NORTH AMERICA

San Francisco

Boston

ATLANTIC OCEAN

Gulf of Mexico

CENTRAL AMERICA

PACIFIC OCEAN

Isthmus of Panama

SOUTH AMERICA

0   2,000 mi
0   2,000 km

LEGEND
...... Panama route
——— Cape Horn route

N
W   E
S

Cape Horn

Whether they went around Cape Horn or through Panama, most travelers usually landed in San Francisco.

American settlers could also travel overland to get to California. Many hired guides like James Beckwourth to help them, or followed routes set by the trailblazers. Most traveled by horse or horse-drawn wagons, and trips could take many months. This type of transportation had its own dangers. Settlers had to cross steep mountains and dry deserts. It was often impossible to carry enough food and water. Maps could be inaccurate, and trails were rough and rocky. The desert heat caused many travelers to become sick. Disease also killed many settlers.

The Donner Party ran into many of these challenges. Traveling to California from Illinois in 1846, they met with dangerous winter storms in the Sierra Nevada. Unable to continue their trip because of heavy snow, they were trapped in the mountains for five months. Those who lived through the winter did not reach California until spring of 1847.

Few settlers traveled these dangerous routes during the early years. But after gold was discovered in California in 1848, many thousands would travel this way. You will read more about this later.

Overland Routes to California

LEGEND
- Jedediah Smith route
- James Beckwourth route
- John Bidwell route

3. ☑ **Reading Check** **Compare and Contrast** Work with a partner and discuss how the sea routes and the overland routes are similar and different.

The Mexican-American War

In the 1840s, many Americans believed that their country was destined to stretch from the Atlantic to the Pacific. They wanted to take control of California and other parts of Mexico. This idea was called Manifest Destiny. One important supporter of Manifest Destiny was President James K. Polk. He wanted California's rich, fertile land to belong to the United States. In fact, he tried and failed to purchase California from Mexico in 1845.

During the 1840s, Mexico and the United States disagreed over their border. Mexico once controlled Texas. American settlers there rebelled and Texas became independent. Then, in 1845, it became part of the United States. But Mexico and the United States did not agree about where the border between Texas and Mexico was. Mexico sent troops across the Rio Grande. Both the United States and Mexico believed they owned this area. This disagreement, along with idea of Manifest Destiny, led to conflict.

The United States declared war against Mexico on May 13, 1846. At that time, there were about 500 Americans living in California. Some of them had already decided they did not want California to be a part of Mexico any longer.

This painting is called "Raising the Bear Flag." It was painted about 100 years after the Bear Flag Revolt. Our state flag today is based on the Bear Flag from 1846. What questions do you have about this painting?

Causes of the Mexican-American War

Cause	Effect
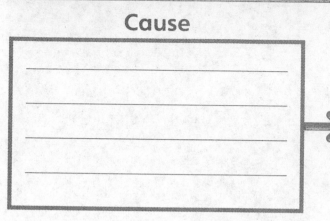 _____ _____ _____ _____	**The Mexican-American War**

At this time, soldier and explorer John C. Fremont was in southern Oregon. When he heard the news that war between the United States and Mexico had broken out, he headed south to Sutter's Fort. There, he encouraged local settlers to challenge Mexican **authorities**.

The settlers took matters into their own hands. They decided to go to the town of Sonoma, near San Francisco, and attack the Mexican authorities there. On June 14, 1846, they revolted and captured Sonoma. The rebels took the local Mexican military and political leader, Mariano Guadalupe Vallejo, prisoner. Vallejo, a Californio, was surprised at his treatment because he had been friendly with the local Americans.

The rebels made a flag with a rough drawing of a grizzly bear and a single red star on it. They raised it, and because of this, their revolt is called the Bear Flag Revolt.

On June 25, Fremont arrived in Sonoma with a small group of soldiers. The rebels asked Fremont to lead the new California Republic. About two weeks later, John Drake Sloat, an American naval commander, moved into the area with his troops. He had heard that the English and the Russians were planning to take control of the area. So, he and his troops captured San Francisco, Sonoma, and Monterey, the capital of Alta California. Facing no opposition from the local people in Monterey, they declared California to be part of the United States, not Mexico. The bear flag came down and was replaced by the American flag. The California Republic had lasted less than a month.

Academic Vocabulary

authority • _n._, a person in control of a place

4. ☑ **Reading Check**
Fill in the graphic organizer by **identifying** two causes of the Mexican-American War.

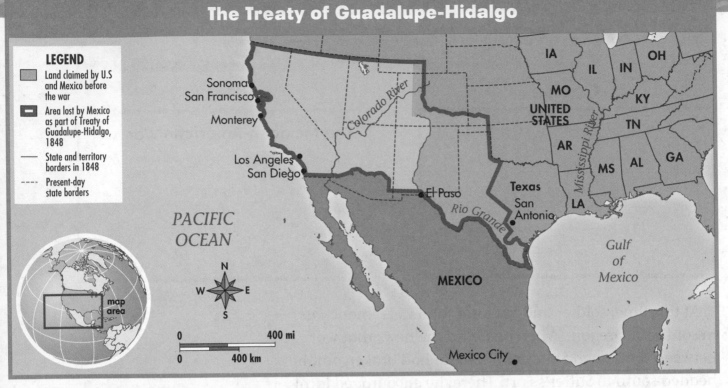

The Treaty of Guadalupe-Hidalgo

LEGEND

Land claimed by U.S and Mexico before the war

Area lost by Mexico as part of Treaty of Guadalupe-Hidalgo, 1848

State and territory borders in 1848

---- Present-day state borders

PACIFIC OCEAN

Sonoma
San Francisco
Monterey
Los Angeles
San Diego

Colorado River

El Paso
Rio Grande

Texas
San Antonio

UNITED STATES

IA
IL IN OH
MO KY
AR TN
MS AL GA
LA

Mississippi River

MEXICO

Gulf of Mexico

Mexico City

N W E S

0   400 mi
0   400 km

map area

---

5. ☑ **Reading Check**

Analyze the map.
Identify the land Mexico and the United States both claimed. Draw an X on that land.

Fighting in California

While most of the Mexican-American War was fought in Mexico, Alta California was not left out of the struggle. The governor of Alta California at this time was a Californio named Pío Pico. Pío Pico was born in Alta California to Mexican parents.

Pío Pico and his military leaders fought to keep Southern California, including Los Angeles, under Mexican rule. American forces were advancing from northern California, however.

After Commodore Sloat and his troops captured Monterey in the summer of 1846, John C. Fremont led his forces south and captured Los Angeles. Pío Pico fled to Mexico to avoid being taken prisoner by the Americans. But his brother, Andrés Pico, defeated the Americans in a fierce battle and took the city back.

In early 1847, however, the Americans recaptured Los Angeles. Mexican forces in Alta California surrendered. Pío Pico would be the last governor of Alta California.

Cannons like this one were used during the Mexican-American War.

The End of the War

By 1848, American forces had invaded Mexico and won the war. It ended in February, 1848, when the two sides signed the Treaty of Guadalupe-Hidalgo. A treaty is an agreement between countries. Under the treaty, the United States took control of much of northern Mexico. California was part of this land, along with much of what is now the southwestern United States. This land became an unorganized territory, not a state. That meant it was run by American military leaders.

According to the treaty, Californios became citizens of the United States. However, they faced many serious challenges. For example, many lost ownership of their land even though the treaty said they could keep it. Among the few who kept their land was Pío Pico. Pico owned hundreds of thousands of acres of land in the Los Angeles area, as well as a fancy hotel.

6. ☑ **Reading Check**
Turn to a partner and **summarize** life for Californios after the end of the war.

☑ **Lesson 1 Check**

 **HSS** 4.3.1, 4.3.2, 4.3.5
ELA RI.4.1, RI.4.3, RI.4.5, RF.4.4

👆 **INTERACTIVITY**

Check your understanding of the key ideas of this lesson.

7. **Compare and Contrast Explain** how the journey to California through Panama was similar to, and different from, the voyage around Cape Horn.

_____

_____

_____

8. **Describe** Fort Ross's location and the people who built and settled it.

_____

_____

_____

9. **Explain** why Mariano Guadalupe Vallejo was jailed during the Mexican-American War.

_____

_____

_____

Distinguish Fact From Fiction

A **fact** is information that can be proved true or false. Texts that inform or educate should contain a lot of facts. You learned many facts in the lesson you just read. For example, you read that the United States and Mexico went to war in 1846. That is a fact that you can check. You can find primary source documents that describe the start of the war, such as newspapers from the time.

Fiction is very different. Fictional stories can tell about imaginary people or events. Fictional stories can include facts, but they do not have to. For example, a writer might tell a story about something that actually happened to her, but she could change the ending if she likes.

Historical fiction is a kind of writing that tells made-up stories set in the past. They may be based on real events, but the story (or part of it) is not real. For example, Sid Fleishman wrote about a boy traveling by sea to California. The passage shown here is from his book, *By the Great Horn Spoon!* It sounds as if it could be true, but Fleishman made it clear that it is historical fiction. It is a story based on history, but it is not a true story.

Historical fiction can help you imagine past events in a new way, and it can be a fun way to read about history. But remember, it is fiction, not fact! Never use historical fiction as your source for learning about a topic or a period from history.

> ▶ **VIDEO**
>
> Watch a video about distinguishing fact from fiction.

A sailing ship with two great sidewheels went splashing out of Boston harbor on a voyage around the Horn to San Francisco. Below decks, in the creaking darkness of her cargo hold, there sat eighteen barrels of potatoes. Inside two barrels, side by side, there squatted two stowaways.

–from *By the Great Horn Spoon!*, by Sid Fleischman

1. Write about something that happened at school last week that is fact and can be proven.

_____

_____

_____

_____

2. Review what you wrote and underline the phrases and sentences that can be proven.

3. Now write about the same event, but add fictional details or characters. Change what you wrote so that it is now fiction and more of a story than fact.

_____

_____

_____

_____

4. Follow your teacher's instructions to research a primary source describing a trip to California by one of the trailblazers you read about. Then compare it with the passage on the previous page. Which one can you use as a source for learning about California's history?

_____

_____

2 The Gold Rush

Unlock The BIG Question

I will know how the Gold Rush affected California, its people, and the world.

Vocabulary

miner
entrepreneur
foreigner
tax
claim
prospector
lode
boomtown

Academic Vocabulary

discover
individual
erode

JumpStart Activity

Play a class game in which someone thinks of an exciting bit of news and whispers it to a classmate. Then, that classmate whispers it to someone else, and so on until everyone in the class has received the news. How fast does the news travel to everyone in your class?

Gold miners came to the American River near Sacramento to mine for gold. They brought picks, shovels, and pans.

Remember that the United States had recently taken control of California. American miners claimed that this meant they should benefit most from the gold discovery. They did not like that miners were coming from other countries.

Americans mistreated **foreigners**, or people from other countries. They forced foreign miners to leave, attacking and robbing those who refused.

California's government treated foreign miners differently from Americans. It began charging a foreign miners' **tax** in 1850. A tax is money paid to a government. Anyone who was not an American had to pay $20 a month to mine for gold. A second tax of $3 per month was passed in 1852. It was aimed at Chinese miners.

American miners used violence against foreign miners. They attacked Spanish-speaking miners from Mexico and Chile. They burned down the houses of Chinese miners, and killed some. As a result of all this, Chinese miners left the mines and began working other jobs. Thousands of Mexican miners returned to their homes because of unfair treatment.

Life as a Miner

As soon as miners arrived, they would "stake their claim." A **claim** is an official right to own something, such as an area of land. Miners had the right to mine for gold on their claim. Miners were also called **prospectors**. A prospector is someone who looks for a natural resource.

Searching for gold was hard, physical work. Miners wrote of moving large rocks for hours, digging in dirt, and wading in ice-cold streams all day. They had to use heavy shovels and picks. They lost fingernails and had their fingers crushed.

Panning is one way of finding gold buried in the dirt beneath a river. Miners would scoop up dirt and water from the river in a flat-bottomed pan and swirl it around. The heavier gold would stay in the bottom of the pan and everything else would wash over the side.

2. ☑ **Reading Check**
Identify and underline one way that the government treated foreign miners differently.

Today, tourists can learn how to pan for gold, just like the Gold Rush miners did.

Academic Vocabulary

individual • *adj.*, single, separate

3. ☑ **Reading Check**
Underline and **identify** the impact of hydraulic mining on the environment.

Few miners got rich. Some miners ended up with just a pinch of gold dust. A "pinch" was what a person could squeeze between their thumb and forefinger. During the Gold Rush, miners paid for things using gold. If a miner was lucky enough to have found gold nuggets, shopkeepers used scales to weigh them.

A **lode** is a deposit of gold or other metal or mineral trapped in rock. A large area rich in minerals is called a mother lode. There was an important mother lode that ran through the Sierra Nevada.

Hydraulic mining became popular in the 1850s, especially in the mother lode area. This was a way of mining under mountains using water from rivers and streams. Large areas could be mined quickly with fewer miners this way, but it ruined farmland, rivers, and streams.

Prospectors could pan for gold by themselves or in small groups. But it took big companies with lots of money to set up hydraulic mines. **Individual** miners could not compete with them. Some of these frustrated miners simply went home when they realized they were not going to get rich. Some were unable to leave California because they could not afford to travel. Some stayed because they found other opportunities.

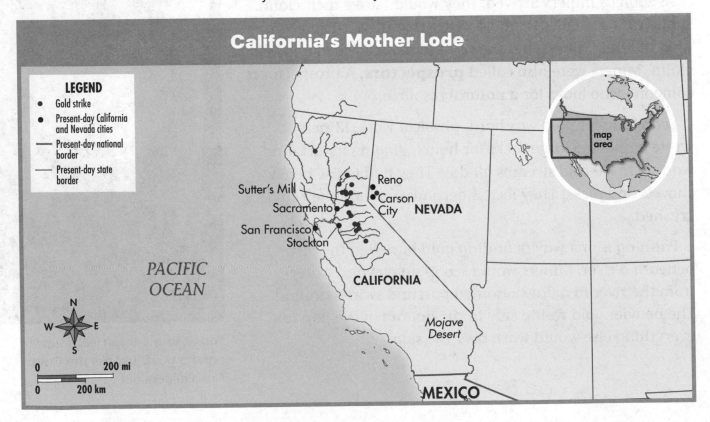

California's Mother Lode

LEGEND
- Gold strike
- Present-day California and Nevada cities
- Present-day national border
- Present-day state border

Sutter's Mill
Reno
Carson City
Sacramento
NEVADA
San Francisco
Stockton
PACIFIC OCEAN
CALIFORNIA
Mojave Desert
MEXICO

N W E S

0   200 mi
0   200 km

map area

Cities and the Economy Grow

The Gold Rush brought sudden wealth to California, and to its major cities in particular. However, California's economy was not ready to meet the needs of thousands of newcomers.

Entrepreneurs Profit

The miners needed everything from mining supplies to tents, food, and clothing. California did not have enough of everything to go around. Prices rose, and miners ended up spending much of what they earned to pay for their supplies. For example, a dozen eggs might cost $90 in today's dollars!

Entrepreneurs saw an opportunity. They started new businesses to support the miners. They opened restaurants and hotels, and produced and sold supplies and clothing. Levi Strauss, a German Jewish immigrant, did not strike it rich as a gold miner. But his tough denim pants with metal rivets were very big sellers with the miners. His company's jeans are still popular today!

San Francisco: The Golden Gate

Even before the Gold Rush, John C. Fremont named the entrance to San Francisco Bay the "golden gate" because he saw the bay as "a golden gate to trade" with countries in Asia across Pacific Ocean. That was in July of 1846.

San Francisco grew rapidly during the Gold Rush and was a busy, bustling city by 1849.

Quest Connections

Study the picture of San Francisco. In what ways does it show how California changed because of the Gold Rush?

INTERACTIVITY

Study a quote from the Gold Rush era.

In 1847, San Francisco was still a small village with 800 people. The discovery of gold turned it into a city almost overnight. Since it was the main port for travelers coming by ship to the gold fields, it filled up with people from all over the world. By December of 1849, it had 25,000 people.

San Francisco during the Gold Rush was a city dotted with shacks and tents instead of houses. Gambling houses, restaurants, and hotels made plenty of money, so these buildings were nicer than others. Politicians and law enforcement tried to gain control over crime and the growing population.

Sacramento: Supply Center

In 1841, John Sutter built his fort in what is now Sacramento. But the city did not exist at that time. It was founded in 1849, fueled by the Gold Rush. Miners stopped there to buy supplies as they went into the mother lode area. The economy grew as stores, hotels, and warehouses for supplies were built. Because the city was located on the American and Sacramento Rivers, supplies could be sent easily by boat.

Negative Effects of the Gold Rush

While a few newcomers to California grew rich from the Gold Rush, Northern California's Indians suffered. Natural resources that provided food and shelter were ruined by mining. Miners forced Indians from their homes. If they refused to leave their land, miners burned down their homes and even killed them. Some Indians fought back and raided mining towns and settlements.

4. ☑ **Reading Check**
Turn to a partner and **discuss** how Sacramento changed during the Gold Rush.

This photo shows a way the Gold Rush impacted California's environment. Trees were cut down for lumber and to make room for mining camps.

In 1850, California passed the Indenture Act. An indentured person is forced to work for someone else for a set period of time. Under this act, California Indians, mostly young people, were forced to work for landowners.

About 100,000 Indians lived in California in 1848 when the Gold Rush started. By 1860, only about 30,000 Indians were left in California. Many died from disease and starvation. Most died from violent attacks.

The Gold Rush hurt the environment. Hydraulic mining **eroded** large areas, turning mountainsides into stones, sand, and mud. These were carried down into valleys by melting snow. Rivers and streams became clogged and polluted. Flooding became a serious problem, hurting farmers. Fish that lived in the rivers died.

Miners needed lumber to build camps, to set up mines, and to build up cities and towns. They cut down trees in the Central Valley to get what they needed.

Academic Vocabulary

erode • *v.*, to gradually destroy

5. ☑ Reading Check Fill in the chart by **identifying** the effects of the Gold Rush.

Effects of the Gold Rush	
How the Gold Rush Affected...	**Effects**
San Francisco	
California Indians	
the environment	

Gender During the Gold Rush

Biddy Mason was a successful entrepreneur.

Most of the forty-niners were men, but women came to California, too. At this time, many jobs were usually done only by men. But because so many men were involved in mining, women in California often did these jobs. Women mined, owned businesses, and became entrepreneurs.

Sarah Royce came to California in 1849 by wagon train with her husband and two-year-old daughter. When they arrived in California, they were unable to make money from mining and struggled. Royce became a school teacher and published a book called *A Frontier Lady* based on a diary she kept.

Biddy Mason was an entrepreneur. She was an enslaved African American born in Mississippi. She moved to California in 1851 and won her freedom there in 1856. She worked as a nurse and eventually became one of the first African American women to own land in Los Angeles. She became wealthy and used her money to help the poor. She helped found Los Angeles's first African American church.

One person who was born female but lived as a man, worked as a stagecoach driver. Charley Parkhurst was one of the best stagecoach drivers in the business and was well-known throughout California. Stagecoaches are a type of wagon used to carry passengers, goods, or mail. Parkhurst survived more than one robbery and even killed a thief. After driving a stagecoach for almost 30 years, Parkhurst died in 1879.

Stagecoaches were an important way for people to travel and communicate.

In 1849, Louise Clapp and her husband moved to San Francisco. They lived in two very rough mining camps that grew quickly into **boomtowns**. Boomtowns are towns that suddenly grow because of new business and population. Very few women lived in boomtowns. Clapp wrote letters to her sister describing her life that are still important to historians.

Another woman whose writing is considered a valuable historical resource is Maria Angustias de la Guerra. She was a Californio who lived through the Mexican-American War and the Gold Rush. In *Occurrences in Hispanic California*, she describes her experiences during these years.

6. ☑ **Reading Check** Imagine you are going to interview a woman who lived during the Gold Rush. **Identify** questions you have about what it was like to live during the Gold Rush. Then turn to a partner and ask them.

The writings of Maria Angustias de la Guerra have helped people learn more about life during the Gold Rush.

☑ **Lesson 2 Check**　🔊 **HSS** 4.3.3, 4.4.2 **ELA** RI.4.1, RI.4.2, RI.4.3, RF.4.4

👆 **INTERACTIVITY**

Check your understanding of the key ideas of this lesson.

7. **Distinguish Fact From Fiction** Re-read the section called "Life as a Miner." **Identify** one fact about a miner's daily life.

_____

_____

8. **Evaluate** whether the Gold Rush was a positive or negative event for California. Cite facts to support your answer.

_____

_____

_____

9. **Understand the** *Quest* **Connections** **Describe** one event that happened during the Gold Rush era that changed California.

_____

_____

Luzena Stanley Wilson '49er

In the spring of 1849, Luzena Stanley Wilson packed her two sons into a wagon and left Missouri with her husband. They were on their way to California to find gold. The family survived hunger, thirst, and disease and made it to California. She became a successful entrepreneur, helping to build a hotel. Wilson told her experiences to her daughter in 1881, and her daughter wrote them down and published them.

This is an artist's view of Luzena Stanley Wilson.

Vocabulary Support

in a place lit by pine torches

rival • *adj.*, competing
precious • *adj.*, very valuable
provisions • *n.*, supplies
permanent • *adj.*, lasting

"I determined to set up a rival hotel. So I bought two boards from a precious pile belonging to a man who was building the second wooden house in town. With my own hands I chopped stakes, drove them into the ground, and set up my table. I bought provisions at a neighboring store, and when my husband came back at night he found, mid the weird light of the pine torches, twenty miners eating at my table. Each man as he rose put a dollar in my hand and said I might count him as a permanent customer. I called my hotel 'El Dorado.'"

— Luzena Stanley Wilson, *Luzena Stanley Wilson '49er; Her Memoirs as Taken Down by Her Daughter in 1881*

Fun Fact

Luzena Stanley Wilson was once offered $10 for a biscuit. Ten dollars in the mid-1800s would be more than $300 today. That's an expensive biscuit!

Close Reading

HSS 4.3.3, 4.3.4, 4.4.2
ELA RI.4.1, RI.4.2, W.4.1

1. What can you **infer** about the town that Wilson lived in from the first sentence? Think about the term *rival hotel*.

_____

2. **Explain** why you think Wilson describes her boards as coming from a "precious pile."

_____

_____

3. **Write** one question you would ask Wilson if you had the chance to interview her.

_____

_____

_____

_____

Wrap It Up

Why do you think Wilson was successful as an entrepreneur during the Gold Rush? Support your opinion by **analyzing** information on other entrepreneurs in Lesson 2 and supporting your reason with details. Use one quotation from the selection shown here.

_____

_____

_____

_____

_____

Lesson 3 — Statehood

INTERACTIVITY

Participate in a class discussion to preview the content of this lesson.

Vocabulary

constitution
constitutional convention
delegate
slavery
compromise
fugitive
civil war

Academic Vocabulary

draft
persist

Unlock The BIG Question

I will know how California became a state and wrote its first constitution.

JumpStart Activity

Work in a group and come up with a new rule for your classroom. After deciding on the rule, discuss with a partner what was challenging and what was fun about working in a group.

After the Mexican-American War, California became part of the United States. But it was not a state yet. If Californians wanted a voice in the United States government, they would have to write a constitution and become a state.

California's flag

California Forms a Government

HSS 4.3.3, 4.3.5 ELA RI.4.1, RI.4.2, RI.4.3, RI.4.4, RF.4.4

During and after the Mexican-American War, California was led by military governors. Bennett Riley was the last one. He called a meeting in 1849 to create a state **constitution**. A constitution is a written plan for government.

At that special meeting, called a **constitutional convention**, 48 people met in Monterey to write California's constitution. These people, called **delegates**, were chosen to make decisions about government. All the delegates were men, and none were California Indians. Six delegates, however, were Californios. Mariano Guadalupe Vallejo was one of the Californio delegates. Remember that he was a Mexican leader imprisoned during the Bear Flag Revolt. The delegates had many important decisions to make. The most pressing issue was slavery.

Slavery is the practice of buying and selling people like property and forcing them to work without pay. In the past, many people from Africa were sold into slavery in the Americas. By the 1800s, most enslaved Africans in the United States worked on large farms called plantations in the south. Southerners wanted slavery to be allowed in the new western lands. Many northerners wanted to end slavery. California's delegates decided they would not allow slavery.

The delegates made other decisions, too. They set California's eastern boundary where it is today. They limited the vote to only white men. Women and non-white men, including California Indians, could not vote. The delegates' decisions were included in the state constitution. Because Californios still had some political power, it was **drafted** in their language, Spanish, as well as in English.

The new California constitution set up three branches of state government. The executive branch included the governor and people who work for the governor. They make sure people follow laws. The legislative branch included the State Assembly and Senate. They make laws. The judicial branch included the state Supreme Court and other courts. They help decide what laws mean. California's government still has these three branches though its constitution was replaced in 1879.

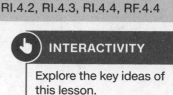
INTERACTIVITY

Explore the key ideas of this lesson.

1. ☑ **Reading Check**
Identify any images or words on the flag that you have already studied by marking them with an X. Turn to a partner and explain the meaning of one of the images or words.

Academic Vocabulary

draft • *v.*, to make an early version or plan of something

California Becomes a State

Once California's constitution was drafted, it had to be approved by the United States government in Washington, D.C. If this happened, California could become a state. The slavery issue, however, **persisted**.

When California's constitution came up for approval, the United States was divided. Fifteen states, called slave states, allowed slavery. Fifteen others, the free states, did not. The United States government wanted to keep this balance. If California became a free state, that would upset the balance.

After almost a year, Congress passed the Compromise of 1850. A **compromise** happens when each side gives up something to reach an agreement. The southern states agreed to accept California as a free state. The northern states agreed to a new law, the Fugitive Slave Act. A **fugitive** is a person trying to escape something, such as slavery. The new law required people in free states to help return any enslaved people who tried to gain their freedom by running away to the north. The California Constitution was approved and California became the 31st state on September 9, 1850.

Academic Vocabulary

persist • *v.*, to continue to exist

2. ☑ **Reading Check**
Summarize Turn to a partner and **discuss** the events that decided whether California would allow slavery.

California: Free State or Slave State?

Step 1: Convention delegates decided that California

_____

_____

⬇

Step 2: The Compromise of 1850 said that California could become a state and that

_____

_____

⬇

Step 3: California became a state on September 9, 1850.

California's state government was different from its governments under Spanish and Mexican rule. In the past, Spanish and then Mexican officials chose California's leaders. Then American military governors led the region. But after statehood, those Californians who could vote chose their own governors.

Californios, California Indians, and Their Land

As you learned, Californios became United States citizens after the Mexican-American War. But, under American rule, they lost much of their land. In 1850, Californios owned about 14 million acres of land. Their land grants, however, had been issued by the Mexican government. In 1851, the United States government passed the Land Act. This law forced Californios to prove land ownership by showing all their paperwork.

Obeying the Land Act was a long and expensive process for Californios. They had to hire costly lawyers to help them. They had to pay new American taxes on their land. Even after doing all this, the government might not approve their land grant.

Californios who did win their land sometimes had no money left after paying lawyers. They had to move off their land anyway. For example, Mariano Guadalupe Vallejo lost almost all of his land even though he was an important Californio leader.

California Indians also lost land after statehood. The government wanted their land for mining and other businesses. It took most of their land except for small reservations, or land recognized as being under Indian control. However, Indian reservations were on very poor land.

Like many Californios, Mariano Guadalupe Vallejo lost his land because of the Land Act of 1851.

Quest Connections

How does Mariano Guadalupe Vallejo's life show how California changed after it became a state?

INTERACTIVITY

Analyze a quote from this era.

California and the Civil War

The Battle of Gettysburg was a key victory for the Union.

In 1861, a **civil war** broke out in the United States. A civil war is a war between two sides within the same country. Several southern states decided to form their own new country, which we call the Confederacy. They fought against the remaining northern states, called the Union. The Civil War lasted from 1861 to 1865. About 620,000 people were killed. Eventually, the Union won and the country was brought back together.

California did not join the Confederacy. Instead, it helped the Union win the war. California sent ships filled with gold from San Francisco to Washington, D.C. This helped the Union pay for supplies it needed. California gold paid for soldiers' food, clothing, and weapons.

California also sent money to the United States Sanitary Commission. This group was responsible for providing medical care for Union soldiers. Many in Washington, including President Abraham Lincoln, were grateful.

Primary Source

I have long desired to see California; the production of her gold mines has been a marvel to me ... nothing would give me more pleasure than a visit to the Pacific shore, and to say in person ... "God bless you for your devotion to the Union."

-Abraham Lincoln, speaking to the Superintendent of Indian Affairs for California, March 25, 1865

Unlike eastern states such as New York or Virginia, California did not send large numbers of troops to fight for either side. However, it sent money to pay for a brigade, or group of soldiers. The soldiers in the California Brigade came from the area around Philadelphia, Pennsylvania, not from California. The California Brigade played an important role in the Battle of Gettysburg.

Although California remained loyal to the Union, many Californians supported the Confederacy. In early 1861, a group came together in Los Angeles and formed the Los Angeles Mounted Rifles to fight for the Confederacy.

Several Union leaders in the war had strong ties to California. You have already read about the trailblazer and soldier John C. Fremont. He served as a Union general. So did William T. Sherman. He was in California when gold was found. He helped check that the gold discovered at Sutter's Mill was real. Then, he spread the word about the discovery. During the Civil War, General Sherman led Union troops in many important battles.

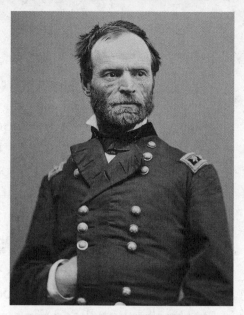

William T. Sherman was an important Union general during the Civil War. Sherman lived and worked in California before the war.

3. ☑ **Reading Check** **Use Evidence From Text** Highlight phrases that **identify** how California helped the Union.

☑ **Lesson 3 Check** 🕐 **HSS** 4.3.5 **ELA** RI.4.1, RI.4.2, RI.4.3, RF.4.4

👆 **INTERACTIVITY**

Check your understanding of the key ideas of this lesson.

4. **Explain** what free and slave states agreed to in the Compromise of 1850.

_____

_____

5. **Summarize** how life for California Indians changed after statehood.

_____

_____

6. **Understand the** *Quest* Connections **Describe** how life changed for Californios after statehood.

_____

_____

Interpret Timelines

VIDEO
Watch a video about interpreting timelines.

All the dates you see in a book about history can be confusing. It can be helpful to see them written down on a timeline. A timeline is a tool that names different events and shows when each event happened. Using a timeline helps you picture the sequence, or order, in which the events happened. Timelines also help you see how events are related.

To read a timeline, first look at its title to learn the topic of the timeline. Read the events and note the date that they happened. The timeline below shows key events in California history. Horizontal timelines run from left to right, which means that the older events are shown on the left and the more recent events are shown on the right. You may see other timelines that run vertically from top to bottom. This means that the older events start at the top, with more recent events at the bottom.

Use this timeline to help you answer the questions on the following page.

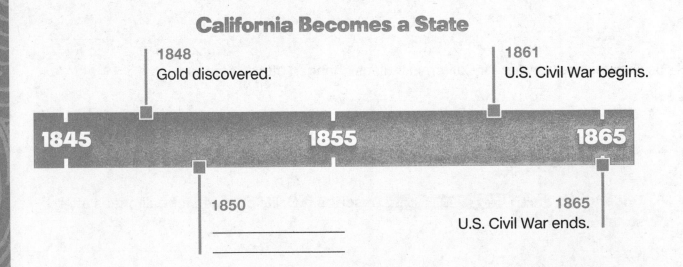

California Becomes a State

1848
Gold discovered.

1861
U.S. Civil War begins.

| 1845 | 1855 | 1865 |

1850
_____
_____

1865
U.S. Civil War ends.

1. There is a very important event in California history missing from the timeline. **Identify** it and write it on the lines provided on the timeline.

2. **Identify** and circle the year on the timeline in which the U.S. Civil War ended.

3. **Identify** how many years passed between when gold was discovered and when California became a state.

_____

4. Which event on the timeline happened first: gold being discovered or the beginning of the U.S. Civil War?

_____

5. In the space below, draw your own horizontal timeline. Fill it in with three or four events from your own life. Be sure to show the year in which each event happened.

★ Citizenship

Quality:
Problem Solving

Bernarda Ruiz

Bernarda Ruiz (1802–1880)
Making Peace in California

Bernarda Ruiz was a Californio who lived through the Mexican-American War. She was known for being both wise and bold. She was educated, a skilled communicator, and from a wealthy family. She worried about her sons, who were in the Mexican army. She wanted to help put an end to the war.

In early 1847, U.S. general John C. Fremont was traveling to Santa Barbara with 400 troops to fight the Mexican army. Ruiz arranged to meet with him before he launched his attack. She convinced him that he should be generous to the Californios. Fremont was an ambitious politician, and he might need their support later, she argued. Her thinking made sense to Fremont, and he took her advice.

Ruiz helped create the peace treaty and organized the meeting between Fremont and General Andrés Pico, the Californio leader. On January 13, 1847, Ruiz looked on as the Treaty of Cahuenga was signed by eight officials, including Fremont and Pico. The treaty brought California's involvement in the war to a peaceful end.

Fremont published his memoirs 40 years later and told the story of how Ruiz helped end the Mexican-American War in California.

Find Out More

1. Identify the problem Bernarda Ruiz was faced with and how she solved it.

_____

_____

_____

2. Bernarda Ruiz helped to solve a problem and end a conflict. Sadly, there are still wars going on in the world today. Follow your teacher's directions to research a current conflict. How did it start? How do you think it could be ended?

4 Visual Review

Use these graphics to review some of the vocabulary, people, and ideas from this chapter.

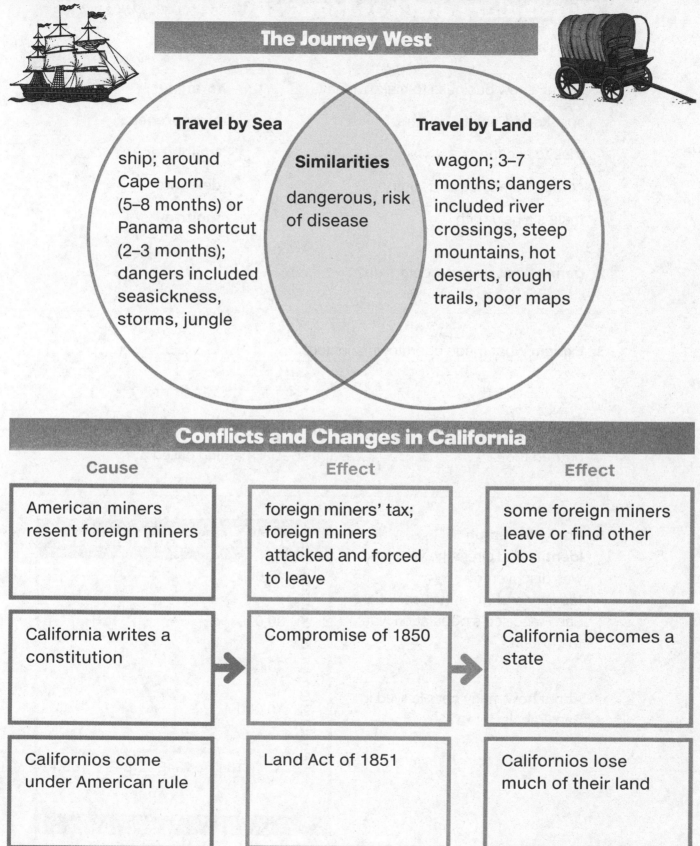

The Journey West

Travel by Sea

ship; around Cape Horn (5–8 months) or Panama shortcut (2–3 months); dangers included seasickness, storms, jungle

Similarities

dangerous, risk of disease

Travel by Land

wagon; 3–7 months; dangers included river crossings, steep mountains, hot deserts, rough trails, poor maps

Conflicts and Changes in California

Cause	Effect	Effect
American miners resent foreign miners	foreign miners' tax; foreign miners attacked and forced to leave	some foreign miners leave or find other jobs
California writes a constitution	Compromise of 1850	California becomes a state
Californios come under American rule	Land Act of 1851	Californios lose much of their land

Vocabulary and Key Ideas

🌀 **HSS** 4.3.3, 4.3.5, 4.4.2 **ELA** RI.4.7

1. Draw a line to match the definitions with the correct words.

starts a new business to make money   **foreigner**

speaks on behalf of others   **entrepreneur**

tries to escape   **trailblazer**

comes from another country   **delegate**

makes a new path   **fugitive**

2. Define What do prospectors do? _____

_____

3. Explain What made boomtowns unique? _____

_____

4. Identify Fill in the blanks to complete the sentence. California delegates

drafted the _____ at a special meeting called a

_____

5. Analyze a Graph
Identify and circle the year gold was discovered.
Identify and write the year where San Francisco's population was the lowest.

_____

About how many people lived in San Francisco in 1850?

_____

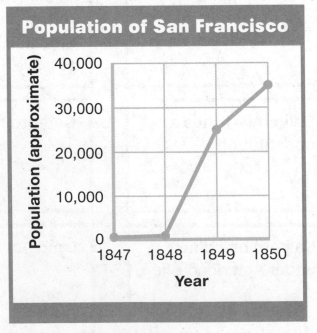

Population of San Francisco

Sources: UCSF, U.S. Census

Critical Thinking and Writing

HSS 4.3.2, 4.3.3, 4.3.4, 4.3.5, 4.4.2
Analysis CST.3 **ELA** W.4.2

6. **Analyze** Fill in the circle next to the best answer.
   Which of the following allowed California to become a state?

   (A) Indenture Act of 1850

   (B) Land Act of 1851

   (C) Compromise of 1850

   (D) Bear Flag Revolt of 1846

7. **Explain** Why did the Bear Flag Revolt happen?

   _____

   _____

8. **Compare and Contrast** How was California's government different during the Spanish and Mexican periods than after statehood?

   _____

   _____

   _____

9. **Analyze** Which way of mining had the most negative effect on the environment? Give an example to support your answer.

   _____

   _____

10. **Revisit the Big Question** How did the Gold Rush create opportunities for women?

    _____

    _____

11. **Writers Workshop: Write Informative Text:** On a separate sheet of paper, write a short paragraph that connects the period in this chapter to the present. What has stayed the same in California? What has changed?

Analyze Primary Sources

HSS 4.3.3, 4.4.2 **ELA** RI.4.1, RI.4.4

The soldiers grumbled . . . about the hardships of standing guard . . . when they might be busy in the mines, putting gold in their leather bags.

-John A. Swan, *A Trip to the Gold Mines of California in 1848*

12. **Explain** what the soldiers described by John A. Swan wanted to do instead of standing guard.

_____

Interpret Timelines

Analysis CST.1 **ELA** RI.4.7

13. **Analyze** the timeline and answer the questions.

 a. Did California hold its constitutional convention before or after the start of the Civil War? _____

 b. The Compromise of 1850 required northern states to accept the Fugitive Slave Act. Did the Civil War begin before or after the compromise was passed? _____

 c. How many years after the Land Act of 1851 did the Civil War begin? _____

California: Statehood and Other Events

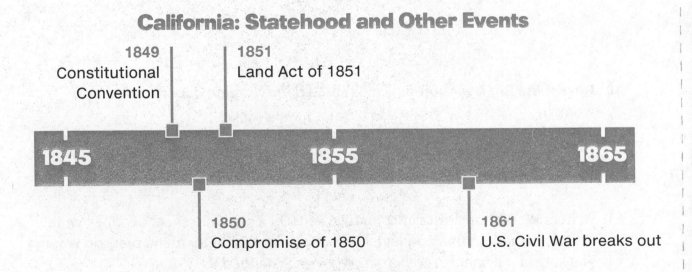

1849 Constitutional Convention

1851 Land Act of 1851

1845   1855   1865

1850 Compromise of 1850

1861 U.S. Civil War breaks out

Quest Findings

Create Your Museum Exhibit

You've read the lessons in this chapter and now you are ready to create your museum exhibit. Remember that the goal of your exhibit is to show how California changed because of the Gold Rush and statehood.

👆 INTERACTIVITY

Use this activity to help you prepare to create your exhibit.

1 Pick Your Items

Work with your team to list ways in which California changed during the Gold Rush and when it became a state. What objects, quotes, or pictures might help show these changes? List several, and then write a sentence explaining why you have listed each one.

2 Build Your Exhibit

Follow your teacher's instructions to build a museum exhibit. Use your notes and your Quest Connections to create the best museum exhibit you can. Make sure your exhibit answers these questions:

• How did California change during the Gold Rush?

• How did it change when it became a state?

• What change does each item in your exhibit represent?

• Why was the change important?

3 Present to the Class

With your team, show your exhibit to the class. Point out all the items on display. Explain why they are important and what changes they show.

4 Listen and Learn

Listen as other groups present their exhibits. What did they do differently? What changes did they show?

5 California After Statehood

GO ONLINE FOR DIGITAL RESOURCES

▶ VIDEO

👆 INTERACTIVITY

🔊 AUDIO

🎮 GAMES

☑ ASSESSMENT

📖 ETEXT

The BIG Question Why do some people leave their homelands?

▶ VIDEO

An illustration of San Francisco in 1893

Lesson 1
Transportation

Lesson 2
Immigration

Lesson 3
Agriculture and Industry

JumPstart Activity 👆 INTERACTIVITY

Look at the image. Boats like those you see here brought immigrants to California. Raise your hand if you and your family have ever moved to a new place. Stand up if you have never moved but would like to. Describe why you moved or would like to move.

_____

_____

_____

_____

_____

HSS 4.4, 4.4.1, 4.4.3, 4.4.4, 4.4.6, 4.4.7 **Analysis** CST.1, CST.2, CST.4, HI.1, HI.3 **ELA** RL.4.1, RI.4.1, RI.4.2, RI.4.3, RI.4.4, RI.4.7, W.4.1, W.4.2, W.4.3, W.4.5, W.4.6, SL.4.1, SL.4.3, SL.4.4, L.4.4

 **AUDIO**

Expansion All Around

Preview the chapter **vocabulary** as you sing the rap:

People need to **communicate**.
Sharing information helps us relate.
Sending a letter meant having to wait.
Our **technology** needed an update.

Wagons and ships were the tools of the day.
Travel was slow and caused much delay.
The **telegraph** system was very quick.
Sending these signals cut down on the long trips.

Transportation, it needed help too,
To move us faster as the country grew.
Builders had an idea for a railroad, a **vision**,
To connect east to west, that was their mission.

Planning it out was fundamental.
Engineers made plans that were instrumental.
The project before them was monumental,
Building a railroad that was transcontinental.

Where did Americans in the 1860s build a railroad that connected California to the East?

The transcontinental railroad made it much easier for people to travel to California.

Transcontinental Railroad

Nebraska

Omaha

Sacramento

California

PACIFIC OCEAN

N
W E
S

Passengers boarded the Central Pacific Railroad at this station in Sacramento.

What happened and When?

Read the timeline to find out how immigration, railroads, and industry changed California.

TODAY
You can still travel from California to the East Coast by train.

1840

1850

1860

1848
California's first public schools open in San Francisco.

1861
Telegraph service reaches California and puts an end to the Pony Express.

Who will you meet?

Collis P. Huntington one of the "Big Four" businessmen who helped build the first railroad to California

Leland Stanford another member of the "Big Four," he later served as a senator and California's governor.

Wong Chin Foo came to San Francisco in 1873 and fought for the rights of Chinese Americans.

Mary Tape fought for the right of Chinese American children to a public education

INTERACTIVITY

Complete the interactive map digital activity.

1870   1880   1890

1869
The transcontinental railroad is completed.

1882
The Chinese Exclusion Act stops Chinese immigration to the United States.

TODAY
More than 4 million Chinese Americans live in the United States.

5 **Quest**
Collaborative Discussion

What's Your Train of Thought?

California went through many changes during the late 1800s. Some happened because of the transcontinental railroad and immigration. Which do you think caused California to change the most?

Quest Kick Off

Your mission is to study California in the late 1800s and decide if the transcontinental railroad or immigration affected the state more. Then you will have a discussion with your classmates about the issue.

Leland Stanford

1 Think About Change

How might your town or city change if a new highway or railroad came to town? How might it change if many new people came from far away?

....

....

....

....

HSS 4.4.1, 4.4.3
Analysis HI.3
ELA W.4.1, W.4.5, SL.4.1, SL.4.3, SL.4.4

2 Plan Your Evidence

What kinds of evidence will you use to help you make a decision? What facts would show that immigration was more important? What facts would show that the railroad was more important?

....

....

....

....

....

INTERACTIVITY

Think about ways the railroad and immigration have changed California since the 1800s.

3 Look for Quest Connections

Turn to the next page to begin looking for Quest Connections that will help you in your discussion.

4 Quest Findings
Discuss It

Use the Quest Findings page at the end of the chapter to help you prepare for your discussion and present your opinion.

1 Transportation

INTERACTIVITY

Participate in a class discussion to preview the content of this lesson.

Unlock
The **BIG**
Question

I will know how changes in communication and transportation affected California.

Vocabulary

communicate
technology
telegraph
engineer
investor

JumpStart Activity

Work with a partner. Brainstorm a list of different ways of getting from place to place, or sending messages to people who are far away. Stand up and model for other students the different things you think of. See if they can guess what you are showing.

Academic Vocabulary

system
vision

A Pony Express rider carrying mail passes men setting up telegraph wires.

Today, **communicating**, or sharing information, with people far away is easy. But in the early 1800s, it was much harder. People could not just dial a phone or send an email. Phones and computers did not exist. Instead, people wrote letters that might take weeks or months to reach someone far away. Traveling long distances also took a long time. People worked to speed up communication and transportation. Some became very rich doing this.

HSS 4.4.1 **Analysis** CST.2, CST.4, HI.1 **ELA** RI.4.1, RI.4.2, RI.4.4, SL.4.1, SL.4.4, L.4.4

INTERACTIVITY

Explore the key ideas of the lesson.

Connecting California

After the Gold Rush, Americans kept moving to California. At this time, most Americans lived in the East. That meant California was thousands of miles away. It also meant that visiting or writing to family and friends left behind would be difficult.

Remember that to get to California, Americans from the East had to either travel a long way by sea or make a difficult land trip. Mail had to go the same way. Both the government and businesses wanted to make this travel faster.

In the 1850s and 1860s, technology made it easier for Californians to communicate with the rest of the United States. **Technology** is the use of scientific knowledge to solve problems.

One company built a route to carry mail by stagecoach. A stagecoach is a type of wagon pulled by horses. The Overland Mail Company carried mail 2,800 miles in 25 days from St. Louis, Missouri, to Los Angeles and finally to San Francisco. The company built roads, bridges, and stations along its route. Two men involved with the company were the bankers Henry Wells and William Fargo. The company name later became Wells, Fargo and Co. While this overland mail service ended, the company still exists today.

An advertisement for the Pony Express, a service that carried mail to California.

1. ☑ **Reading Check** **Draw Inferences** Talk with a partner and **explain** why Americans were interested in creating new communication technology.

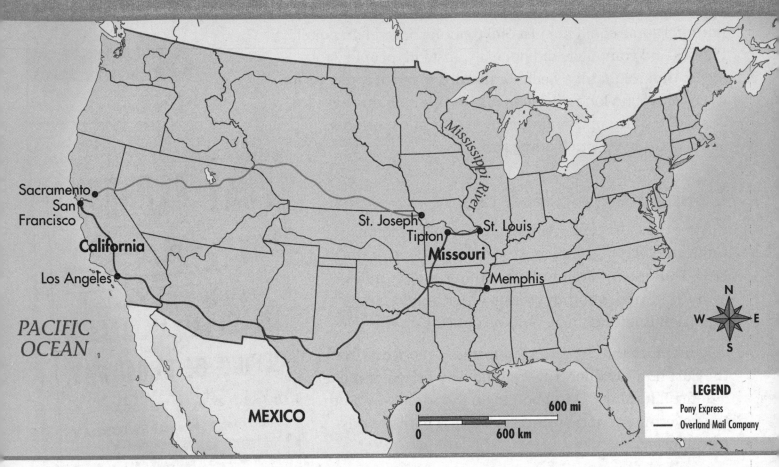

Sacramento
San Francisco
California
Los Angeles

PACIFIC OCEAN

St. Joseph
Tipton
Missouri
St. Louis
Memphis

Mississippi River

MEXICO

0		600 mi
0		600 km

N
W   E
S

LEGEND
— Pony Express
— Overland Mail Company

Academic Vocabulary

system • *n.*, an established way of doing something

2. ☑ **Reading Check**
Analyze Use the map's scale bar to calculate the distances of the two routes shown. Talk with a partner about how you think the routes influenced California.

In 1860 the Central Overland California and Pike's Peak Express Company began running the Pony Express. It carried mail with a **system** that had been used long ago in Asia. The company set up a relay of horse riders. They changed horses every 10 or 15 miles at relay stations. The Pony Express carried mail delivery from St. Joseph, Missouri, to San Francisco in 10 days. Later, the Pony Express was featured in many movies set in the West.

But after only about a year, technology ended the Pony Express. About two decades earlier, Samuel Morse had invented the **telegraph**. It is a machine that uses electric signals to send messages instantly from place to place using wires. At first, it was used in the eastern United States. Then during the 1860s, Western Union Telegraph laid the first telegraph line connecting California to the East. The telegraph is much faster than sending mail on horseback. Western Union still exists, and sent messages by telegraph for more than a century.

Railroads Move West

The telegraph made communication easier, but transportation was still a problem. Stagecoaches were slow and often faced harsh travel conditions.

Railroads have been used for almost two centuries in the United States. At first, they traveled between cities on the East Coast. Railroad technology improved, which allowed people and goods to move faster and farther. Railroad lines grew from east to west. Miles and miles of new tracks were built. Plans were made to build a transcontinental railroad, or a railroad that goes across a continent. It would connect California to the eastern United States.

Many people recognized the need for western railroads. One man, Theodore Judah, was particularly interested. He was an engineer who built railroads. An **engineer** is a person who designs things such as roads, bridges, or machines. He had a big goal. His **vision** was to connect the country from east to west.

Judah explained his reason for wanting to build a transcontinental railroad:

Primary Source

It is an enterprise more important in its bearings and results to the people of the United States, than any other project involving an expenditure [expense] of an equal amount of capital [money]. It connects these two great oceans. It is an indissoluble [permanent] bond of union between the populous States of the east, and the undeveloped regions of the fruitful West. It is a highway which leads to peace and future prosperity.

—Theodore Judah, "A Practical Plan for Building the Railroad," 1857

3. ☑ **Reading Check Predict** how the transcontinental railroad affected California and the rest of the United States.

_____

_____

_____

INTERACTIVITY

Take a closer look at what Theodore Judah said about the transcontinental railroad. Decide which statements are opinions.

Quest Connection

Why did Theodore Judah believe the transcontinental railroad was such an important project?

Academic Vocabulary

vision • *n.*, an idea or goal formed in one's mind

Theodore Judah

Beginning the Transcontinental Railroad

Judah needed **investors** to pay for building a railroad. These are people who give money to a company in exchange for part of what that company earns later. Leland Stanford, Charles Crocker, Collis P. Huntingon, and Mark Hopkins invested in the project. The men became known as the "Big Four." Together, they formed the Central Pacific Railroad Company.

The transcontinental railroad project was so large that the government encouraged two competing companies to lay the tracks. Beginning in Sacramento in January 1863, workers for the Central Pacific Railroad laid track going east. Beginning in July 1865 in Omaha, Nebraska, workers for the Union Pacific Railroad laid track going west. The tracks were laid from both ends and would meet near the middle.

Completing the Transcontinental Railroad

Laying the track and building bridges and tunnels through the mountains was no easy task. Thousands of workers were needed. Officials hired Chinese immigrants, who worked long hours for lower pay than other workers. They were willing to lay tracks in dangerous areas.

4. ☑ **Reading Check**
Identify On the map, trace the route of the Central Pacific Railroad from Sacramento to Promontory Summit, Utah. Circle two areas on the map that would likely be hard to build a railroad through.

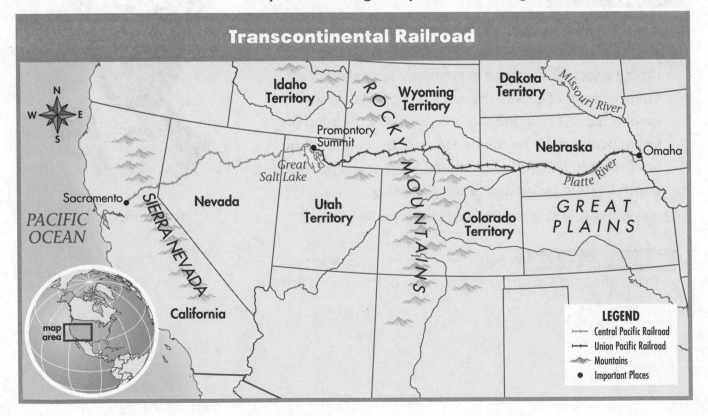

Transcontinental Railroad

LEGEND
- Central Pacific Railroad
- Union Pacific Railroad
- Mountains
- Important Places

Chinese workers had the dangerous job of building tracks through the Sierra Nevada during the 1860s.

The Central Pacific advertised for workers in China. Thousands of Chinese men came to work on the railroad. By 1868 almost 80 percent of the workers for the Central Pacific were Chinese immigrants.

Chinese laborers worked to build tracks through California's Sierra Nevada mountain range. To blast through mountains, workers had to drill holes in the rock and then place explosives in the holes. It was a dangerous job and many were killed. Unlike most other workers, the Chinese workers had to find their own food and tents to live in. Snow and ice in the mountains often caused accidents and led to many deaths.

Many Irish immigrants worked for the Union Pacific. They were sometimes called a sledge-and-shovel army. Most of the track they laid was across the Great Plains.

The more miles of railroad a company could build, the more money they could make. So the Central Pacific and Union Pacific began competing to see who could lay the most tracks in a day. At first, they could lay a mile of track a day. Quickly, the number rose to ten miles in a day.

After six years, the two tracks met at Promontory Summit, Utah, on May 10, 1869. The transcontinental railroad was complete.

Word Wise

Suffixes A suffix is a word part that is added to the end of a word. The word *dangerous* has the suffix *–ous*, which means "full of." What other words can you think of that use the suffix *–ous*?

5. ☑ **Reading Check** **Identify** and underline why railroads preferred to hire Chinese workers over other workers.

The Railroad's Impact

Now the United States had a railroad that went across the country. Even today, trains cross the country. It became cheaper and faster to transport people and goods. New towns grew along the route and existing towns became larger. California farmers could ship their products to eastern markets. The railroad also encouraged trade with Asia. Goods could be shipped across the Pacific to California, then by rail to the East, or go in the other direction. New seaports were built to handle this trade. The Port of Los Angeles was founded in 1907, for example.

But the railroad affected the environment. Tracks cut through many wildlife habitats, harming them. Some kinds of animals struggled to survive. For the buffalo, for example the railroad was very harmful. People killed buffalo to make things from their hides. The railroad passed through areas where buffalo lived and made it easier for hunters to find them. The railroad also provided a way to cheaply transport buffalo hides to markets. So the buffalo largely disappeared.

This railroad carried huge logs to a sawmill to be cut into lumber.

After the completion of the railroad, the Chinese immigrants who worked on the railroad needed new jobs. You will read more about what they did in the next lesson.

Other Railroads in the West

Many local rail lines were built on the West Coast. Railroads connected northern California to the Pacific Northwest, or Oregon and Washington. As you have learned, the northern coast of California has forests with large trees like redwoods. These were needed to build railroads, so the lumber industry grew. As it did, lumber companies built even more railroads to carry their products.

6. ☑ **Reading Check Summarize** how railroads affected northern California.

_____

_____

INTERACTIVITY

Check your understanding of the key ideas of this lesson.

☑ Lesson 1 Check   🌐 HSS 4.4.1 Analysis HI.1 ELA RI.4.1

7. **Draw Inferences** Why were the Pony Express, Overland Mail Company, and Western Union important to California's growth?

_____

_____

_____

8. **Analyze** the reasons why a transcontinental railroad was built.

_____

_____

9. **Understand the** *Quest* **Connections** Based on what you read, do you think Theodore Judah was right to predict that the railroad would benefit the United States? Explain your answer.

_____

_____

The Golden Spike Ceremony

On May 10, 1869, a "golden spike" ceremony was held in Promontory Summit, Utah, to celebrate the completion of the transcontinental railroad. Two primary sources shown here tell about this event. The first is an excerpt from a speech Leland Stanford gave at the event. He was the president of the Central Pacific Railroad. The second is a photograph taken at the ceremony.

Vocabulary Support

things given as symbols of thanks

relating to money

enterprise, *n.*, project
undertaking, *n.*, task

Gentlemen, The Pacific Railroad Companies accept, with pride and satisfaction, these golden and silver tokens of your appreciation of the importance of our enterprise . . . and to the material interests of our whole country, east and west, north and south. . . . Allow me to express the hope that the great importance which you are pleased to attach to our undertaking, may be, in all respects, fully realized.

– Leland Stanford, Account of the "Golden Spike" Ceremony, 1869

Fun Fact
Telegraph signals were sent to San Francisco and New York City as the spike was hit into the track. Why do you think the telegraph was used?

Close Reading

1. **Identify** and circle three words or phrases that show Leland Stanford's feelings about the transcontinental railroad.
2. What details in the photograph show that this was an important event?

_____

_____

_____

Wrap It Up

Do you think the transcontinental railroad had more of an effect on businesses or ordinary citizens? Support your answer with information from the chapter and the photograph and quotation.

_____

_____

2 Immigration

INTERACTIVITY

Participate in a class discussion to preview the content of this lesson.

Unlock The BIG Question

I will know why immigrants came to California in the late 1800s and what challenges they faced.

Vocabulary

racism
discrimination
exclusion
strike
deport

Academic Vocabulary

deny
limit

JumpStart Activity

Immigrants come from many different countries. Take a poll with your classmates about which country the largest number of immigrants comes from today. Your teacher will call on students to name different countries. Stand up when you hear a name you think is correct.

You have read about how people from all over the United States and the world came to California during the Gold Rush. In the years that followed, people kept coming. They came for new opportunities but faced many challenges. California's culture showed the different influences they brought.

Coming to California

In 1860, about 380,000 people lived in California. In 1900, nearly 1,500,000 lived in the state. Where did all these people come from? The transcontinental railroad made it easier for many settlers from New York, Pennsylvania, and the New England states to travel west. Others came from closer western states. Many came from foreign countries. Immigrants came from countries in Europe, including Ireland, Germany, Italy, and Russia. Some came from Mexico and Central America. Others came from Peru and Chile, in South America.

HSS 4.4.3, **Analysis** HI.1
ELA RI.4.1, RI.4.2, RI.4.3, L.4.4

INTERACTIVITY

Explore the key ideas of this lesson.

1. **Reading Check** Work with a partner to find Ireland on a map or globe. **Describe** its relative location compared to California. Do the same for other places listed on this page.

Immigrants came to California on steamships like this one.

INTERACTIVITY

Explore ways immigrants to California were treated and how immigration affected California.

Quest Connection

With a partner, identify which image shows an opportunity for immigrants. Which shows a challenge?

Japanese immigrants pack broccoli on a farm near Guadalupe, California.

Many immigrants also came from Asia. Most were from China and Japan. Smaller numbers came from Korea, India, and the Philippines in the early 1900s.

A group of Japanese families started the Wakamatsu Tea and Silk Colony in 1869. It was a farming community and the earliest Japanese settlement in North America. However, it only lasted for about two years, possibly because of drought. So most of the settlers left and moved to other areas of California. By the 1880s, fewer Japanese people were immigrating to the state.

Opportunities and Challenges

People move to a new place for different reasons. They respond to push and pull factors. Push factors are reasons to leave. Pull factors are reasons to come to a new place. Immigrants to California were pushed by problems in their home countries. These included unemployment and overcrowding. They were pulled to California by opportunities. They could find jobs and land. They could start a new business.

Remember that Chinese immigrants first came to California during the Gold Rush. The discovery of gold was an important pull factor. Many then went on to work on the transcontinental railroad. After that was built, they needed new jobs. They went to work on farms. Many had been farmers in China.

Chinese immigrants worked as sharecroppers on California's large farms. This means they did not own the land but were allowed to grow crops on it. In return, they gave the landowner some of the crops that they grew. Chinese workers were not the only immigrants to work on farms. Immigrants from Japan, the Philippines, and Mexico also worked on farms.

During the 1870s, the American economy grew weaker. There were fewer jobs. Non-Chinese Americans blamed the Chinese for taking jobs that they wanted. Some employers refused to hire Chinese workers. Those Chinese immigrants who had jobs were often mistreated by coworkers. Chinese immigrants faced violent attacks in both cities and rural areas. For example, in Sonoma County in 1870, Chinese farm workers were attacked and forced to leave. In 1871 in Los Angeles, a mob of about 500 mainly white men attacked and killed about 20 innocent Chinese residents.

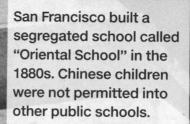

San Francisco built a segregated school called "Oriental School" in the 1880s. Chinese children were not permitted into other public schools.

As this violence shows, Asian immigrants faced racism from their neighbors. **Racism** is the belief that people of other races are not as good as those of your race. Asian immigrants were discriminated against. **Discrimination** is unfair treatment of people based on their race, gender, age, or other characteristic. Asian Americans were not welcome in many places. Chinese people were pushed to live in separate areas of cities. There they opened restaurants, laundries, and other businesses. In San Francisco, "Chinatown" became the only safe place for Chinese immigrants to live.

In the late 1800s, officials in San Francisco also built Chinese schools to segregate Chinese schoolchildren from other children. Mary Tape, a Chinese American woman, fought hard against this. In 1885, she sued the San Francisco School District. A California court ruled that Chinese children must be allowed in public schools. But even with that ruling many schools remained segregated.

Word Wise

Context Clues When you read a word that you do not understand, look for other words or phrases that might give clues to its meaning. Sometimes nearby sentences have words that provide the meaning. What do you think *segregate* means?

2. ☑ **Reading Check** Sequence Underline a sentence that tells you what first brought Chinese immigrants to California. Then draw a circle around what they did next.

Limiting Immigration

Discrimination was something that many Chinese immigrants in California lived with every day. They faced it at work, at school, and when trying to buy a home. Yet these hardships did not stop Chinese immigrants from coming to California. During the 1870s and the early 1880s, Chinese immigrants continued to come. Some joined family members who had already moved to the United States. Most Chinese immigrants settled in areas where there was a large Chinese population such as in Chinatown in San Francisco.

As more Chinese immigrants came to California, racism continued. Non-Chinese Californians rioted against immigrants. A riot is a noisy, violent demonstration.

Many Californians and other Americans called for an end to Chinese immigration. So in 1882, Congress passed the Chinese Exclusion Act. **Exclusion** means keeping a person or group out. Look at the chart here to learn what the Chinese Exclusion Act **denied** to Chinese immigrants.

Academic Vocabulary

deny • v., to refuse

The Chinese Exclusion Act

☐ Chinese immigration was stopped for ten years.

☐ Chinese immigrants already in the United States could not become citizens but were allowed to remain in the country.

☐ Any Chinese people who had left the United States had to receive special permission to return.

☐ People whose ancestors were Chinese were required to carry identification.

An amendment to the Chinese Exclusion Act banned all Chinese immigrants who left the United States from reentering the country. The Chinese Exclusion Act was renewed in 1892 and became permanent in 1902. It took until 1943 for the law to be repealed, or ended.

Asian Americans fought back against racism and discrimination. As you read, Chinese workers were treated unfairly at work. Some went on **strike**, or refused to do their jobs until their demands were met. For example, in 1867 about 5,000 Chinese workers on the transcontinental railroad went on strike. To end the strike, railroad officials kept them from getting food and other supplies. They also threatened the Chinese workers. The strike failed.

After the Chinese Exclusion Act passed, Chinese people protested against it. Some people in China held a boycott of American goods. A boycott is when someone refuses to buy or use something. People use a boycott to show that they do not agree with a decision or action. Some Chinese immigrants also used the United States court system to fight against the Chinese Exclusion Act. They won many cases having to do with unfair treatment.

Some Americans who were not Chinese also fought against the Chinese Exclusion Act. They wrote this petition. A petition is a written request to a government.

Not all Americans were in favor of the Chinese Exclusion Act. Some hoped it would be repealed.

Primary Source

> This nation should be a refuge [shelter] for the oppressed [wronged] of every land. Shall it become instead a land of oppression, persecution, and cruelty? . . . That the Chinese residing [living] in this country up to the time of the passage of the Chinese Restriction Act have as good a constitutional right to be here as any foreign-born resident in the United States.

—Petition protesting the mistreatment of Chinese immigrants, 1885

3. ☑ **Reading Check**
Draw Inferences
Underline the words from the primary source that describe what the petitioners believed the country should be.

Japanese immigrants also faced discrimination. In 1906, Japanese students were segregated from other students in San Francisco schools. The Japanese government protested this treatment. So, in 1907 Japan and the United States reached an agreement. It was called the Gentlemen's Agreement, an informal agreement between the two countries. Japan would stop new immigrants from coming to the United States. In return, the United States would no longer keep Japanese American students apart from other students.

Angel Island Immigration Station closed in 1940. Today, it is a National Historic Landmark that honors the struggles faced by immigrants.

Academic Vocabulary

limit • v., to control

Angel Island

Even after the Chinese Exclusion Act was passed, a small number of Chinese immigrants were still allowed to come to the United States. These included the children of American citizens. Officials wanted to **limit** the number of Chinese people who could come. They built the Angel Island Immigration Station in San Francisco Bay. It opened in 1910. Chinese and other Asian immigrants were held there when they arrived.

Immigrants could be kept at Angel Island for days, weeks, or months. First, they were given medical exams. If they passed, then they were assigned to a living space. Here they lived in crowded conditions while they waited to be questioned by officials. The immigrant was asked about family history, location of his or her village, and many small details. The officials hoped that the person's answers would prove he or she should be returned home. The United States wanted to **deport**, or send back, as many people as possible. In fact, almost 20 percent of Chinese immigrants at Angel Island were sent back to China.

4. ☑ **Reading Check** **Explain** why the United States government built the Angel Island Immigration Station.

_____

_____

☑ **Lesson 2 Check**   🌀 **HSS** 4.4.3 **ELA** RI.4.1, RI.4.2

5. **Draw Inferences** What were the effects of the Chinese Exclusion Act?

_____

_____

_____

_____

6. **Summarize** Which parts of the world did immigrants come to California from in the late 1800s?

_____

_____

7. **Understand the** *Quest* **Connections** How do you think immigration changed California? Explain your answer.

_____

_____

_____

_____

Interpret Graphs

Graphs show information in a visual way. There are different types of graphs. Each shows different kinds of data, or information. On any graph, the first thing to do is to read the title. It tells you what the graph is about.

A line graph uses a line to show information that changes over time. This line graph shows you how the percentage of Sacramento's people who were born in another country changed over time. The labels on the left side show the foreign-born population. The labels on the bottom show the year. Follow the line to see how the numbers changed over time.

A circle graph uses a circle to show the parts that make up a whole. All parts of the circle graph added together equal 100 percent, or the total. On this graph, the whole circle represents all of the immigrants who came to the United States from 1871 to 1920. It is divided into different sections. The sections here represent different regions that immigrants came from. Bigger sections show that more immigrants came from that region. Notice that each section has its own color. You can use the legend to find out what the colors mean.

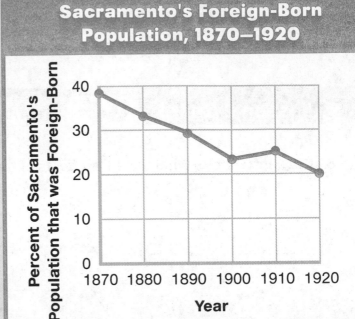

Source: Audrey Singer, Susan W. Hardwick, and Caroline B. Brettell, eds. *Twenty-First Century Gateways: Immigrant Incorporation in Suburban America*, 2008.

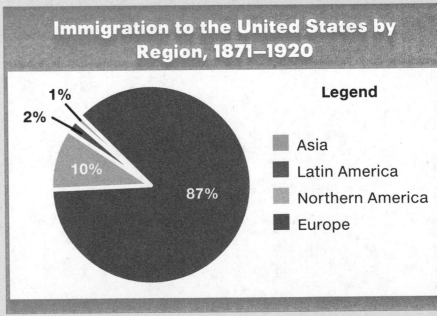

Source: U.S. Census Bureau

Use these graphs to answer the questions.
Apply what you learned to interpret the data.

▶ **VIDEO**

Watch a video about
how to interpret graphs.

1. Look at the line graph. In what year was the percentage
   of foreign-born people in Sacramento the greatest?

   _____

2. Which decade saw an increase in the percentage of foreign-born people
   living in Sacramento?

   _____

3. During which decade did Sacramento's foreign-born population
   decrease the most?

   _____

4. Look at the circle graph. Where did the largest number of immigrants to
   the United States come from during this period?

   _____

5. What percentage of immigrants came from Asia? What have you learned
   that explains this number?

   _____

   _____

6. If you were trying to make a graph showing your height at age 1, age 3,
   age 5, and today, which kind of graph would you use? Why?

   _____

   _____

Lesson 3 Agriculture and Industry

INTERACTIVITY

Participate in a class discussion to preview the content of the lesson.

Vocabulary

aqueduct
reservoir
levee

Academic Vocabulary

former
advocate

Unlock The BIG Question

I will know how California became an agricultural and industrial power in the late 1800s and early 1900s.

JumpStart Activity

Work with your class to show population growth. Some students will stand and hold hands to form California's borders. Your teacher will name economic activities such as farming, mining, and industry. "Come" to California for the activity that interests you. Stand where you think it was important during the late 1800s.

grapes

almonds

lemons

wheat

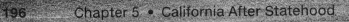

During the late 1800s and early 1900s, California's economy grew. California became an important center for agriculture and manufacturing, or making products. The climate and soil in parts of California made these places perfect for growing many crops. The state's natural resources allowed people to manufacture different kinds of goods. Immigrants from China, Japan, and other countries came to California to work in agriculture, mining, and industry.

California Agriculture

During the 1860s, there were almost 19,000 farms in California. Many were in Southern California or the Central Valley. **Former** miners who had left the gold fields began using California's fertile soil to grow wheat. Wheat does not need a lot of water to grow, which made it a good crop for drier parts of the state. Wheat was an important crop in the 1870s and 1880s, and remained California's leading crop until the 1890s. As the number of farms grew, there was a need for more workers. Farmers often hired immigrant laborers.

HSS 4.4, 4.4.4, 4.4.6, 4.4.7
Analysis CST.4 **ELA** RI.4.1, RI.4.2, RI.4.3, RI.4.4

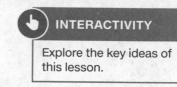

INTERACTIVITY

Explore the key ideas of this lesson.

Academic Vocabulary

former • *adj.*, in the past or before

1. ☑ **Reading Check**
Identify Circle the reason why wheat grew well in California's climate.

A fruit farm in California's Central Valley from the late 1800s

PRIDE OF THE RIVER

Refrigerated train cars helped fruit stay fresh on the long trip from California to the East.

An orange grove in California

California farms grew so large that it was hard to harvest all the crops. Farmers needed better technology. A new machine helped. Called a harvester, it made the job of cutting the grain, separating it, and bagging it into a single job. However, using the soil over and over to grow the same crop caused the soil to become less fertile. Farmers found that the land could no longer produce as much wheat. So they grew more fruits such as grapes, oranges, and lemons. Farmers also grew cotton.

Raising cows for milk also became important in California. As the population grew, so did the demand for dairy products such as milk, cheese, and butter. By the 1890s, dairy farming was a major part of California's economy.

You have read that the transcontinental railroad made it possible for California's farmers to ship their crops to the East. However, farmers faced a problem. How could they keep food from spoiling on the long train trip? New technology helped solve the problem. In the 1870s, a refrigerated railroad car was invented. It kept food cold so it would stay fresh. With refrigerated railroad cars, California's fruits could be shipped to the eastern United States. California had grown into a leader in agriculture.

California Industry and Mining

Starting in the early 1800s, people in Europe and the eastern United States began to make things in a different way. Instead of making goods by hand, people began using machines. Different industries grew, which created lots of new jobs. Workers came to cities where factories were built to find jobs. Immigrants came for work too. Eventually, new industries came to California too.

Food canning grew in California because of agriculture. Canneries, or factories where food is preserved and put into cans, were built throughout the state. By 1900, fruit and vegetable processing was one of the largest industries in California.

You have read about how important mining was during the Gold Rush. It remained important afterwards. Companies tried new ways to get gold and other minerals out of the earth. Mining grew. California workers continued to mine gold and other minerals in the late 1800s. Sand, gravel, and crushed stone became important mining products in the early 1900s. These products were used in construction and helped that industry grow.

Cannery workers in a factory put food into cans.

2. ☑ Reading Check **Main Idea** Underline an industry that grew because of agriculture.

California's Water Projects

3. ☑ **Reading Check**
Identify Circle on the map the aqueducts that bring water to Los Angeles and nearby areas.

The water you drink may come from a nearby well or river. Or it may come from hundreds of miles away. California must move and store water to provide enough for all its people and farms. This is because enough rain for cities and farms falls in some parts the state, but not in others.

Our water systems include aqueducts, dams, and reservoirs. They move and store water. An **aqueduct** is a pipe or other system that moves water from one place to another. For example, the Hetch Hetchy Aqueduct brings water all the way from Yosemite National Park to San Francisco. A **reservoir** is a place where water is collected and stored for use. The water can then be used locally as needed or moved somewhere else.

One early project to move water was the San Diego Flume. Work began on it in 1886. The flume looked a little like a long wooden water slide. It carried water more than 30 miles to San Diego. In 1907, work began on the Los Angeles Aqueduct. It brings water from the Owens River to Los Angeles. More aqueducts were built later on as the city of Los Angeles grew.

In 1901 a project began to bring water to the dry Imperial Valley, in Southern California. Canals and aqueducts bring water to the valley from the Colorado River. The valley became an important place for farming. Today, Imperial Valley farmers grow many kinds of fruits and vegetables.

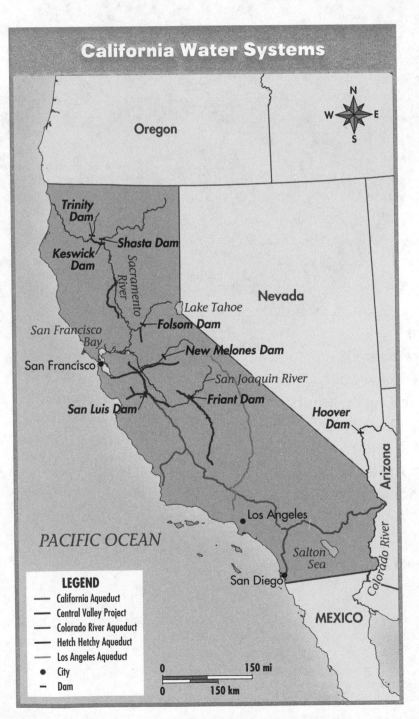

California Water Systems

Oregon

Trinity Dam
Shasta Dam
Keswick Dam
Sacramento River
Nevada
Lake Tahoe
Folsom Dam
San Francisco Bay
San Francisco
New Melones Dam
San Joaquin River
Friant Dam
San Luis Dam
Hoover Dam
Arizona
Los Angeles
PACIFIC OCEAN
Salton Sea
San Diego
Colorado River
MEXICO

LEGEND
— California Aqueduct
— Central Valley Project
— Colorado River Aqueduct
— Hetch Hetchy Aqueduct
— Los Angeles Aqueduct
• City
— Dam

0   150 mi
0   150 km

In the 1930s work on the Central Valley Project began. It was meant to control floods and bring water to the San Joaquin Valley, which is part of the Central Valley. The Central Valley Project is made up of many dams, canals, and reservoirs. Some of its water comes from the California Delta. Remember that this is where the Sacramento and San Joaquin rivers fan out before emptying into San Francisco Bay.

More water systems were built throughout the 1900s. The Colorado River Aqueduct brought water to coastal cities such as San Diego starting in 1941. The California Aqueduct has brought water to Southern California since 1973. In addition, it provides water to the Central Valley.

California's water projects make farming possible in many dry areas of Southern California. Because of that region's warm climate, farmers can grow food there for much of the year. Water projects and the climate both help California farms produce so much food.

Water projects also supported California's cities as they grew larger and larger in the 1900s. California's ability to store and move water has helped the state grow.

4. ☑ **Reading Check** Talk with a partner and **explain** why California needs water systems.

Shasta Dam was built as part of the Central Valley Project. It created Shasta Lake, California's largest reservoir.

Synonyms *Originally*
means "at the beginning."
What is another word or
phrase that means almost
the same as *originally*?

5. ☑ **Reading Check**
Draw Inferences
Underline the words
from California's
constitution that
explain how the state
thinks water should be
used. Then talk with a
partner about why water
rights are included in
California's constitution.

Water Issues

Water is so important to Californians that they sometimes argue over who has the right to use it. The state has laws to decide how water can be used. Originally, the law said that whoever owns the land next to a water source, like a river, can use its water. But during the Gold Rush, miners did not follow this system. They said that whoever claimed a water source first could use its water. In the 1920s, residents of Owens Valley protested over the Los Angeles Aqueduct. Even today, conflicts continue over Owens Valley's right to water.

In 1928, a section was added to the California Constitution. This amendment, or change, had to do with how to use water. Here is part of the amendment:

Primary Source

It is hereby declared that because of the conditions prevailing [existing] in this State ... that the water resources of the State be put to beneficial [helpful] use ... and that the conservation of such waters is to be exercised with a view to the reasonable and beneficial use thereof in the interest of the people and for the public welfare.

—California Constitution, Article X, Section 2, 1928

In the past, the California Delta was marshland filled with wildlife.

Californians' use of water has also led to environmental issues. One of these has to do with marshes, or wetlands, in the California Delta, west of the Sierra Nevada. Starting in the late 1800s, farmers built levees to protect the land from flooding so they could use it for agriculture. A **levee** is a barrier built to keep water from overflowing onto the land.

But now many people **advocate** for returning the area to marshland. They argue that the wetlands support many kinds of animals and plants.

Salt in the Salton Sea is also an issue. The Salton Sea is a human-made lake in the Imperial Valley. It has no outlet, which means its water has nowhere to go. Water evaporates, leaving salt behind. When the lake has too much salt, it hurts animals like the desert pupfish and the brown pelican. People now want to reduce the salt level.

Academic Vocabulary

advocate • *v.*, to speak in favor of

✓ Lesson 3 Check   ⚑ HSS 4.4.1, 4.4.6, 4.4.7 ELA RI.4.1

👆 **INTERACTIVITY**

Check your understanding of the key ideas of this lesson.

6. **Draw Inferences** How have aqueducts, dams, and reservoirs helped California's farmers and city residents?

_____

_____

_____

7. **Analyze** What factors helped California's agriculture and industries grow in the late 1800s and early 1900s?

_____

_____

_____

8. **Identify** some problems caused by California's water projects.

_____

_____

Draw Inferences

When you read, you often draw inferences from the text. An inference is something you figure out based on clues and information that you already know. Sometimes authors do not state everything in the text. You need to "read between the lines," or figure out what the author meant but did not write down.

To draw an inference, look for clues in the text. Make sure you understand what you are reading. Then think about related information you already know. Combine that with the text clues to draw an inference.

Look at the passage and image below. Underline two reasons why Hoover Dam is important to California.

Hoover Dam

Hoover Dam is one of the sources for California's water and electricity. It was built on the Colorado River. Hoover Dam lies on the border of Nevada and Arizona. Construction of the dam began in 1930. Workers used more than 5 million barrels of concrete to build it. It was not until after May 1935 that Hoover Dam started bringing water to parts of Southern California. Today, more than half of the electric power that Hoover Dam makes goes to Southern California, including the city of Los Angeles.

1. Draw an inference by analyzing the last sentence of the paragraph about Hoover Dam.
   Clues: Los Angeles and other parts of Southern California get their power from Hoover Dam.
   What I already know: People need electricity to power lights, refrigerators, televisions, and many other things.
   Inference:

   _____

   _____

2. Reread these sentences from page 197. **Draw an inference** about why wheat became an important crop in California during the late 1800s.

   > During the 1860s, there were almost 19,000 farms in California. Many were in Southern California or the Central Valley. Former miners who had left the gold fields began using California's fertile soil to grow wheat. Wheat does not need a lot of water to grow, which made it a good crop for drier parts of the state. Wheat was an important crop in the 1870s and 1880s, and remained California's leading crop until the 1890s.

   Clues:

   _____

   _____

   What I already know:

   _____

   _____

   Inference:

   _____

   _____

   _____

★ Citizenship

Quality:
Courage

Wong Chin Foo (1847–1898)
Strong Voice for Chinese Americans

Wong Chin Foo was a Chinese immigrant who fought for equal rights for Chinese Americans. He came to the United States in 1867 to attend school and then returned to China in 1871. Two years later, he came to San Francisco. He learned of the discrimination Chinese workers faced. He was determined to speak out against it. He wanted Chinese immigrants to be able to become American citizens. He also worked to promote Chinese culture.

Wong Chin Foo traveled from California to New York. Then in 1883, he started a newspaper called *The Chinese American*. The next year he organized Chinese Americans to protest the Chinese Exclusion Act. He continued to fight against discrimination and was not afraid to stand up for Chinese American's rights. He said:

"We, therefore, appeal for an equal chance in the race of life in this our adopted home–a large number of us have spent almost all our lives in this country and claim no other but this as ours. . . ."

In the late 1890s, Wong returned to China after working for equal rights throughout the United States. The fight for fair treatment went on.

San Francisco's
Chinatown today

Find Out More

1. Wong Chin Foo wrote the words above in 1893 after the Chinese Exclusion Act was passed. Why do you think he said these words?

_____

_____

_____

2. Today, people still protest laws that they believe are unfair, just as Wong Chin Foo protested the Chinese Exclusion Act. Research an issue in your community that people have protested about. Report your findings to the class.

Use these graphics to review some of the vocabulary, people, and ideas from this chapter.

Transcontinental Railroad

- Connected California with the eastern United States
- Made travel to California much faster and easier
- Many workers were Chinese immigrants

Immigration

- Immigrants came from Asia, Europe, Mexico, and South America
- Chinese immigrants came to build the transcontinental railroad
- Asian immigrants suffered discrimination

Agriculture and Industry

- California became a major producer of wheat, fruits, cotton, and dairy products
- Railroads opened new markets in the eastern United States
- Large water projects brought water to farms and cities

☑Assessment

🎮 GAMES

Play the vocabulary game.

Vocabulary and Key Ideas 🔔 HSS 4.4.1, 4.4.3, 4.4.7

1. Draw a line to match the definitions with the correct terms.

unfair treatment of people based on race, gender, or age   **technology**

pipes that brings water from a distance   **discrimination**

keeping someone out of something   **strike**

use of scientific knowledge to solve problems   **exclusion**

refusal to do a job until demands are met   **aqueduct**

2. Use the word *reservoir* in a sentence that shows its meaning. _____

_____

3. **Identify** Fill in the blanks to complete the sentence.

The _____ replaced the Pony Express as a way to

_____ with the eastern United States in 1861.

4. **Interpret a Circle Graph** What percentage of immigrants came from Europe

between 1871 and 1920? _____

5. **Analyze** What is the most likely reason there were so many more immigrants from Europe than from Asia?

_____

_____

_____

Immigration to the United States by Region, 1871–1920

Legend

- Asia
- Latin America
- Northern America
- Europe

1%
2%
10%
87%

Source: U.S. Census Bureau

6. **Analyze** Fill in the circle next to the best answer. How did the economy change in California after the Gold Rush?

  Ⓐ Mining grew and replaced other industries.

  Ⓑ Mining became the main economic activity.

  Ⓒ Agriculture grew and new industries started.

  Ⓓ Logging and mining replaced agriculture.

7. **Draw Inferences** Why did the transcontinental railroad hire Chinese immigrants as workers?

_____

_____

8. **Apply** Why do you think California has made water projects an important part of its planning for the future?

_____

_____

_____

_____

9. **Revisit the Big Question** How did leaving their homelands affect Chinese immigrants to California?

_____

_____

10. **Writer's Workshop: Write Narrative Text** On a separate sheet of paper, write a story about a Chinese family who came to live in California in the late 1800s. Include hopes that family members have for their future and challenges that they must face.

Analyze Primary Sources

Shadowy men worked in the dim light, breath steaming from their mouths as they used hammers and chisels to smooth the walls. At the point where the tunnel began to narrow, men swung pickaxes to widen it chip by chip.

"This is like a battlefield," I said to Father.

"It's war," he grunted. "Because the mountain can kill you in a dozen different ways before you can blink an eye."

–Excerpt from *Dragon's Gate,* by Laurence Yep

11. *Dragon's Gate* is a fictional story about a newly arrived 14-year-old Chinese boy who joins his father and uncle as a worker on the transcontinental railroad. This selection talks about the hardships of laying tracks through the mountains in winter.

Read the selection. Then underline the sentence that tells how the boy feels about where he is and what he is doing. Explain what his father means by his response.

_____

_____

_____

Draw Inferences ● HSS 4.4.7

12. How did the transcontinental railroad and refrigerated rail cars affect Californian's need for water?

_____

_____

_____

Quest Findings

INTERACTIVITY

Use this activity to help you prepare to discuss your opinions and your reasons.

What's Your Train of Thought?

You have read the lessons in this chapter and now you are ready for your discussion. Remember to use facts to support your opinion and to show why you agree or disagree with others. Follow these steps:

1 Form Your Opinion

Which do you think affected California more, the transcontinental railroad or immigration? Think about what you read and your Quest Connections to form an opinion.

2 Gather Evidence

Identify three strong reasons to support your opinion. Then identify three possible objections to your opinion. Use evidence to plan how you might argue against them.

3 Hold the Discussion

Talk with your classmates about the topic. State your opinion and your reasons. Then listen to their opinions and reasons. Be open to new ideas.

California in a Time of Expansion

The BIG Question

▶ VIDEO

How do people respond to good times and bad?

A family facing hard times during the Great Depression

JumpStart Activity

👆 INTERACTIVITY

During World War II, women worked at jobs that mostly men had done before the war. Work with a partner to put a check mark next to the jobs below that you think were jobs that women held during the war.

airplane pilot   _____

journalist   _____

mechanic   _____

welder   _____

telegraph operator   _____

Discuss with your partner why you think women worked at so many new jobs during the war. Why do you think this was important?

HSS 4.4.4, 4.4.5, 4.4.6, 4.4.9, 4.5.2 **Analysis** CST.2, CST.3, CST.4, RE.1, RE.2, HI.1, HI.2, HI.3 **ELA** RI.4.1, RI.4.3, RI.4.4, RI.4.6, RI.4.7, W.4.2, W.4.4, W.4.5, W.4.7, W.4.8, SL.4.1, L.4.4

♪ Rap About It! ♪

 AUDIO

Good Times, Bad Times

Preview the chapter **vocabulary** as you sing the rap:

With **stocks** on the rise, owning was wise

A piece of the prize and a company

To make a profit in the stock market

Buy, then you sell it for more money

Stock market crash, say goodbye to the cash

It was all gone in a flash, a **depression**

With little activity from the business community

With little opportunity people were burdened

Unemployment grew vast, losing jobs fast

The worst hadn't passed. It's the Dust Bowl.

Farmers did what they could, but soil was no good

The place where they once stood was now wasteland

California in a Time of Expansion

Where were ships built in California during World War II?

Many shipyards were located in the Bay Area of northern California.

Locate on the map one place where aircraft were made.

The Richmond Kaiser Shipyards, in Richmond, California, produced 747 ships during World War II.

Richmond

San Francisco • Oakland

Los Angeles

Long Beach

San Diego

TODAY
Richmond Shipyard Number Three is part of the Rosie the Riveter/World War II Home Front National Historic Park.

What happened and When?

Read the timeline to find out about events in California during the time of expansion.

1880

1905

1879
California's second constitution is adopted.

TODAY
The 1879 constitution is still in effect today.

1906
Earthquake and fire destroy much of San Francisco.

Who will you meet?

Hiram Johnson
a progressive politician who brought about change in California in the early 1900s

John Steinbeck
an author who wrote about migrant workers during the Great Depression

Dorothea Lange
a photographer best known for her Depression-era work

Joseph James
an African American leader who fought against discrimination during World War II

INTERACTIVITY

Complete the interactive timeline digital activity.

1931
Severe drought hits the Great Plains, leading to the Dust Bowl.

1945
United States and its allies win World War II.

1930

1955

1929
Stock market crashes; Great Depression begins.

1941
United States enters World War II.

6 Quest

Challenging Times

The 1930s and 1940s were a hard time for California and the nation. In the 1930s, the Great Depression caused many people to lose their jobs and savings. Farmers moved to California from the Midwest when huge dust storms destroyed their land. Then, in 1941, the United States was attacked and Californians stepped up to fight in World War II.

Quest Kick Off

I'm Wendy the Welder. I'm a symbol for California women who worked in factories and shipyards during World War II. We worked long hours to make ships and planes so our country could win the war. Your mission is to study how Californians responded to challenges during the 1930s and 1940s. Then write a short report on what you learn.

1 Ask Questions

What do you think it was like to live during a time when many people could not find jobs, or during a war? Write two questions of your own.

....

....

....

....

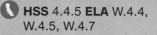
2 Research

Follow your teacher's instructions to find stories or articles about people in California who lived during the Great Depression and World War II. Learn what they have to say about their experiences. In what ways did their lives change?

....

....

....

....

....

INTERACTIVITY

View images of people who lived during the 1930s and 1940s in California and think of what you would like to know about them.

3 Look for Quest Connections

Turn to the next page to begin looking for Quest Connections that will help you write your report.

4 Quest Findings
Write Your Report

Use the Quest Findings page at the end of the chapter to help you write your report.

Lesson 1

Challenges and Reforms

INTERACTIVITY

Participate in a class discussion to preview the content of this lesson.

Vocabulary

corruption
reform

Academic Vocabulary

intent
involve

Los Angeles in 1915

Unlock The BIG Question

I will know how political challenges in the late 1800s led to change in California.

Jumpstart Activity

Work with a partner to list changes you think are needed at your school. For example, do you need better food at lunch? Choose one, and brainstorm one or two solutions. Write the change and solution on the board to share with your class.

You have read that California's population and economy grew in the 1800s. The Gold Rush brought thousands of new migrants. More came in the years afterwards. California's industries expanded and the population boomed. In 1860, there were more than 400,000 people living in California. By 1900, the population was 1.5 million! However, these changes also led to challenges. How did the people of California face them?

The Need for Change

HSS 4.4.4, 4.4.6, 4.5.2
Analysis CST.5 **ELA** L.4.4, RI.4.1, RI.4.3, RI.4.7

Growing industries helped Californians. They created jobs. People had more access to goods and services. However, new industries created problems, too. Some companies began to follow unfair practices. For example, railroads decided to charge high fees to carry goods to make more money. This meant farmers and other producers had to charge more for their goods. Consumers grew frustrated with the rise in prices.

The Central Pacific Railroad company was now part of the Southern Pacific Railroad. As Southern Pacific built tracks throughout California, it used its power to influence lawmakers. The company worked to keep other railroad companies out of California. Southern Pacific wanted to control all of the railroad business in the state. This led to **corruption**, or dishonest and illegal behavior. Southern Pacific would use its power and money to have the government make laws that would help the railroad.

1. ☑ **Reading Check** **Main Idea and Details Identify** and underline in the text one way companies followed unfair practices.

INTERACTIVITY

Explore the key ideas of this lesson.

A New Constitution

To help solve these problems, California adopted a new constitution in 1879. It was the state's second constitution. Although changes have been made to it, it is still in place today. Its goal was to **reform**, or change and improve, California's government.

To fight the corruption of politicians, the new constitution limited the powers of the state legislature. Companies would not try to influence politicians who had little power to change laws. The new constitution also set up new state agencies. These agencies had the power to regulate, or make rules for, the railroad, gas, and other industries. For example, a railroad commission was formed with the **intent** to set fair shipping fees and protect customers. Southern Pacific could no longer charge businesses whatever they wanted to for carrying their freight.

The new constitution lowered taxes for farmers. It gave married women the right to own property. It also made the University of California education system independent from any government control.

The constitution also discriminated against Chinese immigrants. It banned companies and the state from hiring Chinese workers.

Academic Vocabulary

intent • *n.*, goal or purpose

2. ☑ **Reading Check**
Identify a problem and a solution in the chart below. Write one problem that occurred in California in the late 1800s and one solution brought about by the constitution of 1879.

California, Late 1800s

Problem

_____

_____

_____

Solution

_____

_____

_____

Reforms

Despite the new constitution, some problems were not solved. Corporations, including the Southern Pacific Railroad, continued to use their money to influence politics. Corruption remained a problem. In 1910, Californians elected a progressive leader named Hiram Johnson as governor. Progressives were people who supported reforms, like those that limited the power of large companies and fought corruption. They believed reforms would improve people's lives.

Progressives like Johnson wanted to give citizens more power to have a say in government. They believed that people had a right and a responsibility to be **involved** in government and to help fix the state's problems. Under Governor Johnson's leadership, voting laws were changed to allow citizens more control over who got elected. Citizens were also able to vote on some laws directly. They could also vote to remove officials. These reforms are called the initiative, referendum, and recall. You will read more about these later in this book.

Johnson also supported other reforms. At that time, women did not have the right to vote. Johnson supported changing that law. In 1911, California's constitution was changed to give women the right to vote. California was the sixth state in the United States to do this. Progressives like Johnson worked to control railroad companies and stop unfair practices. They also banned gambling in the state.

Governor Hiram Johnson

Academic Vocabulary

involve • *v.*, take part in, include

Women protest for the right to vote.

Growing Cities and New Industries

As California experienced a population boom in the late 1800s and early 1900s, cities such as Oakland, Sacramento, San Jose, and Los Angeles grew. The growth of Los Angeles was in part due to changes in train transportation. In the 1870s, railroads connected the city to San Francisco and in the 1880s, directly to the eastern United States. The city's warm climate and new industries brought many new residents from other parts of the country. When people move from one part of a country to another, it is called internal migration. Immigrant workers from Mexico, Japan, the Philippines, and other countries in Latin America and Asia also poured into the area.

As a result, the city of Los Angeles had a huge jump in population at this time. As you can see from the line graph, in 1850, there were less than 2,000 people living in the city. From 1890 to 1900, the population grew from just over 50,000 to more than 100,000. By 1910, Los Angeles had more than 300,000 residents!

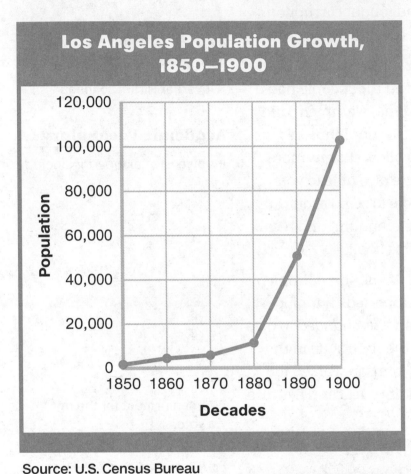

Los Angeles Population Growth, 1850–1900

Source: U.S. Census Bureau

3. ☑ **Reading Check** **Analyze** the graph. Circle the decades when the population increased the most. **Explain** how internal migration led the population to grow.

_____

_____

_____

An early movie being filmed in Los Angeles.

You have read that California built canals and aqueducts to move water. This supported growing cities like Los Angeles during these years.

New industries began to grow in the early 1900s in California. One was the oil industry. The first oil well in California was dug in Pico Canyon, near Los Angeles, in 1876. By the 1920s, California had the largest oil industry in the country. Oil was shipped all over the world from the port of Los Angeles. Demand for oil increased in the United States as a new invention, the automobile, became cheaper to buy. Cars and trucks made it easier for people to move goods, get to work, and travel. They need oil to run. The growing need for oil helped California's economy grow.

Movie making also became very important to the state at this time. American movies were first made on the East Coast in the early 1900s. Soon, however, the film industry moved to Los Angeles. The weather was better for filming outside and costs were cheaper. This new industry brought jobs, money, and tourists to the Los Angeles area. You will learn more about the entertainment industry later.

Word Wise

Multiple Meaning Words
The word *well* has more than one meaning. A *well* is a hole sunk into the earth to reach something underground, like oil. You may also feel or look *well*, meaning good or right. Multiple meaning words have the same pronunciation and spelling.

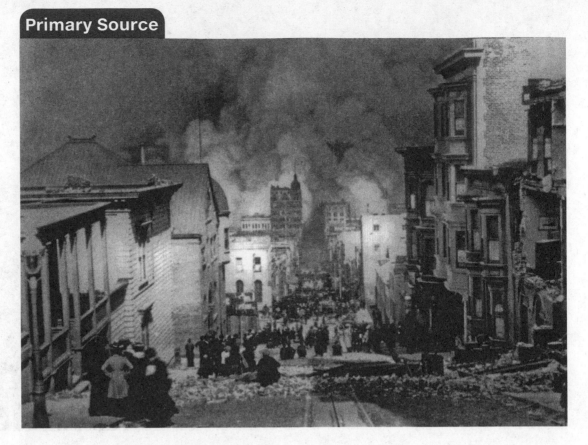

San Francisco was damaged both by the earthquake and the fires it caused.

4. ☑ **Reading Check** **Analyze** the photograph. With a partner, ask a question about what you see.

The San Francisco Earthquake

On April 18, 1906, tragedy struck San Francisco, the largest city in California at that time. A powerful earthquake shook the city. Buildings collapsed and sidewalks buckled. People were trapped in the rubble. Buildings were not strong enough to survive the shaking.

The earthquake broke many of the city's underground gas pipes. The natural gas escaped into the air and caught fire from small sparks. Fires broke out across the city and burned for three days. Homes, stores, and offices burned. The fires could not be put out because the earthquake had also broken water pipes. Fire caused more damage than the earthquake itself.

In all, about 28,000 buildings on nearly 500 city blocks were destroyed. Half of the city's population lost their homes. About 3,000 people died, and many others were injured. In the weeks after the earthquake, survivors slept in tents outside and stood in long lines for food.

This natural disaster led to reforms. In the decades after the earthquake, new laws helped to make buildings stronger, to survive future earthquakes. Construction companies had to follow new rules called building codes to protect property and help save lives.

Chinatown was hit hard by the earthquake. The small neighborhood, packed with about 14,000 people, was completely destroyed. Like the rest of the city, Chinatown was soon rebuilt. In many ways, San Francisco improved itself after the earthquake. It was a safer city. The city was also redesigned in a more beautiful way. But the earthquake is still remembered as the deadliest in American history.

> **INTERACTIVITY**
>
> Check your understanding of the key ideas of this lesson.

☑ Lesson 1 Check

ⓘ HSS 4.4.4, 4.4.6, 4.5.2
Analysis HI.3 **ELA** RI.4.3

5. **Explain** Why did California adopt a new constitution in 1879?

_____

_____

6. **Cause and Effect** Identify three causes of the population boom in Los Angeles in the late 1800s and early 1900s.

_____

_____

_____

7. **Explain** Do you think the progressive leader Hiram Johnson had a positive impact on California? Use evidence from the text to explain why or why not.

_____

_____

_____

_____

Critical Thinking Skills

Ask and Answer Questions

Reading primary and secondary sources can be difficult. Sometimes writers use hard words. Sometimes they talk about things you haven't learned about yet. But asking and answering questions about a text can help you understand it.

Follow these steps to ask and answer questions about anything you don't understand in a source.

1. **Think about what you need to know.** What don't you understand? Are some words confusing? Does the text refer to unfamiliar people or events?

2. **Ask your question.** In your notes, write down a clear question about the text. Try to make it as specific as possible.

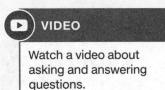

VIDEO

Watch a video about asking and answering questions.

3. **Think about your answer.** Consider where you might find an answer. Do you need to look up words in a dictionary? Should you research an unfamiliar person? Can you read more of the text and find the answer there?

4. **Find your answer.** Now that you've figured out how to find an answer, go find it! Think about how your answer helps you better understand the text.

Read the paragraph below. What questions can you ask to better understand the text?

Many people moved to the city of Los Angeles in the late 1800s and early 1900s. Promoters helped bring people to the area by painting a positive picture of Southern California. They published articles and books about life in Los Angeles. They talked about how the warm, sunny climate could cure sicknesses such as pneumonia. They also described the fertile farmland, which offered new jobs and opportunities. As a result of their efforts, many people moved to the area with the hope of finding a better life.

Your Turn!

1. What questions could you ask about the paragraph on the facing page? In the organizer below, fill in the missing answers. Then write your own question and answer.

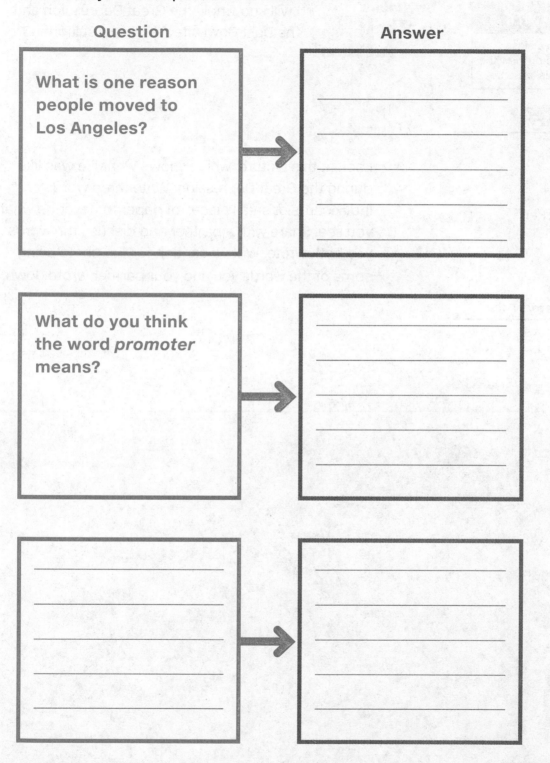

Question

Answer

What is one reason people moved to Los Angeles?

What do you think the word *promoter* means?

2. Reread the section "The San Francisco Earthquake" in Lesson 1. On a separate sheet of paper, write one question and one answer based on the image.

Lesson 2
The Great Depression and Migration

INTERACTIVITY

Participate in a class discussion to preview the content of this lesson.

Unlock The BIG Question

I will know how the Great Depression and the Dust Bowl affected life in California.

Vocabulary

stock
depression
unemployed
migrant worker
drought

Academic Vocabulary

represent
create

JumpStart Activity

Look at this picture, which shows what life was like during the Great Depression. Write three words on index cards or small pieces of paper to describe what you see. Share with a partner and discuss the words you both wrote. Write a caption for the photo using some of the words you and your partner wrote down.

In the early 1900s, California's industries grew. Businesses boomed across the country. In fact, the 1920s are sometimes called the Roaring Twenties, because of how much businesses grew during this period. People had more money to spend on new inventions, such as radios, telephones, cars, and more. They also had money to go to movies and dance halls. But this period of good times came crashing to an end in 1929. What happened? How did it all go wrong?

HSS 4.4.5, 4.4.9
Analysis CST.4, RE.1, HI.3
ELA RI.4.3, RI.4.7

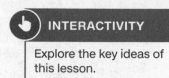

INTERACTIVITY

Explore the key ideas of this lesson.

The Stock Market Crashes

During the 1920s, some Americans bought and sold **stocks**, which are shares or portions of ownership in a company. People buy stocks and then if the company does well, they can sell the stock at a higher price. The stock market is the system through which stocks are bought and sold.

In California, many farm workers and their families lived in camps like this one during the Great Depression.

This California newspaper reported on the 1929 stock market crash like most newspapers in the country.

1. ☑ **Reading Check** **Analyze** the graph. Circle the year with the highest unemployment. **Talk with a partner** about what caused such high unemployment.

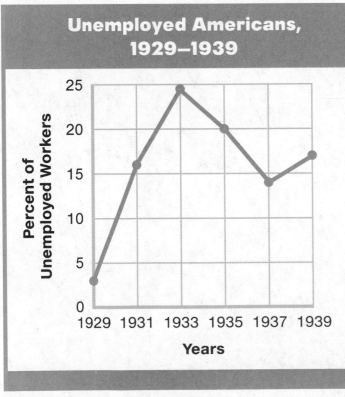

Unemployed Americans, 1929–1939

Source: Bureau of Labor Statistics

In October 1929, the stock market crashed. Prices dropped sharply and quickly. People rushed to sell stocks that no longer had any value. This crash began the Great Depression. A **depression** is a period of time when business activity slows down.

In California and across the country, banks and businesses closed after the stock market crashed. People lost their jobs and became **unemployed**, or without a job. The unemployment rate, a measure of unemployed workers, rose. Many people lost their savings and could not pay back loans. This led to even more businesses closing and more workers losing their jobs. Many Americans lost their homes and farms. The hard times became worse and worse.

The Great Depression in California

California's workers suffered during the Great Depression. Many lost their jobs. Some Californians blamed the hard times on immigration.

Many government officials and non-immigrant workers believed immigrants were taking the few jobs that were available. They also believed the government should not spend money helping poor immigrants. The state had many large farms that hired **migrant workers**, or people who move from place to place for work. Many Mexican and Filipino immigrants had come to California to find jobs as migrant farm workers.

Citizens protest against unemployment during the Great Depression.

The federal government worked with state governments to force some 1 million Mexicans and Mexican Americans to leave for Mexico in the 1930s, including 400,000 from California. The children of Mexican immigrants, who were United States citizens, were deported along with their parents. In 2005, the government of California issued an apology for the illegal removal of Mexican Americans in the state during the Great Depression.

In 1935, Congress passed the Filipino Repatriation Act. It paid for the transportation of Filipinos in the United States back to the Philippines.

During this period, migrant workers, including Mexicans and Filipinos, fought against discrimination. They participated in strikes. As the Depression worsened, unions, such as the Teamsters, grew and became more successful. Unions are organizations of workers that **represent** their members. They argue for higher wages and better working conditions. In the 1930s, the Teamsters represented mostly truck drivers delivering goods for companies.

Academic Vocabulary

represent • *v.*, to speak for someone

The Dust Bowl

create • v., cause something to happen

In the mid-1930s, much of the Great Plains region in the middle of the country experienced a terrible **drought**, or a time of very little rain. The drought **created** serious problems for farmers in Oklahoma, Kansas, and neighboring states. Without rain, the topsoil, or top layer of soil, quickly dried out. When winds blew across dry farmlands, that topsoil blew away and led to huge dust storms. Dust filled the air and settled in thick layers on farms and even inside homes. Farmers could no longer grow crops. The area affected by these dust storms became known as the Dust Bowl.

Families from Dust Bowl states moved west to find jobs and a better life.

Primary Source

"The land just blew away; we had to go somewhere."

–Kansas preacher, June 1936

A dust storm strikes on the Great Plains

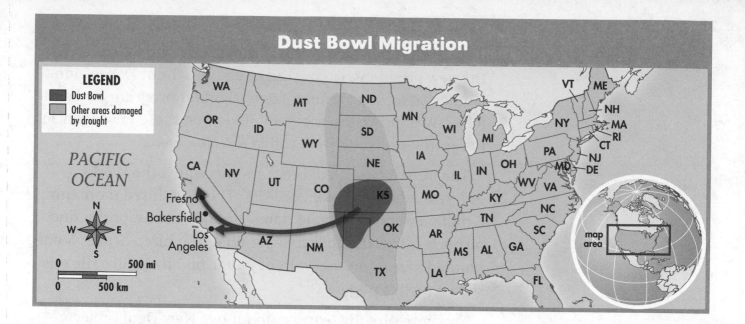

Dust Bowl Migration

LEGEND
- Dust Bowl
- Other areas damaged by drought

PACIFIC OCEAN

Fresno
Bakersfield
Los Angeles

0   500 mi
0   500 km

N W E S

map area

WA, MT, ND, VT, ME, NH, OR, ID, WY, SD, MN, WI, MI, NY, MA, RI, CT, PA, NJ, DE, CA, NV, UT, CO, NE, IA, IL, IN, OH, MD, KS, MO, KY, WV, VA, OK, AR, TN, NC, AZ, NM, MS, AL, GA, SC, TX, LA, FL

2. ☑ **Reading Check** **Study** the map. Which parts of California did people migrate to during the Dust Bowl?

_____

_____

Many farmers in the Dust Bowl area left to find new jobs and homes. By 1940, more than 2 million people had moved out of the Great Plains. About 200,000 of them moved to California to find work on farms and in cities. Whole families packed up and migrated, looking for a new start. They faced tough times. Many did not receive a warm welcome when they arrived. Many could find jobs only as migrant workers. They were paid very little money for the cotton or fruit that they picked. Many migrant workers lived in shacks with no plumbing and few comforts.

The conditions of migrant workers during the Great Depression inspired John Steinbeck to write *The Grapes of Wrath*. This novel told the story of a fictional family's migration from Oklahoma to California. Steinbeck described poverty and homelessness during these years. His story helped readers understand the struggles of this period in American history.

Quest Connections

How do you think children who moved to California because of the Dust Bowl might have felt? Share your response with a partner.

👆 **INTERACTIVITY**

Study the map and historical photo to learn about a family responding to the challenges of the Dust Bowl.

The New Deal

In 1932, Americans elected Franklin Delano Roosevelt as the new president. He worked to end the Great Depression. He started new government agencies and programs to create jobs and improve the economy. Together, these new agencies, programs, and laws were called the New Deal.

The largest New Deal program was called the Works Progress Administration, or WPA. The WPA hired more than 8 million workers to build dams, bridges, roads, parks, and airports across the country. The WPA also hired artists. Some painted murals on the walls of public buildings, like the one shown on this page.

Murals painted by the WPA often focused on work and the economy, like this image of farm workers at Coit Tower in San Francisco.

You have already learned about two New Deal projects that helped California, the Central Valley Project and the Hoover Dam. Many dams, canals, and reservoirs were built as part of the Central Valley Project. They provided water for farms, homes, and factories. The project employed many people. It let farmers grow more crops and farm in new areas. The Central Valley Project played a key role in California's economic recovery.

Thousands of workers helped build the Hoover Dam in these years. The Hoover Dam includes a major power plant that turns waterpower into electricity. Although it is on the Nevada/Arizona border, it provides electricity for Los Angeles, 266 miles away. The Hoover Dam project is an example of how the nation worked to overcome the challenges of the Great Depression.

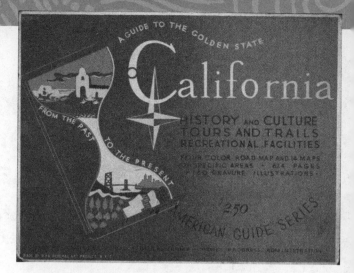

Artists created posters to advertise New Deal programs and projects, such as this poster attracting tourists to California.

3. ✓ **Reading Check** **Summarize Discuss** with a partner the purpose of the New Deal. Why did President Roosevelt start it?

✓ **Lesson 2 Check**   ◆ **HSS** 4.4.5, 4.4.9 **Analysis** HI.1, HI.3 **ELA** RI.4.3

> **INTERACTIVITY**
>
> Check your understanding of the key ideas of this lesson.

4. **Cause and Effect** How did the Great Depression affect life in California and the United States?

_____

_____

5. **Summarize** What did Steinbeck write about in his novel *The Grapes of Wrath*? What might you learn from reading his novel?

_____

_____

_____

6. **Understand the Quest Connections** Based on what you have learned, why did Dust Bowl Farmers move to California?

_____

_____

_____

John Steinbeck, "Dubious Battle in California" and Dorothea Lange, "Migrant Mother"

As you have read, John Steinbeck was an American author. This selection comes from a magazine article he wrote during the Great Depression.

Vocabulary Support

Midwest

made unfit to live in

having used all their money

an old vehicle

nondescript, *adj.*, plain, lacking interesting features

destitute, *adj.*, extremely poor, without possessions

ragged, *adj.*, old and torn

The drought in the Middle West has very recently made available an enormous amount of cheap labor. Workers have been coming to California in nondescript cars from Oklahoma, Nebraska, Texas, and other states, parts of which have been rendered uninhabitable by drought. Poverty-stricken after the destruction of their farms, their last reserves used up in making the trip, they have arrived so beaten and destitute that they have been willing at first to work under any conditions and for any wages offered.

. . . Let us see what the emigrants from the dust bowl find when they arrive in California. The ranks of permanent and settled labor are filled. In most cases all resources have been spent in making the trip from the dust bowl. Unlike the Chinese and the Filipinos, the men rarely came alone. They bring wives and children, now and then a few chickens and their pitiful household goods, though in most cases these have been sold to buy gasoline for the trip. It is quite usual for a man, his wife, and from three to eight children to arrive in California with no possessions but the rattletrap car they travel in and the ragged clothes on their bodies. They often lack bedding and cooking utensils.

- John Steinbeck, from "Dubious Battle in California," 1936

HSS 4.4.5, 4.4.9 **Analysis** RE.1, HI.1 **ELA** RI.4.1, RI.4.3, W.4.9

Dorothea Lange, "Migrant Mother"

Dorothea Lange was a famous photographer who worked during and after the Great Depression. Despite a disability caused by the disease polio, she traveled all over California to take photographs. Her stunning images showed the difficulties of life during the Great Depression. This image, called "Migrant Mother," is her most famous photo.

Close Reading

1. **Identify** and circle words in the text selection that describe the condition of workers arriving in California from the Dust Bowl.
2. **Describe** Lange's photo and what the image suggests about the Great Depression.

_____

_____

_____

Wrap It Up

Did the migrants from the Dust Bowl region have a good chance for a better life in California? Support your answer with information from the chapter. Refer to the image and use one quotation from the selection shown here in your answer.

_____

_____

_____

_____

_____

INTERACTIVITY

Participate in a class discussion to preview the content of this lesson.

Unlock The BIG Question

I will know how World War II affected California and how California helped the United States win the war.

Vocabulary

invasion
defense industry
prejudice
internment camp
rationing

Academic Vocabulary

previously
support

Jumpstart Activity

Talk with a partner about a time when a big event in the country or the world happened. Discuss how you felt about the event. How did it affect your life, or your family or friends? As you read this lesson, think about how events in the war far away affected the people of California and the United States.

You have read about the difficulties of the Great Depression, from lost jobs to dust storms. In the 1940s, the world became even more dangerous. War broke out all over the globe. Our country was attacked. Californians faced many new challenges.

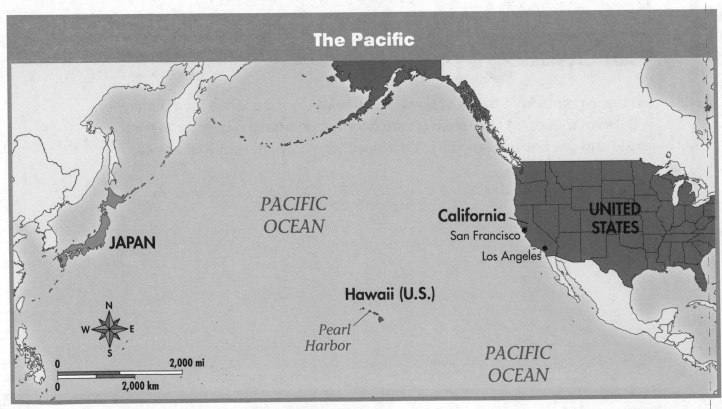

The Pacific

PACIFIC OCEAN

JAPAN

California
San Francisco
Los Angeles

UNITED STATES

Hawaii (U.S.)

Pearl Harbor

PACIFIC OCEAN

N
W · E
S

0   2,000 mi
0   2,000 km

World War II

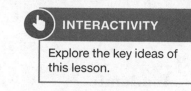

HSS 4.4.5, 4.4.6
Analysis CST.4, HI.3
ELA L.4.4, RI.4.1,
RI.4.3, RI.4.4

In 1937, Japan attacked China. Then, in 1939, Germany attacked its neighbor, Poland. Countries around the world took sides as World War II began. Britain, France, the Soviet Union, and other countries joined together as the Allies. They fought Germany, Japan, and Italy, known as the Axis.

Then, on December 7, 1941, The United States was attacked. On that day, Japanese planes bombed Pearl Harbor, a United States Navy base in Hawaii. Hawaii is an island chain in the Pacific Ocean that is part of the United States. Over 2,000 soldiers and sailors lost their lives, and 180 planes and 19 naval vessels were destroyed or damaged. **Previously**, the United States had stayed out of the war. But the bombing led it to join the Allies and declare war against Japan and the other Axis powers. Over 800,000 Californians served in the armed forces during the war. Nearly 25,000 of them were killed.

After the attack on Pearl Harbor, many Californians feared an **invasion**, that Japanese troops might try to take control of California. Look at the map of the Pacific. You can see that if the Japanese continued towards the United States mainland, they would reach California. Japanese submarines did attack American ships off the California coast.

California residents installed miles of barbed wired on their beaches. Some even placed sandbags in front of their homes and businesses to protect them. Unfortunately, they also treated their Japanese American neighbors unfairly. You will read more about this later in this lesson.

> **INTERACTIVITY**
>
> Explore the key ideas of this lesson.

Academic Vocabulary

previously • *adv.*, at an earlier time; before

Japanese planes bombed Pearl Harbor on December 7, 1941.

1. ☑ **Reading Check** **Study** the picture and map. What might Californians have been afraid of, and why?

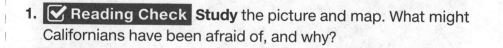

The Home Front in California

To win the war, the United States needed weapons and supplies for its military. The government spent money to produce these things. This spending helped create new jobs, especially in California. Unemployment nearly came to an end. Every American was called on to do his or her part on the "home front," as everyday citizens **supporting** the effort to win the war.

Californians went to work in the **defense industry**, or the businesses that make supplies for the military. They worked in factories, aircraft plants, and shipyards. They made guns, tanks, ships, and planes. The San Francisco Bay area became one of the largest shipbuilding centers in the world.

Women played a huge role in the war effort. Because so many men were away fighting, women went to work in factories and on military bases. Many of these women were working outside of the home for the first time. They did jobs that men had done before they war. "Rosie the Riveter" was a character often seen in government posters and other advertisements. Her image was used to help bring women into the work force to support the war. The effort was very successful. There was even a California version of Rosie the Riveter. Northern California newspapers called the women who worked in shipbuilding plants "Wendy the Welder."

2. ☑ **Reading Check**
Discuss with a partner why you think so many women joined the workforce during the war.

Many California women went to work in factories to help build planes for the war.

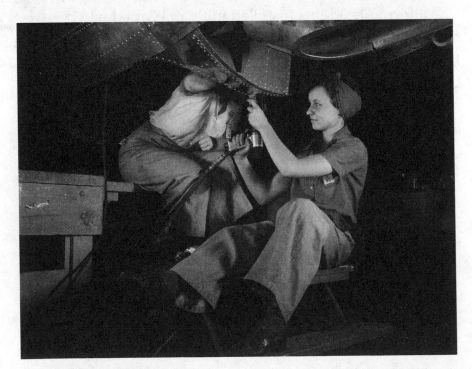

California was central to the effort to defeat Japan in the Pacific. More military bases were located here than in any other state, by far. During World War II, the number of bases in California increased from 16 to 41. This was more than the next five states had combined! Many of these bases were training centers for soldiers and sailors soon to join the war overseas. Camp Roberts, for example, was a huge new training base for the army. Almost half a million troops trained at this base on the central coast during the war. Two-thirds of all troops sent to fight against Japan left from Fort Mason on San Francisco Bay.

Millions of American soldiers and sailors worked or trained on military bases in California during World War II.

Californians also contributed to the war effort as volunteers. They helped to provide for the troops. Even Hollywood stars pitched in. At a restaurant and dance hall called the Hollywood Canteen, they served free food and entertained service members.

California needed workers to work in the defense industry and help run bases. Thousands of new residents came to the state to find work. More than 300,000 African Americans from the southern United States moved to Los Angeles, Long Beach, and other cities during the war. The San Francisco Bay Area saw its African American population increase by 46,000 people between 1941 and 1945.

The sacrifices made by members of the military and citizens on the home front eventually paid off. The United States and its allies won the war, which ended in 1945.

3. ☑ **Reading Check** **Main Idea and Details Identify** one way Californians supported the war effort during World War II.

_____

_____

_____

This poster ordered Japanese Americans to leave an area in California.

Unfair Treatment on the Home Front

Wartime worries led to acts of **prejudice** and racism. Prejudice is unfair dislike or treatment of a group of people.

Japanese American Internment

Shortly after Japan attacked Pearl Harbor, the United States government began to investigate and arrest Japanese Americans. There were many rumors at the time. Newspapers began to say that Japanese Americans were the country's enemies. Many people on the West Coast were afraid of a Japanese invasion. The investigations, rumors, and newspaper attacks made them more afraid.

In February 1942, the government began to make Japanese Americans on the West Coast leave their homes. They were given very little time to gather their belongings. Many had to sell their property and businesses very quickly.

About 120,000 Japanese Americans, including 94,000 in California, were sent to **internment camps**. An internment camp is a place where people are held against their will, often during a war. Many of these Japanese Americans were born in the United States. In fact, more than 60 percent of people at the internment camps were United States citizens.

Japanese Americans were sent to internment camps during World War II.

Japanese American children had to leave their teachers and friends and move to camps with their parents. Inside the camps, Japanese American men, women, and children were held behind barbed wire. They were not allowed to go outside to work or visit their friends.

In 1944, the government decided to close all internment camps. All Japanese Americans were released by the end of 1945. After being released, many found that property they owned before had been stolen or damaged.

Fred Korematsu was a Japanese American citizen who refused to live in an internment camp. He was arrested and then fought for his right to live as a free citizen during the war. His legal case went all the way to the United States Supreme Court. The Court ruled against him in 1944. Decades later, however, the decision was overturned, and Korematsu received a Presidential Medal of Freedom.

Despite the internment camps, more than 33,000 Japanese Americans served in the United States military during World War II. They earned many medals for their service.

Zoot Suit Riots

Mexican Americans also faced mistreatment during the war. In the 1940s, many young Mexican American men liked to wear a kind of suit called a zoot suit. Some people objected to this style of dress. They believed the outfits were too fancy to wear when the nation was at war.

This dislike of zoot suits and prejudice against Mexican Americans turned to violence. In 1943, a group of off duty soldiers attacked young Mexican American men wearing zoot suits in Los Angeles. Thousands joined the attacks. Soldiers and sailors beat Mexican Americans in movie theaters and other public places. These attacks became known as the Zoot Suit Riots, and they lasted for several days before the violence ended.

Quest Connections

How did Fred Korematsu respond to a challenge in his life during World War II?

INTERACTIVITY

Compare Korematsu to others responding to challenges during the war.

4. ☑ **Reading Check**
Cause and Effect Why did the U.S. government set up internment camps during World War II? **Discuss** with a partner.

African American soldiers carrying ammunition in France, 1944.

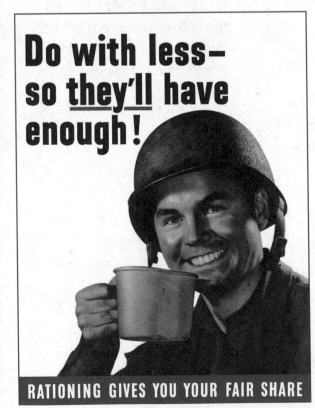

Do with less—
so they'll have
enough!

RATIONING GIVES YOU YOUR FAIR SHARE

Posters and brochures encouraged the public to support rationing during the war.

Discrimination Against African Americans

African Americans also faced discrimination during the war years. As soldiers, they were placed in separate all-African American units. They were not allowed to fight alongside white soldiers. African Americans who worked in the defense industry received lower pay than white workers, for the same work.

Effects of the War on California

Americans had to make sacrifices during the war. Many items needed for the war were in short supply on the home front. **Rationing** became common. Rationing is when the government limits the amount of food or supplies people can buy. Meat, sugar, clothing, and gasoline were some of the items rationed. This made sure the military had the food and supplies it needed to fight the war.

The war hurt California's environment. As more people moved to California and industries grew, air and water pollution got worse. Homes and factories were built over what had once been farms and wetlands.

By the end of the war, California had become the nation's fastest-growing state. As cities became more and more crowded, residents moved into new suburbs outside the cities. Highways and shopping centers were built to serve people who lived in the suburbs.

The war also changed California's economy. Before the war, California's economy was mostly based on farming and mining. After the war, a large part of the economy was based on manufacturing and technology. The growth of the defense industry helped lead to this change. During the war, California produced 17% of all American-made war supplies. The defense industry in California continued to grow after the war. Southern California continued as a center for the design and construction of airplanes.

New industries provided jobs for Californians, including women and African Americans. In addition, in 1942, the U.S. government worked with the Mexican government to create the Bracero program. This program allowed workers from Mexico to work in the United States. They were called *braceros*. More and more Mexican migrant workers came to California. They mostly took jobs on farms. They replaced farm workers who were off fighting in the war. As you read, Mexican migrant workers during the Great Depression were forced out of California. With a need to increase food production during the war, they were invited back.

All of these developments changed California in ways both big and small. By the end of World War II, it had become a very different state.

5. ☑ **Reading Check**
Underline parts of the text that **explain** why so many people moved to California during and after the war.

👆 **INTERACTIVITY**
Check your understanding of the key ideas of this lesson.

☑ Lesson 3 Check   🔊 **HSS** 4.4.5, 4.4.6 **Analysis** HI.1, HI.3

6. **Summarize** the impact of the bombing of Pearl Harbor on life in California.

_____

_____

_____

_____

7. **Identify** some effects of the population growth in California during and after World War II.

_____

_____

_____

8. **Understand the** *Quest* Connections Based on what you have learned, what might it have been like to be a young working woman in California during World War II?

_____

_____

_____

Sequence

Sequence is the order of events. When you understand a sequence of events, you know when events took place in history. Dates are one way to identify a sequence of events. Dates might appear within a text or on a timeline. You can also use clue words, such as *next, first, after, then, finally, during, past, present, future, now, today,* and *later* to know when events took place. Words that describe periods of time can also help. These include *decade* (10 years), *century* (100 years), and *generation* (the time between when parents are born and when their children are born).

VIDEO

Watch a video about sequence.

First, Japan attacked the United States.

Then, Americans fought in World War II.

Finally, the Allies won the war.

World War II

The Japanese attack on Pearl Harbor on December 7, 1941, brought the United States into World War II. One important battle was fought at Midway in June 1942. There, the United States navy defeated the Japanese. Another important event took place on June 6, 1944. On that day, called D-Day, the United States and its allies invaded France to free it from German rule. Finally, Japan and Germany surrendered in 1945, and the war ended. Decades later, the United States built the National World War II Memorial to honor those who fought in the war. It opened in April 2004. Even now, several generations after the war and in a new century, Americans still remember those who fought.

Your Turn!

1. Read and analyze the paragraph on World War II. Underline the words or dates that help you recognize sequence. Then fill in the sequence of events in the chart below.

World War II

2. Work with a partner to tell a story that summarizes the most interesting things you have learned about California's history so far. Use the following words in your story to help show the sequence of events: *past, present, future, decade, century,* and *generation.*

★ Citizenship

Quality:

Respect for the Rights of Others

Joseph James

(1900s, exact years of birth and death unknown)

Fighting for Equal Rights

During World War II, many African Americans found jobs in the defense industry in California. But these workers faced discrimination. They were offered jobs with low wages even if they had the skills and education for higher-paying jobs. Eventually, the federal government admitted there was a problem and worked to end discrimination against African American workers during the war.

Joseph James was a welder in a Sausalito shipyard during the war. He played a large role in working to end this discrimination in California. He became president of the San Francisco branch of the National Association for the Advancement of Colored People (NAACP) in 1943. The NAACP fights for the civil rights of African Americans in the United States. The next year, James won a lawsuit in the California Supreme Court. It stopped a union from discriminating against its African American members. This decision led to more court cases that stopped employers and unions from discriminating based on race.

Find Out More

1. What impact did Joseph James have on the lives of African American workers?

_____

_____

_____

_____

2. Research to find a news article that shows someone who respects or works to protect the rights of others.

Visual Review

Use these graphics to review some of the vocabulary, people, and ideas from this chapter.

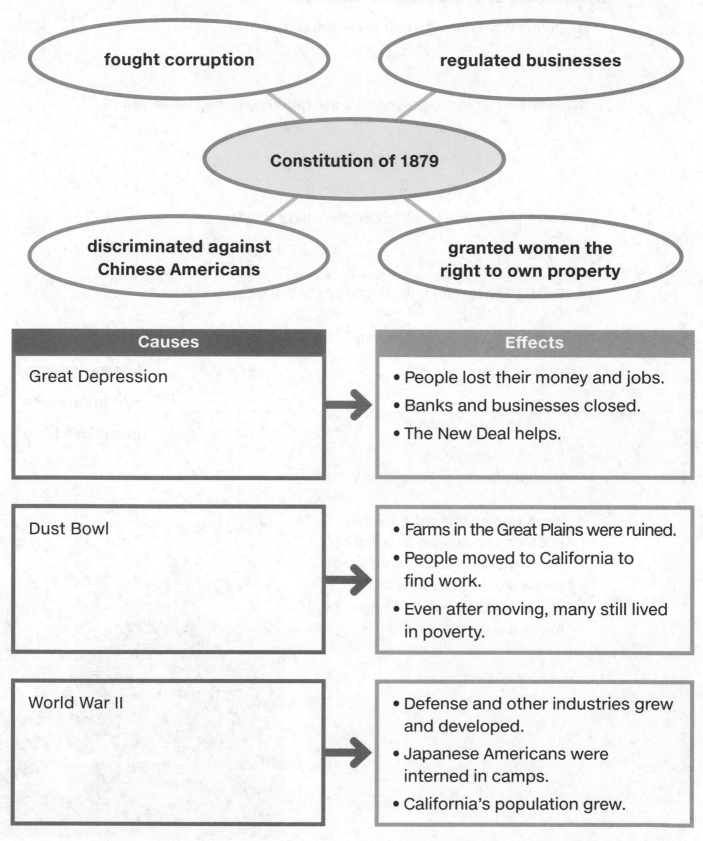

Causes	Effects
Great Depression	• People lost their money and jobs. • Banks and businesses closed. • The New Deal helps.
Dust Bowl	• Farms in the Great Plains were ruined. • People moved to California to find work. • Even after moving, many still lived in poverty.
World War II	• Defense and other industries grew and developed. • Japanese Americans were interned in camps. • California's population grew.

6 ☑ Assessment

Vocabulary and Key Ideas ⓢ HSS 4.4.4, 4.4.5 Analysis RE.1

1. **Define** What does it mean to **reform** something?

   _____

2. **Define** Why did the government use **rationing** during World War II?

   _____

   _____

3. **Identify** Fill in the blank to complete the sentence.

   A powerful _____ shook San Francisco in 1906.

4. **Draw** a line to match the definitions with the correct terms.

   dishonest and illegal behavior   **corruption**

   without a job   **defense industry**

   people who move from   **migrant workers**
   place to place for work
                                                      unemployed
   industry that makes
   supplies for the military

5. **Analyzing an Image** Study the photograph showing an effect of the Great Depression. What words can you use to describe it? What does the image help you understand about this period in history?

   _____

   _____

   _____

   _____

Critical Thinking and Writing

HSS 4.4.4, 4.4.5, 4.5.2
Analysis HI.1, HI.3

6. **Determining Causes** Fill in the circle next to the best answer.
   What was a main reason for California's rapid population growth during the late 1800s and early 1900s?

   (A) The rest of the country was in a depression.

   (B) Canadians crossed the border and stayed.

   (C) People moved to the state to find jobs.

   (D) Trade between California and Japan increased.

7. **Analyze** What was an important way the California state government worked to fix corruption in the late 1800s?

   _____

   _____

   _____

8. **Compare** the Bracero program to the deportation of Mexicans and Filipinos during the Great Depression.

   _____

   _____

   _____

   _____

9. **Revisit the Big Question** Give one example of how people responded to either good times or bad during this period.

   _____

   _____

   _____

10. **Writers Workshop: Write Informative Text** On a separate sheet of paper, write two short paragraphs about life in California during World War II. Choose the perspective of a factory worker, service member, or Japanese American citizen.

"California, California
Here I come too.
With a coffee pot and skillet,
And I'm coming to you.
Nothing left in Oklahoma,
For us to eat or do.
. . . Come to California,
Eat and eat till your full."

–Flora Robertson, "Why We Come to California," 1940

11. In the poem, why did Robertson leave Oklahoma? How did she hope life would be different in California?

_____

_____

_____

Sequence ⓘ **Analysis** CST.1, HI.1

12. The events that occurred in the United States in the late 1800s and early 1900s had a big impact on life in California. Identify a sequence of at least two events that happened during this time and write how they affected life in California.

_____

_____

_____

_____

_____

_____

Quest Findings

INTERACTIVITY

Use this activity to help you write your report.

Write Your Report

You've read the lessons in this chapter and now you're ready to write your report. Remember that the goal of your report is to share how a person or group of people who lived in California during this period responded to challenges. Follow these steps:

1 Prepare to Write

Review what you learned about life during this period. Pick the person or group of people you are going to write about. Take notes about the challenges they lived through and how they responded.

2 Write a Draft

Use your notes to write your report. Make sure your draft answers the following questions:

- What challenges did the person or group face during this period?
- How did the person or group overcome them?

3 Share With a Partner

Exchange your draft report with a partner. Tell your partner what you like about the report and what could use improvement. Be polite when you provide suggestions.

4 Revise

Make changes to your report after meeting with your partner. Correct any grammatical or spelling errors.

GO ONLINE FOR
DIGITAL RESOURCES

▶ VIDEO

👆 INTERACTIVITY

🔊 AUDIO

🎮 GAMES

☑ ASSESSMENT

📖 ETEXT

The **BIG** Question ## How can change create opportunities?

▶ VIDEO

At this ceremony, immigrants to California become United States citizens.

Lesson 1
Expanding Rights and Political Change

Lesson 2
California's Economy

Lesson 3
Immigration and Trade

Lesson 4
Education

Lesson 5
Culture

JumPstart Activity

 INTERACTIVITY

Think about a time when something changed in your life. Maybe a younger brother or sister was born. Maybe you moved to a new city. Walk around and find a partner. Discuss your changes with each other. Then, sit down and think about the effects of your change. What was good about it? What was hard? Make a list of the effects.

_____

_____

_____

_____

HSS 4.4.6, 4.4.8, 4.4.9 **Analysis** CST.1, CST.3, RE.2, HI.2, HI.3, HI.4
ELA L.4.2, L.4.3, L.4.4, RI.4.1, RI.4.2, RI.4.3, RI.4.4, RI.4.5, RI.4.7, W.4.1, W.4.2, W.4.4

Rap About It!

 AUDIO

Driving Change

Preview the chapter vocabulary as you sing the rap:

California has many industries
Just take a listen and we'll name a few of these
Commercial agriculture or farming for profit
Good weather and soil why would you stop it?

Aerospace is another big trade
It's where technology for flying is made
Up into space or wherever you fly
Think California and look to the sky

Trade is a part of the economy
We **export** goods to other countries
Our **ports** are considered to be top grade
Where ships load and unload goods for trade

Entertainment is a major industry
Music you hear, that blockbuster movie
Actors playing characters on TV and screen
Hollywood in Los Angeles is where to be seen

Where do Californians get an education?

This map shows California's public universities.

Locate and circle the university closest to where you live.

University of California Los Angeles

What happened and When?

Read the timeline to learn about important events that have happened in California since World War II ended in 1945, a period called the postwar era.

TODAY
The University of California Los Angeles, or UCLA, has almost 45,000 students.

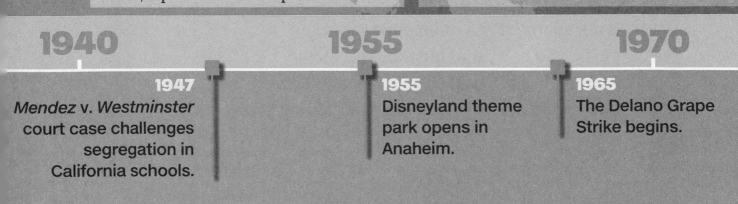

1940	1955	1970

1947
Mendez v. *Westminster* court case challenges segregation in California schools.

1955
Disneyland theme park opens in Anaheim.

1965
The Delano Grape Strike begins.

Who will you meet?

Ronald Reagan A movie star who went on to serve as California's governor and the 40th president of the United States

Dolores Huerta A leader in the struggle for the rights of farm workers who co-founded the National Farm Workers Association with César Chávez

Walt Disney A pioneer in the field of animation who founded Walt Disney Studios and built Disneyland, one of the world's most popular tourist attractions

Louis B. Mayer A Hollywood film producer who co-founded Metro-Goldwyn-Mayer (MGM), a major film studio

👆 **INTERACTIVITY**

Complete the interactive map digital activity.

1985

2000

2015

1990
California's population approaches 30 million.

2013
Hollingsworth v. *Perry* court case legalizes same-sex marriage in California.

Quest
Document-Based Writing

The Spectacular State Awards

Hello! I'm Director Dawn. I'm directing the Spectacular State Awards here in Hollywood. Different states will win awards for achievements in categories like technology, education, and culture.

Quest Kick Off

Your mission is to write an opinion essay. Convince the judges that California should win in one of these categories.

1 Ask Questions

What makes you proud of your state? Why does California deserve an award? Write down questions you have about California's achievements in technology, education, or culture.

....

....

....

....

2 Plan

How can you learn more about California's achievements in technology, education, or culture? What sources can help you? Write down some ideas here.

....

....

....

....

INTERACTIVITY

Explore California's achievements in technology, education, and culture.

3 Look for Quest Connections

Turn to the next page to begin looking for Quest connections that will help you get some ideas about the great things Californians have done.

4 Quest Findings
Write Your Essay

Use the Quest Findings page at the end of the chapter to help you write your essay.

Lesson 1

Expanding Rights and Political Change

INTERACTIVITY

Participate in a class discussion to preview the content of this lesson.

Unlock
The **BIG**
Question

I will know how people struggled for civil rights in California and how the state's politics have changed.

Vocabulary

poverty
civil rights
activist
boycott
movement
segregation

Academic Vocabulary

occupy

Jumpstart Activity

Work in a small group and talk about any changes you would like to see in your school or community. For example, do you feel safe crossing the streets near your school? Do you think your school cafeteria serves healthy food?

In the years after World War II, a flood of new residents arrived in California looking for work and new homes. These new residents came from all across the United States and from many other countries. By 1962, California had more people than any other state in the United States.

Workers on a California farm

260

Changing Population and Politics

ELA RI.4.1, RI.4.4, RI.4.5, L.4.4

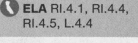

INTERACTIVITY

Explore the key ideas of this lesson.

You have learned that immigrants have been coming to California for a long time. Many more have come to find jobs in the years since World War II, including many from Mexico and Asian countries. The state has become more diverse. The population has grown in part because of immigration. In 1950, California's population was about 10.5 million. In 2015, it was more than 39 million.

As the state's population grew, new Californians needed homes, healthcare, transportation, and other services in order to live. California had trouble keeping up with the demands of all the new people. The rising population led to challenges, including pollution and **poverty**. Poverty is the state of being very poor and in need of resources. Poverty remains an issue in California today. Organizations and concerned citizens work to help people who live in poverty. They may help in finding them good jobs, for example.

Immigrants to California sometimes faced discrimination. They had to work hard for their rights. For example, many immigrants faced discrimination when they tried to get a job, buy a house, or rent an apartment. The state became a center of important **civil rights** struggles during the second half of the 1900s. Civil rights are the rights of all citizens to freedom and equality.

California's politics also affected the nation after World War II. One president during this period, Richard Nixon, was born in California. Another president, Ronald Reagan, had served as California's governor. Reagan moved to California as a young man and became a famous movie star before he entered politics.

1. ☑ **Reading Check**
Use Evidence From Text Identify and underline one way that California's population changed after World War II.

Rights for Farm Workers

Agriculture has been a big business in California for a long time. But farm workers have long faced poor treatment. For example, in the past some workers had to pay a quarter in order to drink a cup of water. Their housing had no heat, kitchens, or indoor plumbing. Children were forced to work. Some workers even died from workplace accidents. They were among the worst-paid people in the country. They also had no job security, which meant they could be fired at any time. They organized to fight for better treatment.

In 1965, the Agricultural Workers Organizing Committee and labor leader Larry Itliong organized a strike against grape growers in the city of Delano. Itliong and many of the farm workers were from the Philippines. Itliong came to the United States in 1929 at the age of 15. He joined his first strike the following year. Beginning in the 1930s, Itliong worked hard to secure fair wages for farm workers.

Activists César Chávez and Dolores Huerta quickly joined Itliong's strike. An activist is someone who works hard for change. César Chávez became well known for his work on behalf of farm workers. He also was a leader in issues important to Mexican Americans. He worked for fairness and equality in immigration, education, and political activity.

Chávez and Huerta had, in 1962, started a different union called the National Farm Workers Association. When Itliong, Chávez, and Huerta joined forces, their combined union was called the United Farm Workers (UFW). The UFW wanted better pay and working conditions for all farm workers. They also wanted to educate people about the challenges farm workers faced.

Dolores Huerta was born in New Mexico but moved to California when she was a child. She became an important labor activist.

César Chávez led striking farm workers.

Chávez, Huerta, and the UFW used nonviolent methods to support their cause. This means they used protests, not violence, and worked to teach people about their cause. For example, Chávez called for a **boycott** of grapes. A boycott is when people refuse to buy something in order to make a point. Millions of Americans refused to buy grapes or grape products. Grape growers started losing money.

The Delano Grape Strike lasted five years. In 1970, the growers agreed to give the workers higher wages and better working conditions. Since then, however, working conditions for farm workers have remained poor. Wages are very low and farm owners do not provide housing. Some farm workers have to sleep outside or in their cars. Today, California farm workers and activists still work to improve life for farm workers. For example, an organization called California Rural Legal Assistance helps farm workers get educational training. With more education, some workers might find higher paying jobs.

This striking UFW member's sign says *huelga*, which means "strike" in Spanish.

2. ☑ **Reading Check** Fill in the graphic organizer and **identify** the missing effects of the struggle for farm workers' rights.

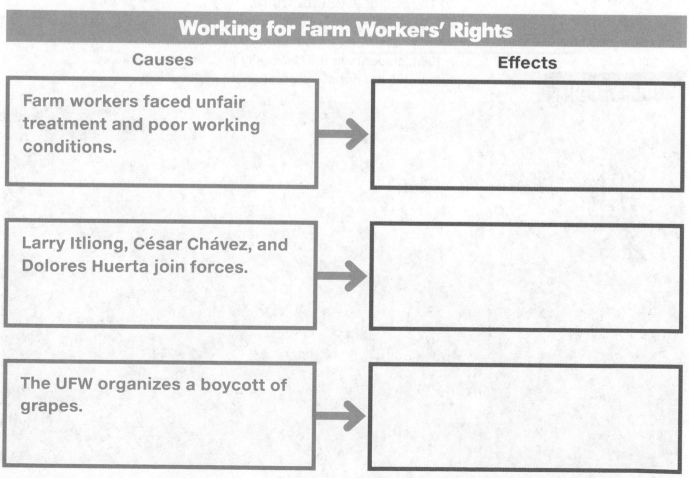

Working for Farm Workers' Rights

Causes	Effects
Farm workers faced unfair treatment and poor working conditions.	
Larry Itliong, César Chávez, and Dolores Huerta join forces.	
The UFW organizes a boycott of grapes.	

Student Activism

Activism was not limited to farm workers. Many people, including students, worked to bring change in California during the 1960s. For example, high school students in Los Angeles demanded that Mexican American history be taught in their classes. They also wanted more Latino teachers and principals.

Students at San Francisco State University and the University of California, Berkeley, also protested for changes. In 1964, students at the University of California, Berkeley, started the Free Speech Movement. A **movement** is a group of people who work together to achieve a goal. At that time, universities limited political protests. Students wanted to speak up about important issues of the time. They demanded the right to protest.

Students also demanded that schools teach more about the history of women and minority groups. Students at San Francisco State University and the University of California, Berkeley, protested until Asian American history was added to the subjects taught there.

3. ☑ **Reading Check**

With a partner, study the photo and **analyze** what it shows about student activism at that time.

In 1964, students at the University of California, Berkeley, demanded the right to protest about political issues.

Primary Source

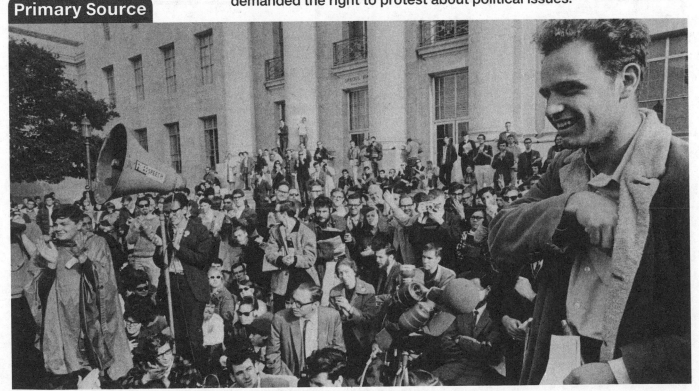

The occupation of Alcatraz Island was a major event in American Indian activism.

Struggles for Equal Rights

As you have read, discrimination against immigrants and minorities has long been a problem. This is true in California and across the country.

In the 1950s, the movement for African American civil rights grew across the nation and in California. African Americans protested against discrimination. They demanded equal rights in schools, housing, the workplace, and society.

Mexican Americans also fought for their rights. In 1947, a court case known as *Mendez* v. *Westminster* challenged racial **segregation** in Orange County. Segregation is the forced separation of people. At that time, Mexican and Mexican American children were forced into separate schools from other children. Five Mexican American men challenged this. The court found that this segregation went against the United States Constitution. The case was an important step on the way to *Brown* v. *Board of Education*. In that 1954 case, the Supreme Court said that school segregation anywhere in America went against the Constitution.

American Indians also struggled for their rights during this time. A group of Indian activists **occupied** Alcatraz Island in San Francisco Bay in 1969.

Word Wise

Suffixes A suffix is a letter or group of letters added to the end of a word to change its meaning. One common suffix is *–tion*. When you add this to a verb, it becomes a noun. Remember that a verb is an action word while a noun is a person, place, or thing. When you add this suffix to *segregate*, for example, you get *segregation*. Find the word *occupation* on this page. What verb does it come from? What do you think *occupation* means?

Academic Vocabulary

occupy • *v.*, to take control of a place

The protestors aimed to bring awareness to the poor living conditions faced by many American Indians. They also wanted to turn the island into a cultural center. The occupation lasted 19 months until the government forced the protestors to leave.

Lesbian, gay, bisexual, and transgender (LGBT) Californians have also had to struggle for their rights for many years. Two important early gay and lesbian rights groups, the Mattachine Society and the Daughters of Bilitis, were founded in California in the 1950s. California gay and lesbian rights groups worked hard to end discrimination. In 1978, activists fought against a proposed law that would have banned gay and lesbian people from working as teachers. The law was defeated. One of the activists who opposed it was Harvey Milk.

Harvey Milk was an outspoken voice in the struggle for gay and lesbian rights. Milk was elected to the San Francisco Board of Supervisors in 1977. He was California's first openly gay public official. While in office, Milk was killed by another member of the board, Dan White.

Until recently, it was illegal for people of the same sex to marry one another. For many years, gay and lesbian couples struggled for their right to get married. They worked to pass laws making marriage for same-sex couples legal. They also argued in court. In the 2010s, the United States Supreme Court ruled on the issue. In the case *Hollingsworth* v. *Perry*, in 2013, the court made marriage for same-sex couples legal in California. Then, in 2015, in the case *Obergefell* v. *Hodges*, the court made it legal throughout the country.

Transgender Californians have made strides towards greater equality in recent years. In 2010, Victoria Kolakowski became California's first openly transgender elected official. Kolakowski became a trial judge in Alameda County, near San Francisco.

4. ☑ **Reading Check**
With a partner, **identify** and **discuss** a key event in the struggle for LGBT rights.

Many Californians have fought hard for their own rights and the rights of others. Activists with different political views continue to hold protests and organize about many different issues.

After the *Hollingsworth* v. *Perry* decision, Sandy Stier and Kris Perry could legally get married.

INTERACTIVITY

Check your understanding of the key ideas of this lesson.

☑ Lesson 1 Check

ELA RI.4.1, RI.4.2

5. **Cause and Effect Explain** the effects of student activism in the 1960s.

_____

_____

_____

6. **Summarize** why *Mendez* v. *Westminster* was an important step in the struggle for equal rights for Mexican Americans.

_____

_____

_____

7. **Cause and Effect** What did the UFW hope to achieve? How did it work to achieve it?

_____

_____

César Chávez, "A Farm-Bred Unionist"

César Chávez and his family were migrant farm workers in California. Migrant workers lived in difficult conditions, and worked hard for little pay. As an adult, Chávez worked to improve conditions for farm workers.

The newspaper article below describes the activist work César Chávez was doing in the 1960s. Notice that Chávez did not write the article. Rather, it includes quotes from him.

fertile, *adj.*, good for growing crops

fledgling, *adj.*, new and inexperienced

contract, *n.*, an agreement to do work for payment

viable, *adj.*, able to grow and develop

Vocabulary Support

speaking softly and with strong belief in himself

organized and energized

Mr. Chavez first came to wide public attention in 1965, when he called a strike of grape pickers in the hot and fertile San Joaquin Valley around Delano. Since then, his fledgling union has won about a dozen contracts with major wine processors.

The struggle, Mr. Chavez himself admits, is far from over. But he has succeeded where others failed for 30 years, in building the foundation for the nation's first viable farm worker union.

"A big job has to be done and we know it," he said. "It will take many years. But," he added with quiet conviction, "we know that a union of farm workers is going to be built somehow because the workers are on the move, and they want a union."

—"A Farm-Bred Unionist", *The New York Times*, March 11, 1968

César Chávez fought for the rights of migrant farm workers.

Close Reading

Analysis RE.2 **ELA** RI.4.1, RI.4.2

1. **Explain** why you think Chávez says that workers "want a union."

_____

_____

_____

_____

2. **Identify** and circle in the article one success of Chávez's union.

3. **Describe** opportunities for farm workers that might have resulted from the changes Chávez and the union made.

_____

_____

_____

_____

Wrap It Up

Re-read the newspaper article. What questions do you have about Chávez and the union?

_____

_____

_____

_____

Lesson 2 California's Economy

INTERACTIVITY

Participate in a class discussion to preview the content of this lesson.

Unlock The BIG Question

I will know how California's economy changed and grew after World War II.

Vocabulary

freeway
suburb
urbanization
hydroelectric power
commercial agriculture
aerospace

Academic Vocabulary

consequence
revenue

JumpStart Activity

Work with a partner and try to list every kind of technology you use daily. Think about everything you do, from the time you get up to the time you go to sleep. Then, make a class list of all the technology everyone uses.

You have read that California's economy changed during World War II. Before the war, California was less developed than some other states. Californians mostly grew crops and produced resources. During and after the war, new industries grew in California. The state became an industrial giant.

California's freeway system connects cities and suburbs.

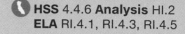

HSS 4.4.6 **Analysis** HI.2
ELA RI.4.1, RI.4.3, RI.4.5

INTERACTIVITY

Explore the key ideas of this lesson.

After the war, millions of Californians moved to suburbs like Glendale. It is a suburb of Los Angeles. How does suburban architecture compare to the architecture of cities that you have seen photos of?

Freeways and Suburbs

California's towns and cities are connected by freeways. A **freeway** is a highway that does not cost money to use. Freeways allow for faster travel than smaller roads. The first freeway in the western United States was built in California. It was built in 1940 and connected Los Angeles and Pasadena. In the years that followed, many more freeways were built, and the state soon had a large freeway system.

The freeway system changed the state in a number of ways. First, it led to the decline of railway systems that connected cities. Instead, people traveled by car. Second, California's industries grew stronger because fast new roads helped California businesses ship their goods. Also, workers could travel to their jobs more quickly.

The freeways changed California's settlement pattern, or where people live. More people chose to live in suburbs. **Suburbs** are communities located near cities. The development of suburbs changed California's landscape. Soon, suburbs popped up all over California. Older suburbs grew larger.

1. ☑ **Reading Check**
Identify and underline two effects that California's freeway system had on the state.

Urbanization and the Environment

Urbanization is when people move from rural areas to towns and cities. During and after World War II, California became more urbanized. This affected the environment. To build freeways and suburbs, people cut down orchards, fields, and farmland. For example, towns and cities in the Santa Clara Valley, like San Jose, grew and expanded onto agricultural land.

Growing towns and cities needed good sources of water and electricity. You have read how Californians built canals, dams, and reservoirs to move water starting in the 1800s. These projects provided drinking water to cities and irrigation water to farms.

However, the state's environment was damaged by all this construction. For example, it polluted wild rivers and watersheds. A watershed is an area of land around a lake or river. In the watershed, all precipitation that falls drains into that body of water. When parts of a watershed are polluted, rain and melting snow may carry that pollution into rivers and lakes. This harms the people and animals that depend on those sources of water.

California has always depended heavily on its ground water, or water we get from underground. In fact, in an average year, it provides almost 40 percent of the state's water. However, using so much ground water over many years has had **consequences**. Some wells have dried up. Some canals collapsed after the water was pumped out. Recently, laws have been passed to control how much ground water is pumped to farms.

Power plants were built to supply towns and cities with electricity. Some of these plants used hydroelectricity. **Hydroelectric power** is electricity created by the force of falling water. In 1893, the first major hydroelectric power plant began working near San Bernardino.

2. ✅ **Reading Check**
With a partner, ask and answer questions that **explain** how urbanization was shaped by California's geography.

Academic Vocabulary

consequence • *n.*, a result or effect

This hydroelectric plant is part of the Hetch Hetchy power system, which provides electricity to San Francisco.

Commercial Agriculture

Agriculture has long been an important part of California's economy. You have read about how California's geography and environment make places like the Central Valley good for growing crops. After World War II, farming became big business. **Commercial agriculture** means farming for profit, rather than to eat what you grow. By 1947, California provided about one third of the country's fruit. The following year, California brought in more **revenue** from agriculture than any other state for the first time.

After World War II, farms in California changed. First, as cities grew, farms were pushed into new areas. For example, when the city of San Jose expanded, fruit farms in that area relocated to the Central Valley.

Another change was the use of new machines to plant, water, and pick crops. Farm owners were looking for ways to grow food faster and more cheaply. Sometimes, machines replaced farm workers. An example of this was tomato harvesting. In 1960, all of California's tomatoes were picked by hand. By 1968, nearly all tomatoes were picked by machines. However, the prediction that machines would replace all farm workers has not come true. Today, agriculture is still one of California's leading industries. Hundreds of thousands of people work in agriculture.

Commercial agriculture affected the environment. Big farming machines polluted the soil and the air. Pesticides polluted water. These are chemicals that help control insects that eat crops.

Californians still work to protect the environment from these and other problems. In 2015, for example, citizens in Los Angeles protested the use of fracking. Fracking is a new way to get oil and natural gas out of the ground. However, many citizens are concerned that fracking pollutes groundwater.

The machine on the right harvests tomatoes. The trailer on the left takes them to where they can be prepared for sale.

Academic Vocabulary

revenue • *n.*, money made by a business

3. ☑ **Reading Check**
Cause and Effect
Identify and underline the effect that large-scale agriculture had on the environment.

Oil and Automobiles

Many other industries developed and grew in California during the second half of the 1900s. One was the oil industry. As you have learned, the oil industry in Southern California began in the late 1800s. Oil production increased to meet demand during World War II and then continued to grow after the war. Oil was needed for all the cars that traveled California's new freeways and brought people to their homes in the suburbs. It was also needed to power new farm machines. California became one of the largest oil producers in the country.

Californians did not just drive cars, they also made and designed them. The state's automobile industry began in the 1900s and continued to grow during and after World War II. However, beginning in the late 1950s, California's auto industry started to contract. Today, far fewer Californians work in car factories. There are several California companies, however, that manufacture electric cars.

Word Wise

Antonyms Find the verb *contract*. Do you know what it means? Its antonym, or opposite, is *expand*. How does that help you understand its meaning?

4. ☑ **Reading Check** **Analyze** the chart. Circle which industry you would most like to work in. Then, turn and talk to a partner about why.

California's Industries

Industry	General Location
Aerospace	Southern California
Communication	Northern and Southern California
Electronics	Northern California
Large-scale commercial agriculture	Central and Southern California
Defense	Northern and Southern California
Oil and automobile	Southern California

Aerospace and Defense

The **aerospace** industry makes airplanes, spacecraft, rockets, and other things that fly. During the 1950s and 1960s, Southern California was a center of the aerospace industry. Cities like Long Beach and Carson were home to companies that manufactured airplanes. Most of these companies were also part of the defense industry. The defense industry builds weapons, airplanes, drones, and other things for the military. Southern California's economy depended greatly on the strength of the defense industry.

Californians helped the United States launch its space program during that same period. By the 1960s, hundreds of thousands of Californians worked in aerospace factories and built equipment for the space program. The first U.S. spacecraft to successfully land on the moon, *Surveyor 1*, was designed and built in California.

Today, fewer Californians work in aerospace and defense factories than in the past. In fact, the number of factory jobs in all industries in California has declined since the 1950s and 1960s.

5. **☑ Reading Check Use Evidence From Text Identify** and underline how the aerospace industry impacted the economy of southern California.

In this photo from the 1970s, workers in the city of Palmdale build a space shuttle.

INTERACTIVITY

Explore an image gallery about the history of the computer.

6. ☑ **Reading Check** Turn to a partner and **discuss** why the electronics and communications industries are important to California.

Electronics, Communication, and Entertainment

California is home to a big electronics industry. The electronics industry includes companies that make computer technology, televisions, and other things that use electricity. California also has a successful communications industry. In the past, communications companies mostly provided services to landline phones in people's homes. Today, they provide Internet and cellular phone services.

Taken together, these two industries employ hundreds of thousands of workers in the state. Some of the biggest names in technology are based in California. These companies include Google, Apple, and Facebook. All three of these companies are located in Silicon Valley. Silicon Valley is an area near San Francisco that has been the center of the electronics and communications industries for many years. The area is called Silicon Valley because companies there use silicon to make chips found inside computers and cell phones.

A technology company's headquarters in Silicon Valley

As you have read, California was the center of the film industry before World War II. After the war, the industry continued to grow. It expanded into a larger entertainment industry that included television and popular music. Television shows were produced in Southern California and became extremely popular in the 1950s. The music industry grew in the Los Angeles area when rock and roll bands began performing and recording albums there. Many thousands of people work in the entertainment industry today. You will read more about this industry later in this chapter.

The Hollywood sign in Los Angeles is a symbol of the entertainment industry.

INTERACTIVITY

Check your understanding of the key ideas of this lesson.

☑ Lesson 2 Check 🔔 HSS 4.4.6 ELA RI.4.1, RI.4.3, RI.4.5

7. **Cause and Effect Identify** one important industry in California and describe its effect on the state.

_____

_____

_____

_____

8. **Explain** why the oil industry grew after World War II.

_____

_____

_____

9. **Understand the** Quest **Connections** How would people's lives be different if cellular phones had not been invented?

_____

_____

_____

_____

Analyze Costs and Benefits

When we are making a decision, we need to analyze the costs and benefits of that decision. A **cost** is what you give up when you decide to do something. A **benefit** is what you gain by making a decision.

VIDEO

Watch a video about analyzing costs and benefits.

Conducting a cost-benefit analysis is a key part of making a decision. For example, when the Oroville Dam was built on the Feather River north of Sacramento in the 1960s, there were both costs and benefits to consider.

One benefit was that it provided a good water supply for local communities and farmers. It also provided hydroelectric power, and floods could be controlled, too. The cost was that it hurt fish that swam in the Feather River. Salmon and steelhead trout lost their natural habitat.

Read the paragraph below that identifies another situation that had costs and benefits.

After World War II, thousands of Californians moved to the suburbs.

After World War II, California's population grew and many people moved to the suburbs. There was, however, a housing shortage. New homes needed to be built. Building new homes provided jobs to people who worked in the construction industry. But valuable farmland was lost in the process. This hurt farmers. Less farmland meant fewer crops for farmers to sell. Construction also destroyed trees and wetlands, killing birds and fish. Still, there were benefits to having so many new homes. Low-cost housing was available to the state's growing population.

1. Use the graphic organizer to analyze the situation described in the paragraph you just read. Include information about costs in the first column and benefits in the second column.

Costs	Benefits

2. Go back to Lesson 2 and re-read the section titled "Urbanization and the Environment." Use the graphic organizer to summarize the costs and benefits of increased urbanization in postwar California. If the costs and benefits are not clearly stated, try to draw inferences.

Costs	Benefits

3. Choose an event that is currently going on in your school or community and conduct a cost-benefit analysis. Use a separate piece of paper and organize your work in a graphic organizer like the ones you completed on this page.

Lesson 3 Immigration and Trade

INTERACTIVITY

Participate in a class discussion to preview the content of this lesson.

Unlock The BIG Question

I will know how California changed as a result of increased immigration and trade.

Vocabulary

refugee
export
port
opposition

Academic Vocabulary

contribute

Jumpstart Activity

Work in a small group and talk about your favorite foods from different countries around the world. Do you know where they come from? Can you find these places on a world map?

In 1965, the United States passed a new law called the Immigration and Nationality Act. This law made it easier for people from different parts of the world to come to this country. Before the act, the law made it hard for non-Europeans to immigrate. But by 2010, nine out of ten immigrants came from outside of Europe. In particular, people came from countries in Latin America and Asia.

In San Diego, people can cross the border into Mexico.

MEXICO

Coming to California

HSS 4.4.6 **Analysis** CST.3
ELA L.4.4, RI.4.1, RI.4.3, RI.4.4, RI.4.5, RI.4.7

Many of the immigrants who arrived in the United States after the law was changed came to California. By 1970, most newcomers to California were coming from other countries rather than from other parts of the United States.

INTERACTIVITY

Explore the key ideas of this lesson.

You have already read about how push and pull factors lead immigrants to move to new places. Pull factors that brought immigrants to California included jobs, freedom, and new opportunities. Because California has so many different industries, it can provide lots of jobs.

Many immigrants came to be reunited with family members. Cities like San Francisco and Los Angeles attract immigrants because they are thought of as socially and culturally free. This means people can freely practice their cultures there.

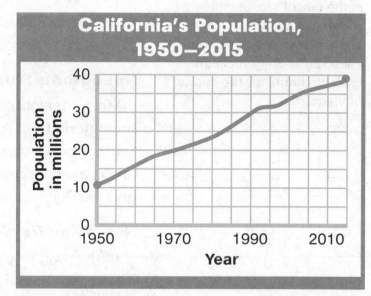

California's location is another a pull factor. Many come from Mexico, which borders California. Others come from countries across the Pacific Ocean. California is closer to these countries than the East Coast is. Southern California's warm climate also attracts immigrants.

Source: U.S. Census

Another law that affected immigration was the Refugee Act of 1980. This was a pull factor for some immigrants. **Refugees** are people who leave their own country for safety, running away from war or violence. This law increased the number of refugees the United States could accept per year. Many refugees chose to settle in California.

1. ☑ **Reading Check Analyze** the line graph and circle the year in which California's population came closest to 30 million.

This Vietnamese market is in the city of Westminster, which has its own Vietnamese neighborhood called Little Saigon. Saigon is an old name for the capital of Vietnam.

Immigrants From Around the World

California is home to more than 10 million immigrants. They come from countries all over the world.

Immigrants From the Americas

Many immigrants have come to California from Mexico. Immigrants from Spanish-speaking countries in Central and South America also made their way to California. They have also come from countries in the Caribbean, such as Cuba, Haiti, and the Dominican Republic.

New Asian Immigrants

In the past, most Asian immigrants to California came from China, Japan, and the Philippines. Many still come from these countries. But in recent years, immigrants from countries like India, Pakistan, Sri Lanka, Bangladesh, and South Korea have also come to California in numbers larger than ever before.

During the 1960s and 1970s, the United States was involved in the Vietnam War. In 1975, Congress passed a law to help refugees from that conflict enter the country. As a result, many immigrants from Vietnam and its neighbors Laos and Cambodia settled in California. The Vietnam War was an important push factor for these immigrants.

Iranians and Armenians Arrive

A major push factor also caused many Iranians to leave their country. In 1979, the country of Iran went through a revolution. A new government took power, and many people including Muslims, Jews, and Armenians, fled from it. Today, California has a large Iranian American population, particularly in the Los Angeles area.

Many Armenian immigrants have also come to California. Armenia is a country in Asia, near Russia and Turkey. Millions of Armenians left that region in the 1900s due to conflicts. Today, there is an Armenian American community in Fresno, and you can visit the "Little Armenia" neighborhood of Los Angeles. The city of Glendale is home to about 80,000 Armenian Americans.

Immigration Past and Present

Immigrants have come to California for many years, and they still come today. Immigration is an example of how some things change while others stay the same. Immigrants have come from Latin America and Asia for a long time. That has not changed. However, in the past, more came from Latin America. Since 2010, that has changed. More immigrants now come from Asia.

2. ☑ **Reading Check** **Summarize** how immigration connects California's past and present.

_____

_____

This woman is celebrating Nowruz the Iranian New Year, at a parade in Los Angeles.

The Pacific Basin

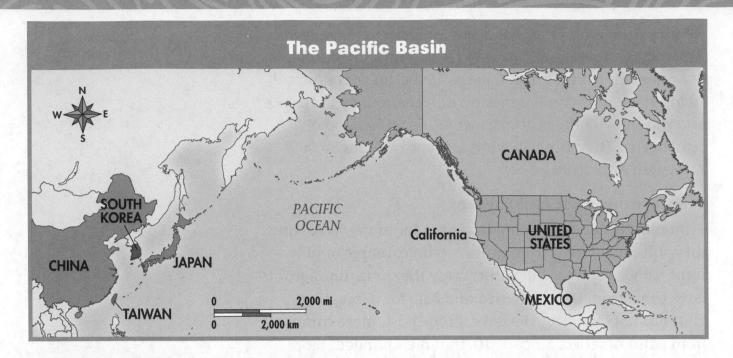

3. ☑ **Reading Check**
Study the map.
Summarize California's connection with other countries of the Pacific Basin by drawing lines from California to the places in Asia it trades with.

Word Wise

Multiple-Meaning Words
Many words in English have more than one meaning. You can see the words *basin* and *rim* on this page. *Basin* can mean a large bowl. *Rim* can mean the edge of a cup or bowl. Why do you think we use these words to describe places near an ocean?

Trade

As you know, California is located on the Pacific Ocean. It is part of the Pacific Basin, which refers to the Pacific Ocean and the countries that surround it. These countries are sometimes called the Pacific Rim, because they are on the rim, or edge, of the ocean. California has important trade links with other Pacific Basin countries.

California's economy benefits from international trade. California companies sell goods and services to places all over the world, but they sell more to Mexico, Canada, and China than to any other countries. They also sell to Japan, South Korea, and Taiwan. These countries lie across the Pacific Ocean. California also sends **exports** to countries in Europe like the Netherlands, Germany, and Great Britain. An export is something sold or traded to another country.

Cities such as Los Angeles and Long Beach have major ports through which goods pass. A **port** is a place where ships load and unload goods for trade. International trade provides jobs in port cities like these.

Trading with countries of the Pacific Basin also affects the state's culture. Californians trade cultural goods, or products, like books, music, movies, and crafts. For example, films from Asia are popular in California. K-pop is also popular in California. It is a type of music that comes from South Korea.

Immigrants Contribute to California

California attracts more immigrants than any other state in the country. More than one quarter of all Californians were born in another country. Immigrants **contribute** new skills and ideas. They do important jobs in many parts of the economy, from agriculture to technology.

Immigrants contribute to California's economy. For example, nearly half of all new businesses opened between 2007 and 2011 were founded by immigrants. Two major technology companies, Yahoo and Google, were founded in part by immigrants. Jerry Yang was born in Taiwan and immigrated to San Jose when he was 10. He helped found Yahoo in 1994. Sergey Brin is a Russian Jewish immigrant. He came to the United States when he was a young boy. Sergey Brin founded Google in 1996 along with Larry Page.

Some immigrants become involved in politics. Dalip Singh Saund was an Indian Sikh immigrant from the Punjab region of South Asia. He attended the University of California, Berkeley. In 1957, he became the first Asian American to serve in the United States Congress.

Arnold Schwarzenegger, a famous movie star, was born in Austria and immigrated to the United States when he was 21 years old. From 2003 to 2011, he served as governor of California.

Academic Vocabulary

contribute • *v.*, to give something to a larger whole

Jerry Yang co-founded Yahoo in 1994.

Primary Source

Everything I have, my career, my success, my family, I owe to America. In this country, it doesn't make any difference where you were born . . . America gave me opportunities, and my immigrant dreams came true.

-Governor Arnold Schwarzenegger, 2004

Immigrants also contribute their unique cultures to California. This includes different foods, languages, and religious beliefs. Visiting an immigrant neighborhood like Little Saigon offers the chance to enjoy Vietnamese foods. In Little Armenia, you will hear people speaking Armenian.

4. ☑ **Reading Check**
Compare and Contrast
With a partner, **compare** two of the people mentioned in this section.

Challenges for Immigrants

Even though many immigrants have found opportunities in California, immigrants have also faced opposition. **Opposition** is organized disagreement. You have read about discrimination against immigrants in the 1800s already. More recently, California residents voted on two important propositions that dealt with immigrants in the state. In California, a proposition is a proposed law that voters can choose to pass or reject. Propositions are referred to by their numbers.

In 1986, Californians voted in favor of Proposition 63. It said that English would be the state's official language. This proposition was written in response to the growing number of immigrants—and languages spoken—in California. Opponents claimed that the law was unfair and would exclude many immigrants who did not speak English. They said it would make it hard for people who did not speak English to talk to government officials.

Proposition 187 was approved in 1994. This law said that undocumented immigrants could not go to public schools or get non-emergency medical care. Undocumented immigrants are immigrants who do not have the government's approval to come to the country. They do not have the documents, or paperwork, needed for legal immigration.

Both propositions made many immigrants feel unwelcome in California. In the end, however, neither Proposition 63 or 187 went into effect. A federal court ruled that Proposition 63 was not legal. Most parts of Proposition 187 were also rejected by a court.

Many people protested against Proposition 187.

Immigration Propositions

Proposition 63 (1986)   **Proposition 187 (1994)**

_____

_____

_____

5. ☑ **Reading Check** Complete the Venn diagram by **comparing** and **contrasting** Propositions 63 and 187.

☑ **Lesson 3 Check** 🕐 **HSS** 4.4.6 **ELA** RI.4.1, RI.4.3, RI.4.5

👆 **INTERACTIVITY**

Check your understanding of the key ideas of this lesson.

6. **Cause and Effect Explain** how California's relative location affects international trade.

_____

_____

7. **Explain** why immigration is important to California.

_____

_____

8. **Identify** some contributions immigrants made to California.

_____

_____

Cause and Effect

Analyzing a cause and its effect helps us understand what we read. A cause tells why something happened. An effect is what happened. Sometimes writers use the words *cause* and *effect* to show readers how events are related. Other times, you have to look for clue words such as *because*, *if*, *then*, *so*, and *changed* to help you identify the cause and effect.

VIDEO

Watch a video about analyzing cause and effect.

Historical events usually have multiple, or many, causes and effects. This means that more than one thing causes an event. That event then has more than one effect.

Read the following passage about Asian immigration to California after World War II. As you read, look for multiple causes and effects.

At the end of the Vietnam War, many refugee families came to California.

Postwar California saw an increase in the number of Asian immigrants. One of the causes of this was the Immigration and Nationality Act of 1965. This law allowed more people from Asia to come to the United States. The Vietnam War was another cause of this change. It led many people from Vietnam, Laos, and Cambodia to leave their homes as refugees. Many came to California. These new immigrants from Asia changed California. They had to fight discrimination, which led to new movements for equal rights. Also, they brought their culture to communities like Little Saigon in Huntington Beach and Koreatown in Los Angeles.

Your Turn!

Analysis HI.3 ELA RI.4.1, RI.4.3, RI.4.5

1. Using what you read on the previous page, fill in the graphic organizer with multiple causes and effects of Asian immigration in California since World War II.

Asian Immigration

CAUSES	EFFECTS

2. Re-read the section in Lesson 3 called "Trade." Fill in the graphic organizer with the causes and effects of California's international trade. Try to draw inferences if the causes and effects are not all clearly stated.

International Trade

CAUSES	EFFECTS

3. Research an event that occurred in California after World War II. On a separate sheet of paper, take notes on the multiple causes and effects of that event. Then, fill in a graphic organizer like the ones shown here with the causes and effects of that event.

INTERACTIVITY

Participate in a class discussion to preview the content of this lesson.

Vocabulary

public school
district
private school
university
higher education
campus
research
trade school

Academic Vocabulary

accessible

Unlock The BIG Question

I will know how California's educational system grew and created new opportunities for Californians.

JumPstart Activity

Work in a small group and talk about your experiences in school up until now. Then, talk about what you think school will be like when you are older. What will high school be like? Do you think you want to go to college?

Elementary schools in California educate children starting in kindergarten.

California's Schools

California's first free public school opened in 1851, the year after California became a state. **Public schools** are schools funded, or paid for, by the government.

Today, there are more than 6 million students attending public schools in California. They attend from kindergarten through high school. California has more public school students than any other state.

The state's public schools are divided into hundreds of **districts**. A district is a part of the government set up to run a certain thing in a specific area. For example, the Los Angeles Unified school district runs the public schools in Los Angeles and many nearby communities. It is the state's largest school district with more than 900 schools and nearly 650,000 students.

California also has many **private schools**. These are paid for by private groups or individuals rather than the government.

INTERACTIVITY

Explore the key ideas of this lesson.

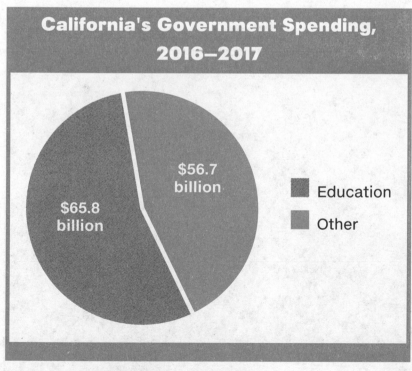

California's Government Spending, 2016–2017

$56.7 billion

$65.8 billion

■ Education
■ Other

Source: California Department of Finance

1. ☑ **Reading Check**
Analyze the graph. Then turn to a partner and **discuss** the following question: How do you know that California believes education is important?

Colleges and Universities

 Connection

In what ways could a college education affect a person's life?

INTERACTIVITY

Answer a question about the state's education system.

Education does not end when students graduate from high school. They can go on to one of many different colleges and **universities** in California for their **higher education**. A university is an educational institution designed for advanced learning. Higher education refers to education beyond high school.

Just as California has public and private schools, it also has public and private colleges and universities. In fact, it has the largest system of public state colleges and universities in the country. California's state higher education system is organized in three parts: the University of California system, the California State University system, and the California Community Colleges system.

The University of California was the state's first public university. It was founded in Berkeley in 1868. Today, the system includes 10 different campuses throughout the state and serves nearly 240,000 students. A **campus** is the land and buildings of a school.

The campus of Stanford University today

The University of California system is widely admired and is a model for the rest of the nation. A recent study that compared public universities around the country found that six of the top ten were part of this system.

Founded in 1960, the California State University system has become the largest four-year public university system in the country. It includes 23 campuses and serves more than 460,000 students. The California Community Colleges system is the largest system of higher education in the world. It includes 113 community colleges and serves more than 2.4 million students.

Stanford University is a private university located in the San Francisco Bay area. It was founded by Leland Stanford in 1885. Stanford is one of the top-rated private universities in the United States. Graduates include 21 astronauts, 51 winners of the Nobel Prize, and many members of Congress.

Sally Ride

Colleges and universities are centers of **research**. Research is deep study of a particular subject. For example, the University of California has an entire research program that works to find a cure for cancer.

Many people educated in California have gone on to achieve great things. The astronauts Sally Ride and Ellen Ochoa are good examples. An astronaut is someone trained to go into space. Sally Ride attended both the University of California, Los Angeles (UCLA), and Stanford University. She became the first American woman and the youngest American astronaut to go into space. Ellen Ochoa graduated from both San Diego State University and Stanford University. In 1993, she became the first Hispanic woman ever to go into space.

Primary Source

I tell students that the opportunities I had were the result of having a good educational background. Education is what allows you to stand out.

–Ellen Ochoa

Ellen Ochoa

2. ☑ **Reading Check** **Identify** and underline the names of two people who benefited from California's universities.

Education for All

California's schools educate people in many different subjects. They prepare students to work in fields that require highly educated workers. People who work in computer technology, the aerospace industry, science, and agricultural research need strong educations. California's economic development, businesses and industries need workers who are highly educated.

Colleges and universities are not the only places that offer higher education to Californians. **Trade schools** teach technical skills required for a specific job. At a trade school, people can learn to be auto mechanics, electricians, or video game designers. Some high schools teach these trade skills, too.

Trade schools are part of California's effort to offer opportunities for everyone. Both immigrants and Californians who were born here can benefit from the state's educational system. Education has long provided an opportunity for people to learn skills they need at work and in everyday life. California works to make education **accessible** to immigrant children. For example, schools that serve immigrant children can receive extra money to help students who are learning English.

At some high schools, students can learn skills like auto repair.

Academic Vocabulary

accessible • *adj.*, available

3. ☑ **Reading Check** **Summarize** how California's educational system creates opportunities for everyone.

_____

_____

_____

Some California schools offer programs that teach technology skills, like robotics.

☑ Lesson 4 Check

🕐 **HSS** 4.4.8 **ELA** RI.4.1, RI.4.5

4. **Cause and Effect Explain** why a student might choose to attend a trade school.

_____

_____

_____

5. **Describe** the difference between a public and a private school.

_____

_____

_____

6. **Understand the** Quest **Connections** How does California's education system contribute the state's success?

_____

_____

_____

Lesson
5 Culture

INTERACTIVITY

Participate in a class discussion to preview the content of this lesson.

Unlock The BIG Question

I will know that California's movies, television shows, museums, and music are famous around the world.

Vocabulary

popular culture
trend
Hollywood

Academic Vocabulary

responsible

JumpStart Activity

What is your favorite movie? Work with a partner and write down where the movie takes place. Is it in space? In a desert? In a city? Wherever your favorite movie is set, there is a good chance it was made in California.

California is home to some of the world's most famous artists, filmmakers, and musicians. Movies, music, television shows, and art from California are famous all over the world.

California's Cultural Impact

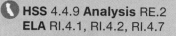

HSS 4.4.9 **Analysis** RE.2
ELA RI.4.1, RI.4.2, RI.4.7

INTERACTIVITY

Explore the key ideas of this lesson.

Since the beginning of the 1900s, California has had an important cultural impact on the United States. It has often been the birthplace of our country's **popular culture**. Popular culture refers to cultural products aimed at everyday people. Movies, books, television programs, video games, and pop music are all part of popular culture.

More movies and television shows are produced in California than in any other state. California has a busy music scene, as well. Many musicians begin their careers in the state. Also, many new **trends**, or ideas that are popular or fashionable, begin in California before spreading to the rest of the country. For example, skateboarding became popular in California and then spread across the country.

1. ☑ **Reading Check** **Summarize** what sometimes happens to trends that start in California.

_____

_____

_____

A skateboarder in California

Quest Connection

How does the quote from Louis B. Mayer show that California has had great cultural achievements?

INTERACTIVITY

View a gallery of images that show California's entertainment industry.

The entertainment industry is one of California's biggest and most well-known industries. The entertainment industry includes making movies, television, and music. People from all backgrounds contribute to the industry as filmmakers, writers, musicians, and actors. Today, many thousands of people work in the entertainment industry. It is also a reason many tourists visit California. They come to tour movie studios, for example, and to see television shows being recorded.

Movies and Television

You have read that moviemaking has a long history in California. Since the early 1900s, **Hollywood**, an area of Los Angeles, has been the center of filmmaking in the United States. The first permanent movie studio was built in Los Angeles in 1909. The area was popular for filmmaking because the weather was mild and sunny. This meant that filmmakers could film outside all year. Also, the land was cheap and movie studios were big and needed a lot of space.

In the years after World War II, the size and influence of movie studios grew. One person who helped the studios grow was Louis B. Mayer. Mayer was a Russian Jewish immigrant who helped found Metro-Goldwyn-Mayer (MGM) studios. By using business skills, Mayer and other studio leaders made the movie industry a big business.

This poster advertised a movie starring the famous actor John Wayne. He often stared in movies set in the west, called "Westerns."

Primary Source

Hollywood brings the world to the United States and the United States to the world. This interchange - of writing brains, talent, music, traditions - is important to world peace. It is equally important to good entertainment which knows no geography and has no international boundary lines.

–Louis B. Mayer

Walt Disney created animated cartoons that are still loved today.

Another person who helped build California's movie industry was Walt Disney. He was one of the first people in the entertainment industry to make cartoons for film and television. He created the character of Mickey Mouse. In 1937, Disney made the first full-length animated film, *Snow White and the Seven Dwarfs*. Beginning in the 1950s, *The Wonderful World of Disney* aired on television and highlighted Disney's Burbank studio. In 1955, he opened the Disneyland theme park in Anaheim, which still attracts millions of visitors to California every year.

George Lucas, born in Modesto, is a pioneer in the use of computers and special effects in films. His *Star Wars* films are some of the most popular movies ever made. They are also among the most successful, in terms of the number of tickets sold.

In the years after World War II, television became very popular. Television shows were, and still are, filmed at Hollywood studios. Today, movies and television are an important part of the state's economy. The industry is **responsible** for more than half a million jobs in Los Angeles County alone.

A scene from Walt Disney's *Snow White and the Seven Dwarfs*

Academic Vocabulary

responsible • *adj.*, being the cause of something

2. ☑ Reading Check With a partner, **analyze** either the movie poster or the *Snow White* image. What questions do you have about these images?

Art and Music

California is home to many famous art museums. Visitors can see famous paintings and sculptures at the Getty Museum in Los Angeles and the de Young Museum and Palace of Fine Arts in San Francisco. The state also has museums dedicated to Asian art and Latin American art. The work of California photographers Ansel Adams and Dorothea Lange is also on view at the San Francisco Museum of Modern Art, or SFMOMA, and the Oakland Museum of California.

Music began to be recorded on flat discs called records in the 1890s. In the early 1900s, Americans started buying and listening to their favorite music on records. The record industry became a big business. In the postwar era, Los Angeles became an important center for this part of the entertainment industry. Today, the city is an important center of rock, hip-hop, rap, and electronic music. Artists record their music in recording studios in the Los Angeles area. People can also listen to classical music and see operas at many concert or opera halls in California.

3. ☑ **Reading Check** Turn to a partner and **summarize** how the music industry grew in the postwar era and how it thrives today.

The Los Angeles Philharmonic performs concerts at Walt Disney Concert Hall.

Sports in California

Professional sports are very popular in California. Sports, like movies and television, are an important part of popular culture. Many Californians enjoy watching games and cheering for their favorite teams. Most major cities, including San Francisco, Los Angeles, Sacramento, and San Diego, have professional teams. In fact, California has more professional teams than any other state.

The San Diego Padres play baseball at this stadium.

4. ☑ **Reading Check** Turn to a partner and **identify** as many professional sports teams in California as you can name.

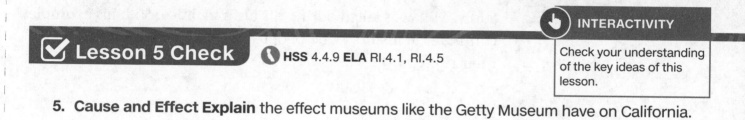

☑ **Lesson 5 Check**   🕐 **HSS** 4.4.9 **ELA** RI.4.1, RI.4.5

⬇ **INTERACTIVITY**

Check your understanding of the key ideas of this lesson.

5. **Cause and Effect Explain** the effect museums like the Getty Museum have on California.

_____

_____

6. **Explain** why Louis B. Mayer was a significant person in the entertainment industry.

_____

_____

_____

7. **Understand the** _Quest_ **Connections** How does the entertainment industry affect people's lives?

_____

_____

_____

★ Citizenship

Quality:
Honesty

Harvey Milk (1930–1978)
Honest and Brave

Harvey Milk was a Jewish gay American civil rights leader. As you learned, in 1977, he became the first openly gay man in California to win an election for public office. At that time, gay and lesbian people faced severe discrimination and prejudice across the country. Many stayed "in the closet," which means that they did not tell others that they were gay or lesbian. Not Harvey Milk, though.

Milk was born in New York in 1930. He moved to San Francisco in 1972 and started a business there. During his time in San Francisco, he became active in the gay and lesbian community. He encouraged gay and lesbian people to be honest about themselves and "come out of the closet." He supported gay- and lesbian-owned businesses so they would have more power and influence. He passionately fought for gay rights.

Sadly, Milk was killed during his term in office. Still, his example continues to inspire LGBT people today to stand up for their rights.

Find Out More

1. How did Harvey Milk demonstrate, or show, honesty?

_____

_____

_____

2. Talk to your parents, grandparents, or any older family member about why honesty is important.

Visual Review

Use these graphics to review some of the vocabulary, people, and ideas from this chapter.

California in the Postwar Era

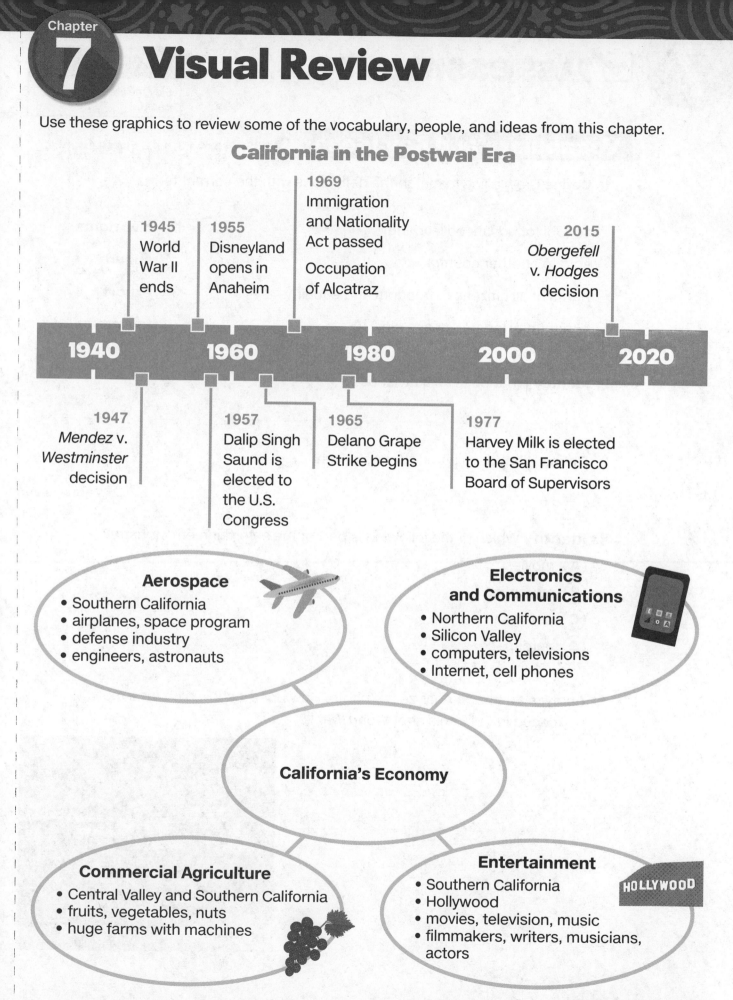

1945 World War II ends

1947 *Mendez* v. *Westminster* decision

1955 Disneyland opens in Anaheim

1957 Dalip Singh Saund is elected to the U.S. Congress

1969 Immigration and Nationality Act passed

Occupation of Alcatraz

1965 Delano Grape Strike begins

1977 Harvey Milk is elected to the San Francisco Board of Supervisors

2015 *Obergefell* v. *Hodges* decision

1940 1960 1980 2000 2020

Aerospace
- Southern California
- airplanes, space program
- defense industry
- engineers, astronauts

Electronics and Communications
- Northern California
- Silicon Valley
- computers, televisions
- Internet, cell phones

California's Economy

Commercial Agriculture
- Central Valley and Southern California
- fruits, vegetables, nuts
- huge farms with machines

Entertainment
- Southern California
- Hollywood
- movies, television, music
- filmmakers, writers, musicians, actors

HOLLYWOOD

☑ Assessment

🎮 GAMES

Play the vocabulary game.

Vocabulary and Key Ideas

🔋 HSS 4.4.6, 4.4.8, 4.4.9 **ELA** RI.4.4, RI.4.7

1. **Define** Draw a line to match the definitions with the correct terms.

school for advanced learning   **civil rights**

sold to another country   **suburb**

rights of all citizens to freedom and equality   **export**

community located near a city   **university**

2. **Identify** What does an activist do?

_____

3. **Define** What does a trade school teach? _____

_____

4. **Identify** Which of the following is part of the entertainment industry?
   (A) movies
   (B) education
   (C) politics
   (D) aerospace

5. **Analyze an Image** Analyze the photo. How does it show a change that happened in California after World War II?

_____

_____

_____

Critical Thinking and Writing

HSS 4.4.6, 4.4.8, 4.4.9 **Analysis** CST.3
ELA RI.4.1, RI.4.3, RI.4.5, W.4.2

6. **Cause and Effect** Which of the following most directly led to Californians moving to suburbs?

   (A) high-quality public education system

   (B) large-scale engineering projects

   (C) the entertainment industry

   (D) a statewide freeway system

7. **Analyze** What are some ways California's industries affect your life?

   _____

   _____

8. **Form Opinions** Which industry has impacted California the most: technology or entertainment? Explain your answer.

   _____

   _____

   _____

9. **Cause and Effect** What was one reason for the increase in Asian immigrants to postwar California?

   _____

10. **Revisit the Big Question** How did the changes you read about in this chapter create an opportunity? **Identify** one example.

    _____

    _____

    _____

11. **Writer's Workshop: Write Informative Text** On a separate sheet of paper, write two or three paragraphs explaining how some things in California have changed over time and others have stayed the same. Consider immigration, industries, struggles for equal rights, or another topic. Support your findings with details from the chapter.

Every moment is an organizing opportunity, every person a potential activist, every minute a chance to change the world.   -Dolores Huerta

12. Rephrase what Dolores Huerta said here in your own words.

_____

_____

_____

Cause and Effect ⓘ HSS 4.4.8 Analysis HI.3 ELA RI.4.1, RI.4.3, RI.4.5

13. California built the University of California campus in Merced for many reasons. The building of the campus had many effects. Read the paragraph below. Then, list the multiple causes and effects in the graphic organizer.

Until 2004, the University of California (UC) had nine campuses across California. However, building a tenth campus was discussed as long ago as 1988. University officials knew there were more students statewide who wanted to attend one of the universities in the UC system. They also wanted to provide opportunity to people living in the San Joaquin Valley. Planning began in 1998, and by 2004, the University of California, Merced, was open to students. Today, the UC Merced campus is home to more than 7,000 students. It serves many communities in the San Joaquin Valley, like the city of Fresno.

University of California, Merced

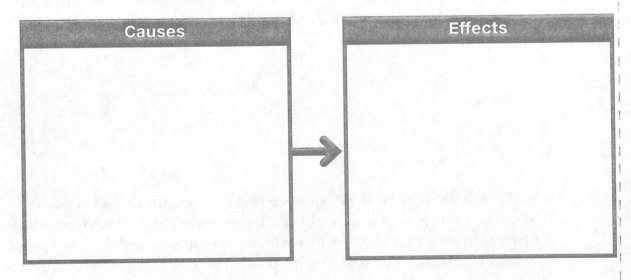

Causes	Effects

Quest Findings

👆 INTERACTIVITY

Use this activity to help you prepare to write your essay.

Write Your Essay

You've read the lessons in this chapter and now you're ready to write your opinion essay. Remember that your goal is to persuade the judges that California deserves a Spectacular State Award in one of three categories: technology, education, or culture. Make sure to provide facts to support your opinion.

1 Prepare to Write

Write your three strongest arguments for why you picked the category you did. Add facts to support your arguments. Use these notes to help you write your essay.

2 Write a Draft

Use your notes and the evidence from your Quest Connections to write a draft of your opinion essay. Make sure your essay answers the following questions:

- Which category did you choose?
- What has California achieved in this area?
- Why is this worth celebrating?
- What effect did the achievement have on California and the country?

3 Share With a Partner

Exchange your draft with a partner. Tell your partner what you like about his or her essay and what could use improvement. Be polite when you provide suggestions.

4 Revise

Make changes to your essay after meeting with your partner. Correct any errors in grammar or spelling.

8 California's Government

GO ONLINE FOR
DIGITAL RESOURCES

▶ VIDEO

👆 INTERACTIVITY

🔊 AUDIO

🎮 GAMES

☑ ASSESSMENT

📖 ETEXT

The **BIG** Question

What should the goals of government be?

▶ VIDEO

California's legislature meets in the State Capitol building in Sacramento. The governor has offices there as well.

Jumpstart Activity

👆 INTERACTIVITY

With a partner, play a game where one of you hides an object and your partner finds it. Set rules for the game before you start. Switch roles, and play another round of the game with no rules. Describe what happened when you played without rules. Explain why rules are important.

_____

_____

_____

_____

🔊 AUDIO

Our Government

Preview the chapter **vocabulary** as you sing the rap:

There are many principles in the Constitution,
which was written after the American Revolution.

The **rule of law**, no one is above it,
not even the leaders of the government.

The national government's power is shared.

The fifty states have power declared.

Federalism, as it is known
allows the states to make rules of their own.

California's constitution gives voters a voice.

They can pass **initiatives** of their own choice.

These proposals for laws need signatures to move.

Collected on **petitions**, a written request to approve.

Sacramento

American River

5

California State Capitol

Sutter's Fort

McKinley Park

50

City Historic Cemetery

50

5

Sacramento Zoo

99

William Land Park

Sacramento River

Where is California's State Capitol building?

It is located in Sacramento, California's state capital, which you can see on this map.

On the map, what landmark is closest to the California State Capitol building?

_____

If you stood under the dome at the California State Capitol building, you would see this view.

What Happened and When?

Read the timeline to find out about the events surrounding the creation of California's constitution.

1790

1788
U.S. Constitution ratified.

TODAY
The U.S. Constitution has been amended 27 times.

Who will you meet?

Governor Jerry Brown served from 1975 to 1983. He was elected again in 2010. The governor leads the executive branch.

Chief Justice Tani Gorre Cantil-Sakauye took office in 2011. The Supreme Court is part of the judicial branch.

Attorney General Kamala D. Harris served from 2011 to 2017. The attorney general is part of the executive branch.

Eric Garcetti, Mayor of Los Angeles, was elected in 2013 for a four-year term. Mayors lead local governments.

👆 **INTERACTIVITY**

Complete the interactive timeline digital activity.

1850

1849
California's first constitution drafted.

1880

1879
California's second constitution approved.

TODAY
California's constitution has been amended more than 500 times.

311

Quest

Project-Based Learning

Changing My Community: One Letter at a Time

I'm Lisa, and I'm a news reporter in your community. I'm always discovering issues that need to be addressed. When I find a problem, I let local political officials like the mayor know. Will you help me?

Quest Kick Off

Your mission is to identify an issue in the community where you live. Write a letter to convince a local political official to help address the issue. Explain the issue, how you propose to address it, and what type of help you might need.

1 Identify Issues

Think about where you live. What issues can you identify? Write down one issue and why you think it's important to address.

....

....

....

....

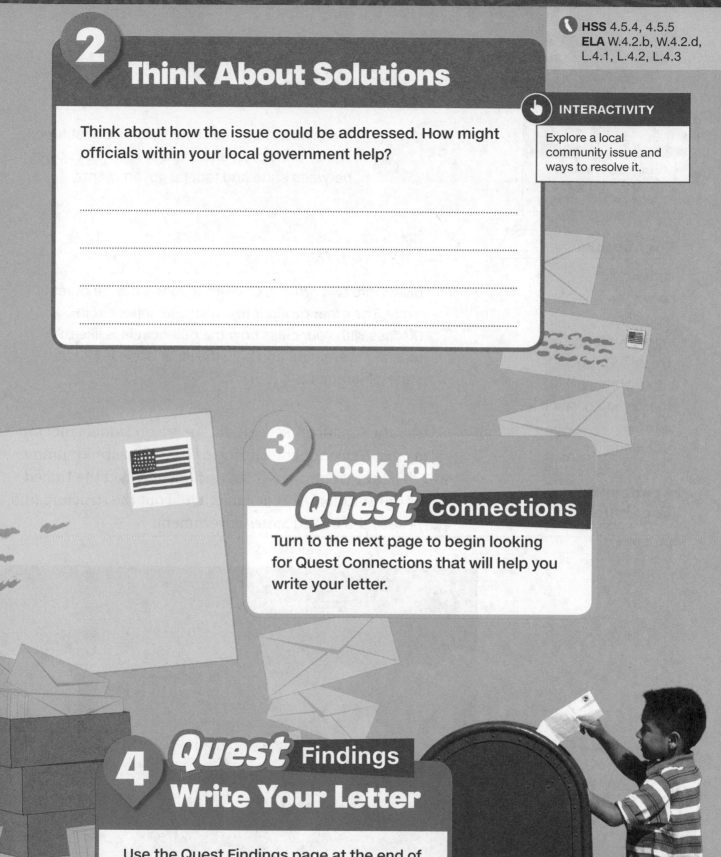

HSS 4.5.4, 4.5.5
ELA W.4.2.b, W.4.2.d,
L.4.1, L.4.2, L.4.3

2 Think About Solutions

Think about how the issue could be addressed. How might officials within your local government help?

INTERACTIVITY

Explore a local community issue and ways to resolve it.

....

....

....

....

3 Look for *Quest* Connections

Turn to the next page to begin looking for Quest Connections that will help you write your letter.

4 *Quest* Findings
Write Your Letter

Use the Quest Findings page at the end of this chapter to help you write your letter.

The United States Constitution

Unlock
The **BIG**
Question

I will understand the United States Constitution, its key principles, and the way it divides power between state and federal governments.

Vocabulary

democracy
rule of law
federalism
legislative branch
executive branch
judicial branch
checks and balances
veto
amendment

Academic Vocabulary

propose

JumPstart Activity

Divide into two groups. One group forms a large outer circle. The other group forms a smaller inner circle. Discuss with your class how the outer circle is like the federal government and how the inner circle is like the state government.

After the American Revolution, American leaders met to form a new government. During a hot Philadelphia summer in 1787, they created a written document called the United States Constitution. This document laid out the structure and purpose of the United States government.

Delegates signed the United States Constitution on September 17, 1787.

Principles of the Constitution

🛈 HSS 4.5, 4.5.1, 4.5.3 Analysis CST.3, RE.2 ELA L.4.4.b, RI.4.1, RI.4.2, RI.4.3, RI.4.4, RI.4.5, RF.4.4.a

The United States Constitution is built around several principles, or key beliefs. One of these principles says that our government is a democracy. In a **democracy**, the power of the government comes from the support of the people. Our government is also limited. Government leaders cannot do whatever they want. They are subject to the **rule of law**. This means that everyone has to follow the law, including government leaders.

👆 **INTERACTIVITY**

Explore the key ideas of this lesson.

Another principle says that the federal, or national, government shares power with state governments. This sharing of power is called **federalism**. According to the Constitution, the federal government has more power in many ways. Still, state governments have their own important powers. You will read more about these in the next lesson.

As you learned, California has its own constitution, just like every other state. This constitution applies only to the state of California, while the United States Constitution applies to the entire country. The two constitutions are alike in many ways, which you will also learn about in the next lesson.

1. ☑ **Reading Check Use Evidence From Text** Underline what the rule of law means.

The Three Branches and Their Responsibilities

The Constitution structures the federal government as three branches, or parts. These are the legislative, executive, and judicial branches. The **legislative branch** of government makes laws. At the federal level, the Senate and the House of Representatives make up the legislative branch. Together, they form the United States Congress. Voters elect two senators from each state. The number of representatives a state has in the House depends on a state's population. California has 53 representatives. It has more people than any other state, so it also has more representatives.

The **executive branch** of government is responsible for enforcing laws, or making sure people follow them. The president of the United States leads the federal executive branch. This branch also includes many people who work for the president. The president is the leader of the United States military.

2. ☑ **Reading Check**
This illustration shows our nation's capital, Washington, D.C. **Identify** and circle the branch of government that makes laws.

The **judicial branch** of government is responsible for interpreting laws. It decides what laws mean when people disagree about them. It is made up of courts and judges. At the federal level, the Supreme Court is the highest court. People who disagree with other federal court decisions can appeal to the Supreme Court. This means that they ask the Supreme Court to make a different decision.

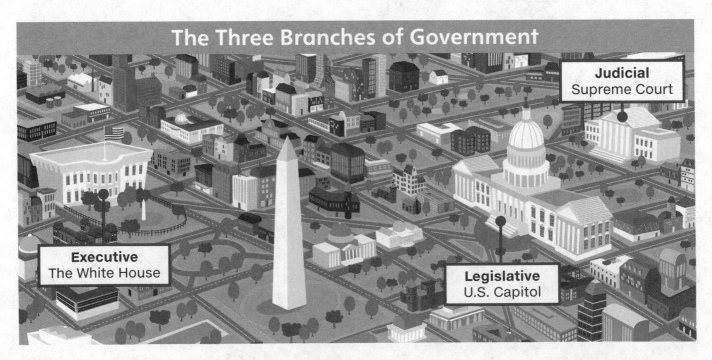

The Three Branches of Government

Judicial
Supreme Court

Executive
The White House

Legislative
U.S. Capitol

Federal Branches of Government

Executive	Legislative	Judicial
Who? _____ _____	**Who?** Congress	**Who?** _____ _____
Role: enforces laws	**Role:** _____ _____	**Role:** settles disagreements about laws

Checks and Balances

In our system of government, power is balanced among the three branches you just read about. This balance of power is known as the system of checks and balances. **Checks and balances** means each branch is allowed to check, or limit, the powers of the others. This prevents any one branch from gaining too much control.

Every branch has a certain jurisdiction, or area of control, as you learned. Congress creates and passes laws. However, if Congress passes a law that goes against the Constitution, the judicial branch can say a law is unconstitutional and cancel it. The president can **veto**, or reject, laws that Congress passes. And while the president **proposes** judges for the Supreme Court, the Senate must approve these selections.

4. ☑ **Reading Check** **Identify** one example of how Congress can check, or limit, the power of the president.

_____

_____

_____

3. ☑ **Reading Check** **Describe** the federal branches of government by filling in the chart.

Word Wise

Prefixes When you see an unknown word, try using prefixes to understand the meaning. For example, read the word _unconstitutional_. The prefix _un-_ means "not," or "the opposite of." What do you think _unconstitutional_ means?

Academic Vocabulary

propose • _v._, to suggest

Federal, State, and Local Powers

In our country, power is shared among the federal, state, and local governments. Each level has its own job to do. Sometimes, responsibilities overlap, however.

Federal Powers

The federal government created by the Constitution has power over national issues. It has many different functions, or roles. The federal government prints the dollars you use to buy things anywhere in our country. It defends the United States and runs the military. It meets with governments of other countries, takes care of our national parks, oversees the United States Postal Service, and more.

State Powers

State governments, including California's, have their own powers and functions. They are responsible for educating children and keeping the public safe. States manage driver's licenses and license plates, organize local governments, manage elections, and more.

5. ☑ **Reading Check**
Identify whether the images represent federal, state, or local responsibility.

Local Powers

Local governments have power over local issues. A local issue is one that affects a specific area, like a city or town. Local government functions include providing services that protect people, such as police and fire departments.

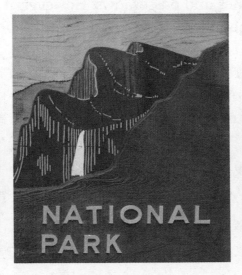

Comparing Powers

Federal, state, and local governments are alike in some ways. Both state and federal governments set up courts and collect taxes, for example. Both have legislative, executive, and judicial branches. Both have their own constitutions. Federal, state, and local governments are all responsible to the people they serve.

But these governments are also different. The federal government can send the military to fight wars, for example, while state governments cannot. The federal government can also pass laws that affect the whole country. State governments can only pass laws that affect their states. They cannot pass laws that disagree with federal laws.

Rights and Responsibilities

Citizens of the United States have rights and responsibilities. Some of our rights are laid out in the United States Constitution. The Constitution was approved in 1789, but it is not the same as when it was first written. This is because we have added **amendments**, or changes to the Constitution.

The first 10 amendments are called the Bill of Rights. They protect some of our most important rights, including the right to speak freely, as you can see in the First Amendment below. Without this protection, the government could punish people for saying things with which leaders disagree.

Primary Source

Congress shall make no law ... abridging [taking away from] the freedom of speech, or of the press; or the right of the people peaceably to assemble, and to petition the Government for a redress [correction] of grievances [problems].

—First Amendment to the U.S. Constitution

6. ✓ Reading Check **Identify** and circle the phrase in the First Amendment that supports our right to gather as a group.

Quest Connection

Highlight sentences that tell how you can make positive changes in your community.

👆 **INTERACTIVITY**

Learn how to match solutions to problems or issues in your community.

Voting is both a right and a responsibility.

Voting is both a right and a responsibility for citizens who are 18 years and older. This right is also protected by the United States Constitution. Voting allows us to choose leaders and participate in decisions that affect our communities. In our system of government, power comes from the citizens. Our democracy would not work if citizens did not vote.

We have other responsibilities as citizens, too. Citizens must obey the law and pay taxes, for example. Taxes help the government pay for things like roads, fire departments, schools, teachers, and the military.

Citizens also have a responsibility to participate in government. This means learning about issues that affect our country, state, or community, and taking action. Citizens can ask government officials to solve problems. They can protest. They can also volunteer to help solve problems in their community. They can clean up a park or a road, for example.

You have responsibilities as a young citizen, too, such as going to school and obeying the law. Even though you have to be 18 years or older to vote, you can still get involved in your community. One way you can participate is by writing a letter to your local government asking a leader to help solve a problem. You will learn more about citizenship in your community in Lesson 3.

7. ✅ **Reading Check** With a partner, **identify** one more way to volunteer in your community.

_____

One way to be involved in your community is to volunteer at a community garden.

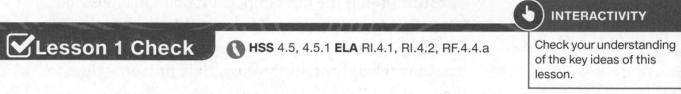

✅ **Lesson 1 Check**   🔵 **HSS** 4.5, 4.5.1 **ELA** RI.4.1, RI.4.2, RF.4.4.a

👆 **INTERACTIVITY**

Check your understanding of the key ideas of this lesson.

8. **Explain** the principle of federalism.

_____

_____

_____

9. **Explain** one reason why the United States Constitution is important to you.

_____

_____

_____

10. **Understand the** _Quest_ **Connections** What change do you think needs to happen in your school or neighborhood? Why is it important?

_____

_____

Identify Main Idea and Details

"I like reading about the government, but sometimes it's hard for me to follow."

"It's not always easy, but it can help if you find the main idea and details as you are reading."

VIDEO

Watch a video about identifying main ideas and details.

A **main idea** is the most important point in a passage. **Details** support the main idea. Identifying the main idea will help you better understand what you read, but finding the main idea is not always easy. Here are some clues to help you:

- The main idea is often (but not always) stated at the beginning of a passage.
- If the main idea is not stated, you can use the important details to figure out the main idea.
- Details give supporting information about the main idea, like facts and examples.

Federal and state governments are alike in some ways. Both state and federal governments set up courts and collect taxes, for example. Both have legislative, executive, and judicial branches. Both have their own constitutions. Federal and state governments are both responsible to the people they serve.

Your Turn!

1. What are the main ideas and details of the paragraph on the facing page? Fill in the organizer showing the main ideas and details of the paragraph.

Federal and State Governments

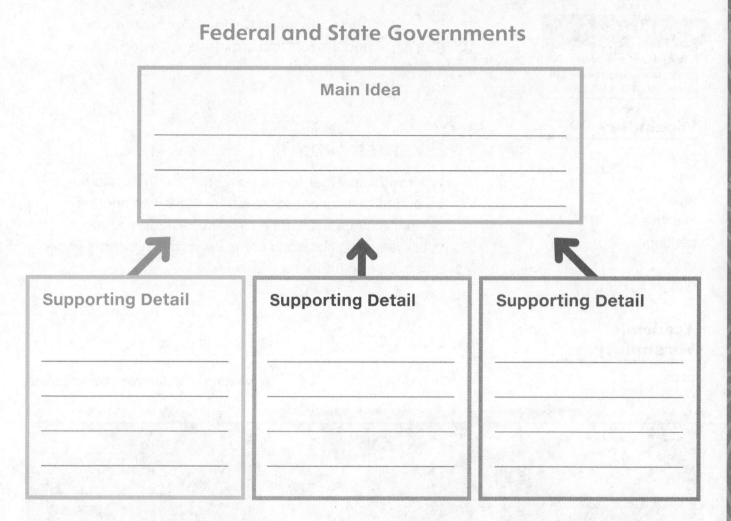

Main Idea

_____

_____

_____

Supporting Detail

_____

_____

_____

_____

Supporting Detail

_____

_____

_____

_____

Supporting Detail

_____

_____

_____

_____

2. Read the paragraphs in Lesson 1 under the heading "The Three Branches and Their Responsibilities." Analyze the information and identify the main idea. Then identify one supporting detail. Write a statement that summarizes the content.

_____

_____

_____

_____

_____

_____

Lesson 2 California's State Government

INTERACTIVITY

Participate in a class discussion to preview the content of this lesson.

Unlock The BIG Question

I will understand California's constitution and the role and structure of California's government.

Vocabulary

preamble
article
recall
initiative
petition
bill
budget

Academic Vocabulary

plan

JumpStart Activity

Work with a partner to write one rule you think should be added to a school constitution. Work with another partner to write a rule for a class constitution. Share your ideas as a class and come up with mini school and class constitutions.

A meeting of California's State Senate

As you have read, California has its own constitution, like all other states. It is like the United States Constitution in many ways. Both are written documents. Their purpose is to set up a plan for government. Both divide the government into three branches. Both are based on the same principles, like the rule of law. Both governments get their power from the people. But the United States Constitution applies to the whole country. California's constitution sets up a government for California.

HSS 4.5, 4.5.2, 4.5.3, 4.5.4
Analysis HI.1 ELA L.4.4, RI.4.1, RI.4.2, RI.4.3, RI.4.4, RI.4.5, RF.4.4.a

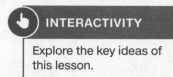

INTERACTIVITY

Explore the key ideas of this lesson.

The California Constitution

Like the United States Constitution, the California Constitution begins with a **preamble**, or introduction. **Articles**, or sections, follow the preamble. There is a Declaration of Rights in the California Constitution that is similar to the Bill of Rights. The state constitution explains how spending, voting, and education will be handled.

As you learned, California adopted a new constitution in 1879. That constitution is still in place today. It has so many rules that it is one of the longest constitutions in the world.

California's constitution is different from some other states' constitutions because it gives voters the power to **recall** officials. Citizens can remove and replace a government official, such as a governor, before the official's time in office has ended. The United States Constitution does not allow voters to recall federal officials.

California's first constitution was approved in 1849.

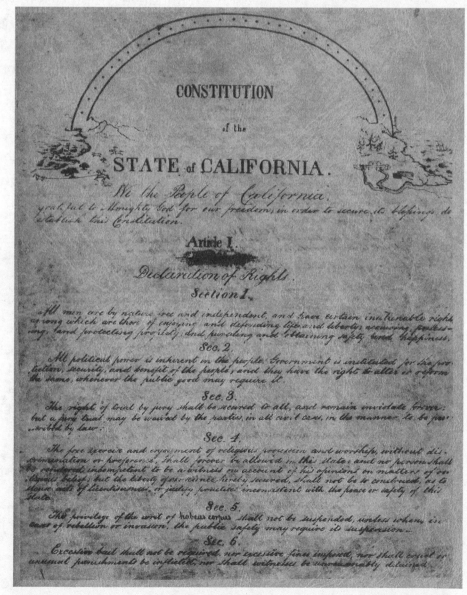

California citizens signing a petition

California also allows voters to pass their own **initiatives**. An initiative is a process in which voters vote on a proposed new law. First, supporters of the proposed law gather voters' signatures on a **petition**. With enough signatures, the proposed law is put on the ballot. To put something on the ballot allows voters to vote on it in an election. If more than half of the voters approve it, the initiative becomes law. Changes can be made to the state constitution the same way.

1. ☑ **Reading Check** **Sequence** the following steps needed to pass an initiative. Number them in order from 1 to 5.

Passing an Initiative

Step	Order
More than half of voters vote in favor of the initiative.	_____
Supporters collect signatures on a petition.	_____
Voters vote on the proposed law.	_____
The proposed law is put on the ballot.	_____
The initiative becomes law.	_____

Governing Our State

Recall that the federal government has three branches: legislative, executive, and judicial. California's state government is organized the same way.

The Legislative Branch

The state legislature is California's legislative branch. The legislature is made up of two parts, called houses. Both meet at the California State Capitol building in Sacramento. One is the Senate and the other is the Assembly. Members of the state legislature are called legislators, or lawmakers. Voters elect them. Their job is to make laws.

Legislators meet and write bills. **Bills** are proposals for new laws, which help to solve problems or **plan** for the future. Legislators vote for or against passing bills into laws. Laws passed by the legislature must follow rules that are in the state constitution. They must also follow the United States Constitution. State legislators make many important decisions. They decide how state taxes will be spent. They vote on amendments, or changes, to the Constitution.

The Executive Branch

The governor leads the state's executive branch. The executive branch makes sure people follow the law. The governor's responsibilities include approving bills passed by the legislature so that they can become law. He or she appoints, or picks, people to different positions. The governor also creates a **budget**, or plan for spending money, for the state, which the state legislature then approves.

The attorney general is another important member of the executive branch. He or she is the state's lawyer and highest law enforcement official. This means that he or she makes sure that people follow state laws. Other officials in the executive branch include the treasurer and the controller. They help manage the state's money.

2. ☑ **Reading Check**
Identify and circle the leader of the state executive branch.

California's State Assembly

The Judicial Branch

Our state's judicial branch includes the California Supreme Court, 6 courts of appeals, and 58 lower courts. One function of courts is to decide legal cases about crimes. For example, if a person accuses someone of stealing his or her bicycle, a court looks at the evidence and decides if that is true. If it is, the court decides how to punish the thief. Courts also settle many disagreements between people over legal issues.

Lower courts hear cases first. Decisions in a lower court can be appealed to a higher court. Then the higher court can decide if it agrees with the lower court's decisions. California's Supreme Court is the state's highest court. Its decisions cannot be appealed to any other state court.

Checks and Balances

You have read about the constitutional principle of checks and balances at the federal level. The state government also has checks and balances. The legislature can pass a bill, but the governor can choose to veto it. The courts can also decide that a law is unconstitutional and cancel it.

3. ☑ **Reading Check**
On the diagram, **identify** and circle the branch that makes laws.

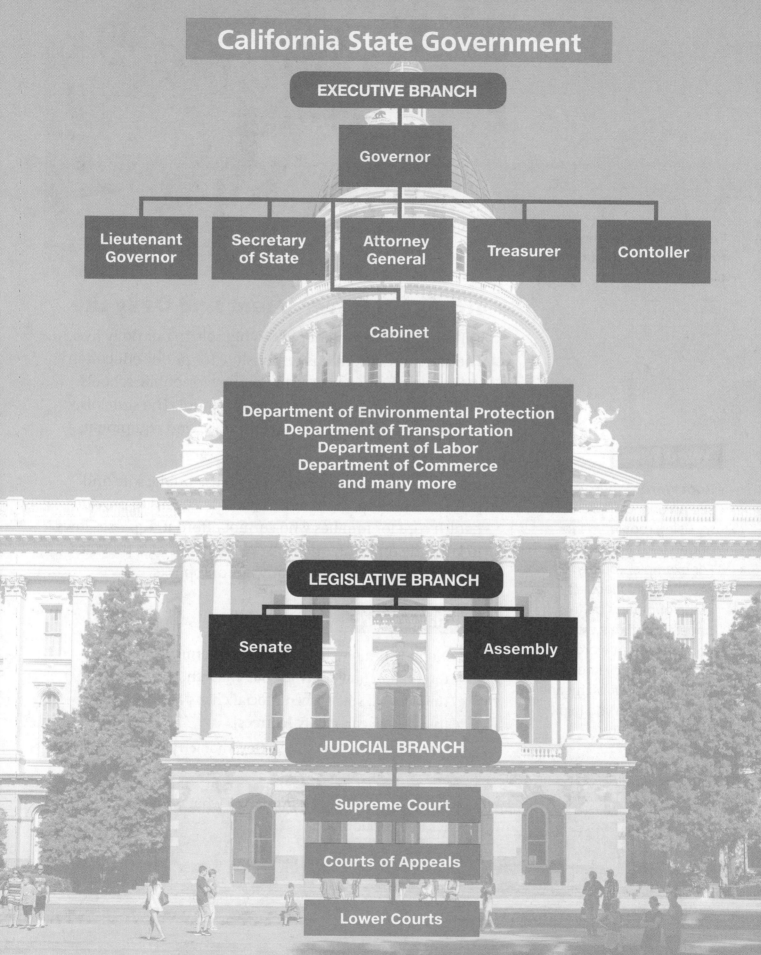

California State Government

EXECUTIVE BRANCH

Governor

| Lieutenant Governor | Secretary of State | Attorney General | Treasurer | Contoller |

Cabinet

Department of Environmental Protection
Department of Transportation
Department of Labor
Department of Commerce
and many more

LEGISLATIVE BRANCH

Senate   **Assembly**

JUDICIAL BRANCH

Supreme Court

Courts of Appeals

Lower Courts

The state provides money for things like computers in classrooms.

The State Government and Daily Life

The state government plays a big role in our daily lives. The state of California is responsible for public education. It provides the majority of the money for public schools. It decides what gets taught in your school. The state also contributes money to schools for books and equipment, such as computers.

States are responsible for keeping the public safe and healthy. The state government runs programs to provide health care for families who cannot afford it. It passes laws to keep the air clean and conserve water. It also provides money to maintain state highways and parks.

Primary Source

Nothing is more determinative [determines] of our future than how we teach our children. If we fail at this, we will sow growing social chaos and inequality that no law can rectify [correct].

—Governor Jerry Brown, 2013

4. ✅ **Reading Check** **Summarize** what Governor Brown says in this quotation.

_____

_____

_____

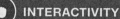
INTERACTIVITY

Check your understanding
of the key ideas of this
lesson.

☑ Lesson 2 Check

🔔 **HSS** 4.5, 4.5.4 **ELA** RI.4.1, RI.4.2, RF.4.4.a

5. **Summarize** what each branch of state government does.

_____

_____

_____

_____

_____

_____

6. **Identify** two ways the state government affects your daily life.

_____

_____

_____

_____

_____

_____

7. **Analyze** and **explain** the difference between lower courts and the state supreme court.

_____

_____

_____

_____

_____

_____

California Constitution: Article III

California's constitution is made up of articles, which are divided into sections. Article III (3), Section 1, defines California's relationship with the federal government. Article III, Section 3, lists the three branches of California's government.

Vocabulary Support

authority in one of the three branches of government

inseparable • *adj.*, cannot be separated

charged • *v.*, given a task or power

SEC. 1. The State of California is an inseparable part of the United States of America, and the United States Constitution is the supreme law of the land.

SEC. 3. The powers of state government are legislative, executive, and judicial. Persons charged with the exercise of one power may not exercise either of the others except as permitted by this Constitution.

– California Constitution, Article III

Fun Fact

At 110 pages, California's constitution is one of the longest constitutions in the world!

The governor's mansion in Sacramento

Close Reading

HSS 4.5.2 ELA RI.4.1, RI.4.2, W.4.1.b

1. Analyze and explain what Article III, Section 1, means.

_____

_____

_____

_____

2. Describe how Article III, Section 3, relates to the idea of the rule of law.

_____

_____

_____

_____

Wrap It Up

Draw Conclusions Why do you think it is important to have checks and balances and the rule of law in our government? Support your answer with information and examples from the primary source and lessons you have read.

_____

_____

_____

_____

_____

California's Local Governments

Unlock
The **BIG**
Question

I will understand California's local governments and what they do.

Vocabulary

city council
mayor
reservation
rancheria
tribal council
school board
superintendent

Academic Vocabulary

agree

JumpStart Activity

With a partner or small group, act out what you think it means to be a good citizen in your community. When it is your turn, identify what other groups are doing to show good citizenship.

Los Angeles County Board of Supervisors in a meeting

If you wanted to ask the government for a new playground at a local park, who would you ask for help? Would you write to the president or the governor? No, you would go to a local government official. Like federal and state governments, local governments serve and protect the people. However, they are smaller and respond to local issues. Local governments have their own structures, powers, and functions.

INTERACTIVITY

Explore the key ideas of this lesson.

County Government

Counties are one level of local government. California is divided into 58 counties. Counties are large areas within a state that have their own governments. A county usually includes several cities within its borders. All of the land in California is part of a county. Los Angeles County has more people than any other county in the country.

In most counties, voters elect five people to serve on the county board of supervisors. This group makes decisions about county property, budgets, and programs that serve the community. The group acts as both the legislative and executive branches of the county. The county administrator is the county's top official. He or she is responsible for the day-to-day functions of the county and prepares the annual budget for the board of supervisors to approve.

The California Constitution and state laws say how much power a county has. Counties, just like the state, may charge taxes to help pay for services. Counties can use tax money to provide fire and sheriff departments and other services such as trash collection. When there is an emergency, a county worker answers the 911 call and sends an ambulance. Counties also run many of the hospitals in California.

County governments, like city governments, may provide schools, libraries, and parks. County laws and decision cannot go against state laws or the state constitution.

1. **Reading Check** **Use Evidence From Text** Underline services county governments provide.

California's Counties

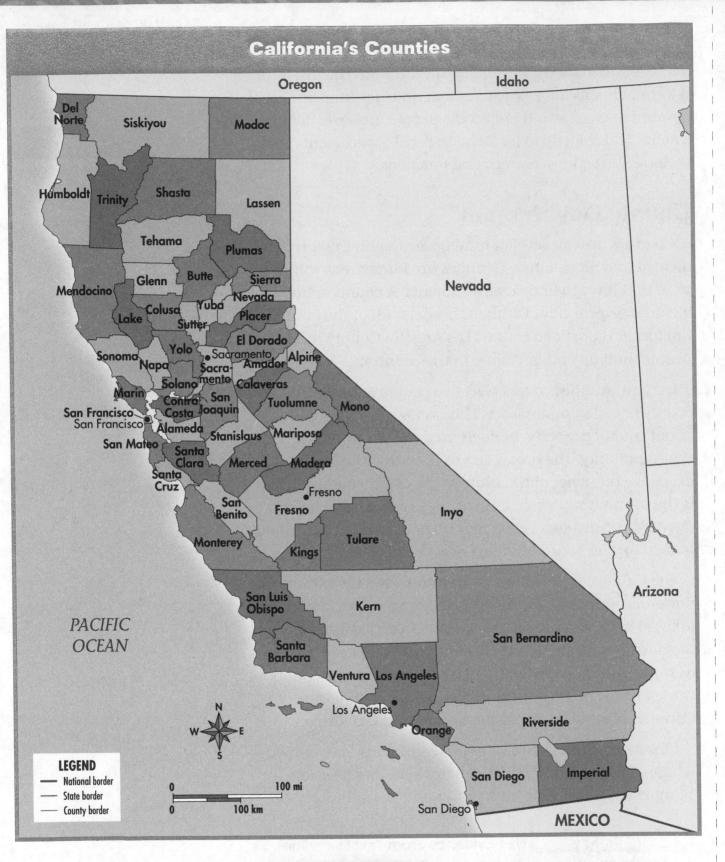

2. ☑ Reading Check Identify and circle on the map the county in which you live.

City and Town Government

Municipal governments serve cities and towns. *Municipality* is another word for a town or city. California has almost 500 municipalities. A town is smaller than a city. Cities and towns are treated the same under California law.

Not all communities have a municipal government. Some are run directly by a county. Local residents can vote for or against becoming a town or city. Incorporating, or setting up a municipal government, makes a town or city more independent from the county government. This means it has more control over land use and services like trash removal and police departments. But being incorporated may also mean having to pay more for services.

There are different forms of municipal governments in California. Most cities elect a **city council**, a group of people who make laws for the city. Towns elect a town council. In some cities and towns, the city or town council chooses one of its members as **mayor**, the leader of a city or town. In other cities or towns, the mayor is elected. The city or town council might also hire a city or town manager to help run the city or town. The mayor heads the city or town executive branch and may run council meetings.

The 43rd mayor of San Francisco, Mayor Edwin M. Lee

The mayor and the city council work together to serve the community. Because cities and towns are much smaller than the state, municipal governments work closely with the people in the community. Cities provide police departments and most have their own fire departments. Cities also hire people to keep roads and parks clean and construction workers to repair roads.

Cities and towns can charge taxes to pay for different services. City laws and decisions must follow state laws and the state constitution.

City workers repair a road in downtown Los Angeles.

3. ☑ **Reading Check** **Compare** county and municipal governments by filling in this diagram with one characteristic of each government and one shared feature.

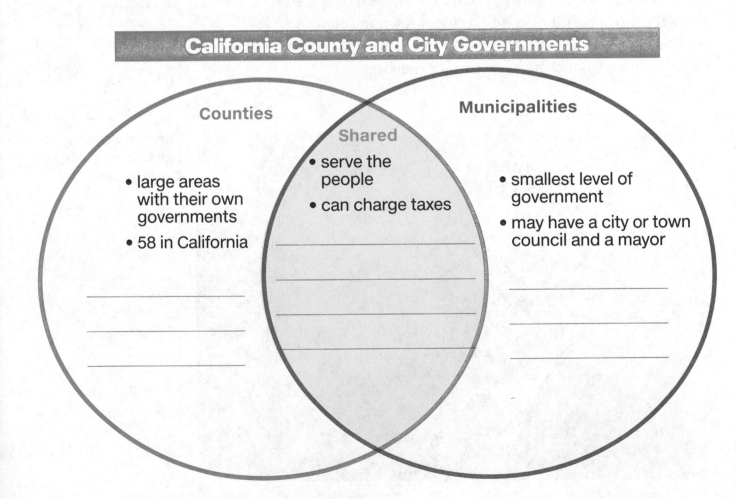

California County and City Governments

Counties

- large areas with their own governments
- 58 in California

_____

_____

Shared

- serve the people
- can charge taxes

_____

_____

_____

_____

Municipalities

- smallest level of government
- may have a city or town council and a mayor

_____

_____

California Indian Governments

American Indian groups have their own governments with specific powers. They are considered sovereign. This means they have the power to govern themselves. The federal government recognizes more than 100 American Indian groups, sometimes called tribes, in California. This is more than in any other state in the country. There are also 45 California Indian groups that are recognized by the state but not the federal government.

Tribal governments make decisions about tribal property, budgets, and who is a member of the group. Protecting the group's people, land, and culture are some of their important responsibilities. Many tribal governments provide their own health care and schools. Some seek help from the state or federal governments on these issues. Tribal governments strengthen the economy of the group by helping develop new businesses. They also teach members of the group how to best use natural resources.

The areas controlled or owned by California Indians can be called reservations or rancherias. A **reservation** is an area of land controlled by a sovereign American Indian group. A **rancheria** is a small piece of land set aside by the government for Indian families.

A tribal administrator works to protect Morro Rock, a sacred site to the Northern Chumash.

Greg Sarris, Miwok Tribal Chairman

Academic Vocabulary

agree • *v.*, to have the same opinion

Many tribal governments have their own constitutions. Their constitution and laws must **agree** with the United States Constitution. These governments have branches similar to the state and federal governments. A tribal chair, or leader, is the head of the executive branch and the community. The chair may also be called a president. A **tribal council** makes up the legislative branch. The council makes rules and solves problems within the group. It might meet with neighboring cities or counties to solve common problems. A tribal court system is the judicial branch. Some California Indian groups choose not to have a constitution or separate branches. They have only a tribal council led by a tribal chair.

Primary Source

It is time, again, for us to start thinking about finding a home here and to start taking care of it. Again, that is what I think we need to do. We need to start to appreciate and understand the past. In the past was a proud model, a beautiful model, that there are so many amongst us today that have survived.

–Greg Sarris, Miwok Tribal Chairman

4. ☑ **Reading Check** **Infer** In his speech, Greg Sarris refers to preserving his group's culture. Why do you think it is important for California Indian cultures to be preserved?

_____

_____

_____

_____

School Districts

Did you know that your school has its own government? Most public schools are part of a school district. A district is an area of a state, county, or city marked off for a special purpose. A school district oversees all of the schools in its area. There are more than 1,000 school districts in California.

California has three types of school districts. Most are unified districts, which include kindergarten through twelfth grade together in one district. Elementary districts are responsible for kindergarten through eighth grade. High school districts run ninth through twelfth grades. District boundaries can change. Schools may be moved to new districts. Districts can be split apart or joined together. The local school board sets these boundaries.

A **school board** is a group of people, elected by local citizens, that manages schools in an area. The board chooses a **superintendent**, who is the top executive in the school district. The superintendent makes decisions about spending and hires people, including school principals. The principal makes sure students and teachers follow the rules set by the superintendent and school board. Principals are also responsible for working with teachers, students, and other members of the community to make sure the school is meeting the community's needs. Anyone who lives in the school district can attend most meetings of the school board.

John Deasey (left) was the superintendent of the Los Angeles Unified School District. It is the largest school district in the state.

5. ☑ Reading Check

Summarize What is the superintendent's responsibility to your school district?

_____

_____

_____

_____

_____

Citizenship in Your Community

You have learned that members of a community can practice good citizenship by voting, volunteering, obeying laws, and writing to officials about important issues and problems. This is true at the federal, state, and local levels.

Many cities and school districts have community meetings where people can suggest changes or talk about problems. Community members can work together to clean up parks or other public areas. Citizens can work to raise money to build parks or playgrounds.

You can make a difference yourself. You can work together with your classmates or neighbors to start a recycling program or clean up school grounds. Even though you will not be able to vote in elections until you are older, you can still be a good citizen in many ways.

6. ☑ **Reading Check Discuss** with a partner how you could help in your community. Write two ideas on the lines below.

_____

_____

Quest Connection

Draw a picture of a challenge your school or community faces. How might a local official be able to help?

👆 **INTERACTIVITY**

See examples of which officials or departments can help with certain issues.

A young girl helps in her California community by helping to paint a wall.

✅ Lesson 3 Check

🌐 **HSS** 4.5, 4.5.4, 4.5.5 **Analysis** HI.1 **ELA** RI.4.1, RI.4.2, RI.4.3, RF.4.4

7. **Summarize** how a tribal government is similar to the state government.

_____

_____

_____

_____

8. **Describe** the main function of a school district.

_____

_____

_____

_____

9. **Understand the**  **Connections** Based on the problem you identified in the Quest Connection, which local official would you contact for help? Explain your answer.

_____

_____

_____

_____

Use and Interpret Evidence

▶ **VIDEO**

Watch a video about how to use evidence to support a claim.

Evidence is important because it proves that something is true. When you are asked to give your opinion or to make a claim about a certain subject, you should support your ideas with evidence. The following questions will help you use and interpret, or understand, evidence:

• What evidence should I look for to support my opinion or claim?

Tribal council meeting

• How does the evidence support my opinion or claim?

• What else does this evidence tell me?

Answering these questions will help you understand how to use evidence to support your ideas.

Read the paragraph below. Evidence that might support a claim has been highlighted.

Many tribal governments have their own constitutions. Their constitution and laws must agree with the United States Constitution. These governments have branches similar to state and federal governments. A tribal chair, or leader, is the head of the executive branch and the community. The chair may also be called a president. A tribal council makes up the legislative branch. The council makes rules and solves problems within the group. It might meet with neighboring cities or counties to solve common problems. A tribal court system is the judicial branch. Some California Indian groups choose not to have a constitution or separate branches. They only have a tribal council led by a tribal chair.

1. What claim could you make with the highlighted evidence?
   What evidence supports the claim?

   _____

   _____

   _____

   _____

   _____

2. What other claim could you make using the evidence from the text
   on the previous page?

   _____

   _____

   _____

   _____

3. Find a paragraph from Lesson 3 where evidence clearly supports a
   claim. Write the claim and the evidence below.

   _____

   _____

   _____

   _____

Quality:
Individual
Responsibility

First Lady Pat Nixon (1912–1993)
Volunteering for Her Country

Pat Nixon was the First Lady of the United States from 1969 to 1974. Her husband Richard was the nation's 37th president. As First Lady, she strongly supported volunteerism.

Pat Nixon grew up in California. Her childhood was not easy. She had to take care of her mother who was sick with cancer. Later, when her father became sick, she had to work to support her family.

She attended college in California and became a teacher before marrying Richard Nixon, who was a lawyer at the time. When Richard was elected president and Pat became the First Lady, she visited hospitals, schools, orphanages, and senior citizen homes.

In 1969, Pat announced a national recruitment program asking for thousands of volunteers to get involved and help their communities. She said, "Our success as a Nation depends upon our willingness to give generously of ourself for the welfare [well-being] and enrichment of the life of others."

Find Out More

1. **Identify** ways that Pat Nixon showed individual responsibility.

   _____

   _____

   _____

2. Today, there are ways that you can be responsible by volunteering in your school or community. Ask someone who works for a local organization, or look in the newspaper or online for ideas. Then invite a friend or family member to volunteer with you!

Use these graphics to review some of the vocabulary, people, and ideas from this chapter.

Comparing the U.S. Constitution and the California Constitution

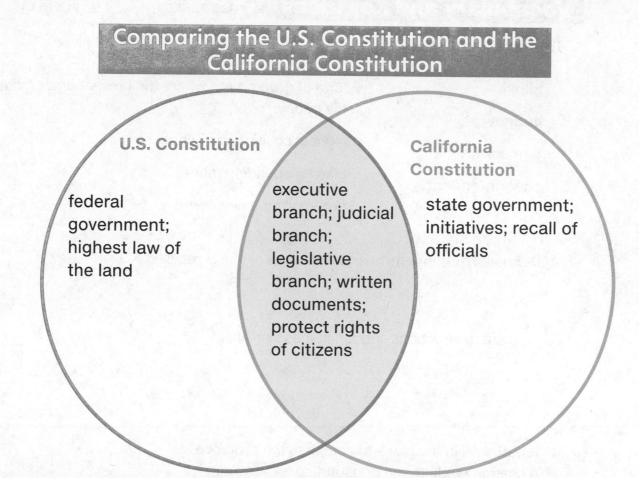

U.S. Constitution

federal government; highest law of the land

(overlap) executive branch; judicial branch; legislative branch; written documents; protect rights of citizens

California Constitution

state government; initiatives; recall of officials

Powers and Responsibilities of Government

Federal Government	State Government	Local Government
• Print money	• Issue licenses and license plates	• Education
• Use the military	• Hold elections	• Police
• Enter into agreements with other countries	• Organize local governments	• Firefighters
• Make laws for the whole country	• Conduct elections	• Local issues

Vocabulary and Key Ideas

🕭 HSS 4.5, 4.5.1, 4.5.2, 4.5.3 **ELA** RI.4.7

1. **Draw** a line to match the vocabulary words with their correct definitions.

   bill   form of government where the power comes from the people

   budget
                                 highest position in a school district
   democracy
                                 plan for spending money
   superintendent
                                 proposal for a new law

2. **Define** What happens to an official if he or she is recalled?

   _____

3. How are reservations and rancherias similar?

   _____

   _____

4. **Identify** Fill in the blank to complete the sentence.
   A change made to the Constitution is called a(n) _____.

5. **Analyze Images** Identify the branch of state government represented in each image.

_____   _____   _____

6. **Identify** Fill in the circle next to the correct answer.
   Which part of local government has mayors?

   Ⓐ Indian rancherias and reservations

   Ⓑ cities and towns

   Ⓒ states

   Ⓓ counties

7. **Explain** the rule of law.

   _____

   _____

8. **Analyze** Why might a community decide to incorporate as a city or town?

   _____

   _____

9. **Apply** How does the California state government affect your daily life? Include examples to support your answer.

   _____

   _____

   _____

10. **Revisit the Big Question** What do you think should be the goals of California's government?

    _____

    _____

    _____

11. **Writer's Workshop: Write Informative Text** On a separate sheet of paper, write two short paragraphs comparing and contrasting federal and state governments. Include details and examples that explain how the levels of governments are similar and different.

SEC. 2. (a) Every person may freely speak, write and publish his or her sentiments [thoughts] on all subjects, being responsible for the abuse of this right. A law may not restrain or abridge [shorten] liberty of speech or press.

-California Constitution, Article I Declaration of Rights

12. What do you think is meant by the phrase "not restrain or abridge liberty of speech or press"? How does this section of the California Constitution illustrate both rights and responsibilities?

_____

_____

_____

_____

_____

Use and Interpret Evidence ◐ HSS 4.5.5 **Analysis** RE.2 **ELA** RI.4.7

Pinoleville Pomo Nation: Mission Statement

"The Nation is dedicated to developing and maintaining co-operative alliances [partnerships] that benefit the Nation and local community. The Nation provides for the health, safety, and general welfare of its citizens, while promoting economic self-sufficiency and personal independence."

13. Analyze the evidence and answer the question. The Pomo Nation is a tribal government, and a mission statement lays out goals for the group. How does the mission statement show the roles and responsibilities of a tribal council?

_____

_____

_____

_____

Quest Findings

☝ **INTERACTIVITY**

Use this activity to help you write your letter to a local official.

Write Your Letter

You've read the lessons in this chapter, and now you're ready to write a letter to a local official. Remember that the goal of your letter is to convince or persuade the official to help you address an issue in your community. Follow these steps:

1 Prepare to Write

Create an outline that includes the issue you think is most important to address in your community, why it is important, and how you think your local government can help.

2 Research Your Local Government

Research your local government online to find which official might best be able to help address the issue you have identified. You will address your letter to this person.

3 Write a Draft Letter

Use your outline and the answers from your Quest Connections to write the most persuasive letter you can. Make sure your letter answers the following questions:

- What issue in your community do you want to address?
- Who does it affect?
- Why is it important to address it?
- How can local government officials help?

4 Share With a Partner

Exchange your draft letter with a partner. Invite your partner to ask questions about your letter and to make suggestions. When it is your turn, do the same for your partner.

5 Revise

Make changes to your letter after sharing it with your partner. Correct any grammatical or spelling errors.

The Declaration of Independence

In Congress, July 4, 1776
The Unanimous Declaration of the Thirteen
United States of America

The first part of the Declaration of Independence is called the Preamble. A preamble is an introduction, or the part that comes before the main message. The Preamble states why the Declaration was written.

The second paragraph lists the basic rights that all people should have. The founders called these **unalienable** rights, meaning that these rights cannot be taken or given away. If a government cannot protect these rights, the people must change the government or create a new one.

1. According to the Declaration, what are three "unalienable rights"? Circle these words in the text.

The third paragraph introduces the List of Grievances. Each part of this list begins with the words, "He has...." These words refer to King George III's actions in the colonies. To prove that the king had abused his power over the colonies, this list of 27 complaints described how the British government and the king had treated the colonists.

When in the Course of human events it becomes necessary for one people to dissolve the political bands which have connected them with another, and to assume among the powers of the earth, the separate and equal station to which the Laws of nature and of nature's God entitle them, a decent respect to the opinions of mankind requires that they should declare the causes which impel them to the separation.

We hold these truths to be self-evident, that all men are created equal, that they are endowed by their Creator with certain unalienable Rights, that among these are Life, Liberty and the Pursuit of Happiness. That to secure these rights, Governments are instituted among Men, deriving their just powers from the consent of the governed; That whenever any Form of Government becomes destructive of these ends it is the Right of the People to alter or to abolish it, and to institute new Government, laying its foundation on such principles and organizing its powers in such form, as to them shall seem most likely to effect their Safety and Happiness. Prudence, indeed, will dictate that Governments long established should not be changed for light and transient causes; and accordingly all experience hath shown, that mankind are more disposed to suffer, while evils are sufferable, than to right themselves by abolishing the forms to which they are accustomed. But when a long train of abuses and usurpations, pursuing invariably the same Object evinces a design to reduce them under absolute Despotism, it is their right, it is their duty, to throw off such Government, and to provide new Guards for their future security.

Such has been the patient sufferance of these Colonies; and such is now the necessity which constrains them to alter their former Systems of Government. The history of the present King of Great Britain is a history of repeated injuries and usurpations, all having in direct object the establishment of an absolute Tyranny over these States. To prove this, let Facts be submitted to a candid world.

He has refused his Assent to Laws, the most wholesome and necessary for the public good.

He has forbidden his Governors to pass Laws of immediate and pressing importance, unless suspended in their operation till his

Assent should be obtained; and when so suspended, he has utterly neglected to attend to them.

He has refused to pass other Laws for the accommodation of large districts of people, unless those people would relinquish the right of Representation in the Legislature, a right inestimable to them and formidable to tyrants only.

He has called together legislative bodies at places unusual, uncomfortable, and distant from the depository of their Public Records, for the sole purpose of fatiguing them into compliance with his measures.

He has dissolved Representative Houses repeatedly, for opposing with manly firmness his invasions on the rights of the people.

He has refused for a long time, after such dissolutions, to cause others to be elected; whereby the Legislative powers, incapable of Annihilation, have returned to the People at large for their exercise; the State remaining in the mean time exposed to all the dangers of invasions from without, and convulsions within.

He has endeavored to prevent the population of these States; for that purpose obstructing the Laws for Naturalization of Foreigners; refusing to pass others to encourage their migration hither, and raising the conditions of new Appropriations of Lands.

He has obstructed the Administration of Justice, by refusing his Assent to Laws for establishing Judiciary powers.

He has made Judges dependent on his Will alone for the tenure of their offices, and the amount and payment of their salaries.

He has erected a multitude of New Offices, and sent hither swarms of Officers to harass our people and eat out their substance.

He has kept among us in time of peace, Standing Armies, without the Consent of our legislatures.

He has affected to render the Military independent of, and superior to, the Civil Power.

He has combined with others to subject us to a jurisdiction foreign to our constitutions, and unacknowledged by our laws; giving his Assent to their Acts of pretended Legislation:

For quartering large bodies of armed troops among us;

For protecting them, by a mock Trial, from punishment for any Murders which they should commit on the Inhabitants of these States;

In the List of Grievances, the colonists complain that they have no say in choosing the laws that govern them. They say that King George III is not concerned about their safety and happiness. They list the times when the king denied them the right to representation. The colonists also state that the king has interfered with judges, with the court system, and with foreigners who want to become citizens.

2. There are many words in the Declaration that may be unfamiliar to you. Circle three words you do not know. Look the words up in the dictionary. Write one word and its meaning on the lines below.

_____

_____

_____

_____

_____

_____

_____

This page continues the colonists' long List of Grievances.

3. In your own words, briefly sum up three grievances.

_____

_____

_____

4. Match each word from the Declaration with its meaning. Use a dictionary if you need help with a word.

abolishing	tried to achieve
plundered	changing
suspending	doing away with
altering	stopping for a time
endeavored	robbed

Statement of Independence
After listing their many grievances, the signers begin their statement of independence. Because the king has refused to correct the problems, he is an unfair ruler. Therefore, he is not fit to rule the free people of America.

For cutting off our Trade with all parts of the world;

For imposing Taxes on us without our Consent;

For depriving us, in many cases, of the benefits of Trial by Jury;

For transporting us beyond Seas to be tried for pretended offenses;

For abolishing the free System of English Laws in a neighboring Province, establishing therein an Arbitrary government, and enlarging its Boundaries so as to render it at once an example and fit instrument for introducing the same absolute rule into these Colonies;

For taking away our Charters, abolishing our most valuable Laws, and altering fundamentally the Forms of our Governments;

For suspending our own Legislatures, and declaring themselves invested with Power to legislate for us in all cases whatsoever.

He has abdicated Government here, by declaring us out of his Protection, and waging War against us.

He has plundered our seas, ravaged our Coasts, burned our towns, and destroyed the lives of our people.

He is at this time transporting large Armies of foreign mercenaries to complete the works of death, desolation and tyranny, already begun with circumstances of Cruelty and perfidy scarcely paralleled in the most barbarous ages, and totally unworthy the Head of a civilized nation.

He has constrained our fellow Citizens taken Captive on the high Seas to bear Arms against their Country, to become the executioners of their friends and Brethren, or to fall themselves by their Hands.

He has excited domestic insurrections amongst us, and has endeavored to bring on the inhabitants of our frontiers the merciless Indian Savages whose known rule of warfare, is an undistinguished destruction of all ages, sexes, and conditions.

In every stage of these Oppressions We have Petitioned for Redress in the most humble terms. Our repeated Petitions have been answered only by repeated injury. A Prince, whose character is thus marked by every act which may define a Tyrant, is unfit to be the ruler of a free People.

Nor have We been wanting in attentions to our British brethren. We have warned them from time to time of attempts by their legislature to extend an unwarrantable jurisdiction over us. We have reminded them of the circumstances of our emigration and settlement here. We have appealed to their native justice and magnanimity, and we have conjured them by the ties of our common kindred to disavow these usurpations, which, would inevitably interrupt our connections and correspondence. They too have been deaf to the voice of justice and of consanguinity. We must, therefore, acquiesce in the necessity, which denounces our Separation, and hold them, as we hold the rest of mankind, Enemies in War, in Peace Friends.

We, therefore, the Representatives of the United States of America, in General Congress, Assembled, appealing to the Supreme Judge of the world for the rectitude of our intentions, do, in the Name, and by the Authority of the good People of these Colonies, solemnly publish and declare, That these United Colonies are, and of right ought to be Free and Independent States; that they are Absolved from all Allegiance to the British Crown, and that all political connection between them and the State of Great Britain, is and ought to be totally dissolved, and that as Free and Independent States, they have full Power to levy War, conclude Peace, contract Alliances, establish Commerce, and to do all other Acts and Things which Independent States may of right do. And for the support of this Declaration, with a firm reliance on the protection of Divine Providence, we mutually pledge to each other our Lives, our Fortunes, and our sacred Honor.

New Hampshire:
Josiah Bartlett
William Whipple
Matthew Thornton

Massachusetts Bay:
John Hancock
Samuel Adams
John Adams
Robert Treat Paine
Elbridge Gerry

Rhode Island:
Stephan Hopkins
William Ellery

Connecticut:
Roger Sherman
Samuel Huntington
William Williams
Oliver Wolcott

New York:
William Floyd
Philip Livingston
Francis Lewis
Lewis Morris

New Jersey:
Richard Stockton
John Witherspoon
Francis Hopkinson
John Hart
Abraham Clark

Delaware:
Caesar Rodney
George Read
Thomas M'Kean

Maryland:
Samuel Chase
William Paca
Thomas Stone
Charles Carroll of
    Carrollton

Virginia:
George Wythe
Richard Henry Lee
Thomas Jefferson
Benjamin Harrison
Thomas Nelson, Jr.
Francis Lightfoot Lee
Carter Braxton

Pennsylvania:
Robert Morris
Benjamin Rush
Benjamin Franklin
John Morton
George Clymer
James Smith
George Taylor
James Wilson
George Ross

North Carolina:
William Hooper
Joseph Hewes
John Penn

South Carolina:
Edward Rutledge
Thomas Heyward, Jr.
Thomas Lynch, Jr.
Arthur Middleton

Georgia:
Button Gwinnett
Lyman Hall
George Walton

In this paragraph, the signers point out that they have asked the British people for help many times. The colonists hoped the British would listen to them because they have so much in common. The British people, however, paid no attention to their demand for justice. This is another reason for why the colonies must break away from Great Britain.

In the last paragraph, the members of the Continental Congress declare that the thirteen colonies are no longer colonies. They are now a free nation with no ties to Great Britain. The United States now has all the powers of other independent countries.

5. List three powers that the signers claim the new nation now has.

_____

_____

_____

_____

_____

_____

6. The signers promised to support the Declaration of Independence and each other with their lives, their fortunes, and their honor. On a separate sheet of paper, tell what you think this means. Then explain why it was a brave thing to do.

United States Constitution

PREAMBLE

This **Preamble** gives the reasons for writing and having a Constitution. The Constitution will form a stronger and more united nation. It will lead to peace, justice, and liberty and will defend American citizens. Finally, it will improve the lives of people.

We the People of the United States, in Order to form a more perfect Union, establish Justice, insure domestic Tranquility, provide for the common defense, promote the general Welfare, and secure the Blessings of Liberty to ourselves and our Posterity, do ordain and establish this Constitution for the United States of America.

ARTICLE I

Section 1. Congress
The legislative branch of government makes the country's laws. Called the Congress, it has two parts, or houses: the House of Representatives and the Senate.

Section 1.

All legislative Powers herein granted shall be vested in a Congress of the United States, which shall consist of a Senate and House of Representatives.

Section 2. The House of Representatives
Members of the House of Representatives are elected every two years. Representatives must be 25 years old and United States citizens. They must also live in the states that elect them.

The number of Representatives for each state is based on the population, or number of people who live there.

1. Why do some states have more Representatives in Congress than other states?

_____

_____

_____

_____

Over the years, the Constitution has been altered, or changed. These altered parts are shown here in gray type.

Section 2.

1. The House of Representatives shall be composed of Members chosen every second Year by the People of the several States, and the Electors in each State shall have the Qualifications requisite for Electors of the most numerous Branch of the State Legislature.

2. No Person shall be a Representative who shall not have attained to the age of twenty-five Years, and been seven Years a Citizen of the United States, and who shall not, when elected, be an Inhabitant of that State in which he shall be chosen.

3. Representatives and direct Taxes shall be apportioned among the several States which may be included within this Union, according to their respective Numbers, which shall be determined by adding to the whole Number of free Persons, including those bound to Service for a Term of Years and excluding Indians not taxed, three fifths of all other Persons. The actual Enumeration shall be made within three Years after the first Meeting of the Congress of the United States, and within every subsequent Term of ten Years, in such Manner as they shall by Law direct. The Number of Representatives shall not exceed one for every thirty Thousand, but each State shall have at Least one Representative; and, until such enumeration shall be made, the State of New Hampshire shall be entitled to choose three, Massachusetts eight, Rhode Island and Providence Plantations one, Connecticut five, New York six, New Jersey four, Pennsylvania eight, Delaware one, Maryland six, Virginia ten, North Carolina five, South Carolina five, and Georgia three.

4. When vacancies happen in the Representation from any State, the Executive Authority thereof shall issue Writs of Election to fill such Vacancies.

5. The House of Representatives shall choose their Speaker and other Officers; and shall have the sole Power of Impeachment.

Section 3.

1. The Senate of the United States shall be composed of two Senators from each State chosen by the Legislature thereof for six Years; and each Senator shall have one Vote.

2. Immediately after they shall be assembled in Consequences of the first Election, they shall be divided, as equally as may be, into three Classes. The Seats of the Senators of the first Class shall be vacated at the Expiration of the second Year; of the second Class, at the Expiration of the fourth Year; and of the third Class, at the Expiration of the sixth Year; so that one-third may be chosen every second Year; and if Vacancies happen by Resignation, or otherwise, during the Recess of the Legislature of any State, the Executive thereof may make temporary Appointments until the next Meeting of the Legislature, which shall then fill such Vacancies.

3. No Person shall be a Senator who shall not have attained to the Age of thirty Years, and been nine Years a Citizen of the United States, and who shall not, when elected, be an Inhabitant of that State for which he shall be chosen.

4. The Vice President of the United States shall be President of the Senate but shall have no Vote, unless they be equally divided.

5. The Senate shall choose their other Officers, and also a President pro tempore, in the Absence of the Vice President, or when he shall exercise the Office of President of the United States.

6. The Senate shall have the sole Power to try all Impeachments. When sitting for that Purpose, they shall be on Oath or Affirmation. When the President of the United States is tried, the Chief Justice shall preside: And no Person shall be convicted without the Concurrence of two thirds of the Members present.

7. Judgment in Cases of Impeachment shall not extend further than to removal from Office, and disqualification to hold and enjoy any Office of honor, Trust, or Profit under the United States: but the Party convicted shall nevertheless be liable and subject to Indictment, Trial, Judgment and Punishment, according to Law.

A state governor calls a special election to fill an empty seat in the House of Representatives.

Members of the House of Representatives choose their own leaders. They also have the power to impeach, or accuse, government officials of crimes.

Section 3. Senate

Each state has two Senators. A Senator serves a six-year term.

At first, each state legislature elected its two Senators. The Seventeenth Amendment changed that. Today, the voters of each state elect their Senators.

Senators must be 30 years old and United States citizens. They must also live in the states they represent.

2. How is the length of a Senator's term different from a Representative's term?

_____

_____

The Vice President is the officer in charge of the Senate but only votes to break a tie. When the Vice President is absent, a temporary leader (President Pro Tempore) leads the Senate.

The Senate holds impeachment trials. When the President is impeached, the Chief Justice of the Supreme Court is the judge. A two-thirds vote is needed to convict. Once convicted, an official can be removed from office. Other courts of law can impose other punishments.

Section 4. Elections and Meetings of Congress
The state legislatures determine the times, places, and method of holding elections for senators and representatives.

Section 5. Rules for Congress
The Senate and House of Representatives judge the fairness of the elections and the qualifications of its own members. At least half of the members must be present to do business. Each house may determine the rules of its proceedings and punish its member for disorderly behavior. Each house of Congress shall keep a record of its proceedings and from time to time publish the record.

3. Why is it important for Congress to publish a record of what they do?

_____

_____

_____

_____

_____

Section 6. Rights and Restrictions of Members of Congress
The Senators and Representatives shall receive payment for their services to be paid out of the Treasury of the United States. Members of Congress cannot be arrested during their attendance at the session of Congress, except for a very serious crime, and they cannot be arrested for anything they say in Congress. No person can have a government job while serving as a member of Congress.

Section 4.

1. The Times, Places and Manner of holding Elections for Senators and Representatives, shall be prescribed in each State by the Legislature thereof; but the Congress may at any time by law make or alter such Regulations, except as to the Places of choosing Senators.
2. The Congress shall assemble at least once in every Year, and such Meeting shall be on the first Monday in December, unless they shall by Law appoint a different Day.

Section 5.

1. Each House shall be the Judge of the Elections, Returns and Qualifications of its own Members, and a Majority of each shall constitute a Quorum to do Business; but a smaller Number may adjourn from day to day, and may be authorized to compel the Attendance of absent Members, in such Manner, and under such Penalties, as each House may provide.
2. Each House may determine the Rules of its Proceedings, punish its Members for disorderly Behavior, and, with the Concurrence of two thirds, expel a Member.
3. Each House shall keep a Journal of its Proceedings, and from time to time publish the same, excepting such Parts as may in their Judgment require Secrecy; and the Yeas and Nays of the Members of either House on any question shall, at the Desire of one fifth of those Present, be entered on the Journal.
4. Neither House, during the Session of Congress, shall, without the Consent of the other, adjourn for more than three days, nor to any other Place than that in which the two Houses shall be sitting.

Section 6.

1. The Senators and Representatives shall receive a Compensation for their Services, to be ascertained by Law, and paid out of the Treasury of the United States. They shall in all Cases, except Treason, Felony, and Breach of the Peace, be privileged from Arrest during their Attendance at the Session of their respective Houses, and in going to and returning from the same; and for any Speech or Debate in either House, they shall not be questioned in any other Place.
2. No Senator or Representative shall, during the Time for which he was elected, be appointed to any civil Office under the Authority of the United States, which shall have been created, or the Emoluments whereof shall have been increased during such time; and no Person holding any Office under the United States, shall be a Member of either House during his Continuance in Office.

Section 7.

1. All Bills for raising Revenue shall originate in the House of Representatives; but the Senate may propose or concur with amendments as on other Bills.

2. Every Bill which shall have passed the House of Representatives and the Senate, shall, before it become a law, be presented to the President of the United States: If he approve, he shall sign it, but if not he shall return it, with his Objections to that House in which it shall have originated, who shall enter the Objections at large on their Journal, and proceed to reconsider it. If after such Reconsideration two thirds of the House shall agree to pass the Bill, it shall be sent, together with the Objections, to the other House, by which it shall likewise be reconsidered, and if approved by two thirds of that House, it shall become a Law. But in all such Cases the Votes of both Houses shall be determined by Yeas and Nays, and the Names of the Persons voting for and against the Bill shall be entered on the Journal of each House respectively. If any Bill shall not be returned by the President within ten Days (Sunday excepted) after it shall have been presented to him, the Same shall be a law, in like Manner as if he had signed it, unless the Congress by their Adjournment, prevent its Return, in which Case it shall not be a Law.

3. Every Order, Resolution, or Vote to which the Concurrence of the Senate and House of Representatives may be necessary (except on a question of adjournment) shall be presented to the President of the United States; and before the Same shall take Effect, shall be approved by him, or, being disapproved by him, shall be repassed by two thirds of the Senate and House of Representatives, according to the Rules and Limitations prescribed in the Case of a Bill.

Section 8.

The Congress shall have Power

1. To lay and collect Taxes, Duties, Imposts and Excises to pay the Debts and provide for the common Defense and general Welfare of the United States; but all Duties, Imposts and Excises, shall be uniform throughout the United States;

2. To borrow Money on the credit of the United States;

3. To regulate Commerce with foreign Nations, and among the several States, and with the Indian Tribes;

4. To establish an uniform Rule of Naturalization, and uniform Laws on the subject of Bankruptcies throughout the United States;

Section 7. How Laws are Made

All bills for raising money shall begin in the House of Representatives. The Senate may suggest or agree with amendments to these tax bills, as with other bills.

Every bill which has passed the House of Representatives and the Senate must be presented to the President of the United States before it becomes a law. If the President approves of the bill, the President shall sign it. If the President does not approve, then the bill may be vetoed. The President then sends it back to the house in which it began, with an explanation of the objections. That house writes the objections on their record and begins to reconsider it. If two thirds of each house agrees to pass the bill, it shall become a law. If any bill is neither signed nor vetoed by the President within ten days, (except for Sundays) after it has been sent to the President, the bill shall be a law. If Congress adjourns before ten days have passed, the bill does not become a law.

Section 8. Powers of Congress

Among the powers of Congress listed in Section 8 are:
- establish and collect taxes on imported and exported goods and on goods sold within the country. Congress also shall pay the debts and provide for the defense and general welfare of the United States. All federal taxes shall be the same throughout the United States.
- borrow money on the credit of the United States;
- make laws about trade with other countries, among the states, and with the American Indian tribes;
- establish one procedure by which a person from another country can become a legal citizen of the United States;
- protect the works of scientists, artists, authors, and inventors;
- create federal courts lower than the Supreme Court;

- declare war;
- establish and support an army and navy;
- organize and train a National Guard and call them up in times of emergency;
- govern the capital and military sites of the United States; and
- make all laws necessary to carry out the powers of Congress.

4. The last clause of Section 8 is called "the elastic clause" because it stretches the power of Congress. Why do you think it was added to the Constitution?

_____

_____

_____

_____

_____

_____

_____

5. To coin Money, regulate the Value thereof, and of foreign Coin, and fix the Standard of Weights and Measures;

6. To provide for the Punishment of counterfeiting the Securities and current Coin of the United States;

7. To establish Post Offices and post Roads;

8. To promote the Progress of Science and useful Arts, by securing, for limited Times to Authors and Inventors the exclusive Right to their respective Writings and Discoveries;

9. To constitute Tribunals inferior to the supreme Court;

10. To define and punish Piracies and Felonies committed on the high Seas, and Offences against the Law of nations;

11. To declare War, grant Letters of Marque and Reprisal, and make Rules concerning Captures on Land and Water;

12. To raise and support Armies; but no Appropriation of Money to that Use shall be for a longer Term than two Years;

13. To provide and maintain a Navy;

14. To make Rules for the Government and Regulation of the land and naval Forces;

15. To provide for calling forth the Militia to execute the Laws of the Union, suppress Insurrections and repel Invasions;

16. To provide for organizing, arming, and disciplining the Militia, and for governing such Part of them as may be employed in the Service of the United States, reserving to the States respectively the Appointment of the Officers, and the Authority of training the Militia according to the discipline prescribed by Congress;

17. To exercise exclusive Legislation in all Cases whatsoever, over such District (not exceeding ten Miles square) as may, by Cession of Particular States, and the Acceptance of Congress, become the Seat of the Government of the United States, and to exercise like Authority over all Places purchased by the Consent of the Legislature of the State in which the Same shall be, for the Erection of Forts, Magazines, Arsenals, Dockyards and other needful Buildings;—And

18. To make all Laws which shall be necessary and proper for carrying into Execution the foregoing Powers and all other Powers vested by this Constitution in the Government of the United States, or in any Department or Officer thereof.

Section 9.

1. The Migration or Importation of such Persons as any of the States now existing shall think proper to admit, shall not be prohibited by the Congress prior to the Year one thousand eight hundred and eight, but a Tax or duty may be imposed on such Importation, not exceeding ten dollars for each Person.

2. The Privilege of the Writ of Habeas Corpus shall not be suspended, unless when in Cases of Rebellion or Invasion the public safety may require it.

3. No Bill of Attainder or ex post facto Law shall be passed.

4. No Capitation, or other direct, Tax shall be laid, unless in Proportion to the Census of Enumeration herein before directed to be taken.

5. No Tax or Duty shall be laid on Articles exported from any State.

6. No Preference shall be given by any Regulation of Commerce or Revenue to the Ports of one State over those of another: nor shall Vessels bound to, or from, one State, be obliged to enter, clear or pay Duties in another.

7. No Money shall be drawn from the Treasury, but in Consequence of Appropriations made by Law; and a regular Statement and Account of the Receipts and Expenditures of all public Money shall be published from time to time.

8. No Title of Nobility shall be granted by the United States: And no Person holding any Office of Profit or Trust under them, shall, without the Consent of the Congress, accept of any present, Emolument, Office, or Title, of any kind whatever, from any King, Prince, or foreign State.

Section 10.

1. No State shall enter into any Treaty, Alliance, or Confederation; grant Letters of Marque and Reprisal; coin Money; emit Bills of Credit; make any Thing but gold and silver Coin a Tender in Payment of Debts; pass any Bill of Attainder, ex post facto Law, or Law impairing the Obligation of Contracts, or grant any Title of Nobility.

2. No State shall, without the Consent of the Congress, lay any Imposts or Duties on Imports or Exports, except what may be absolutely necessary for executing its inspection Laws; and the net Produce of all Duties and Imposts, laid by any State on Imports or Exports, shall be for the Use of the Treasury of the United States; and all such Laws shall be subject to the Revision and Control of the Congress.

Section 9: Powers Denied to Congress

Congress cannot
- stop slaves from being brought into the United States until 1808;
- arrest and jail people without charging them with a crime, except during an emergency;
- punish a person without a trial; punish a person for something that was not a crime when he or she did it;
- pass a direct tax, such as an income tax, unless it is in proportion to the population;
- tax goods sent out of a state;
- give the seaports of one state an advantage over another state's ports; let one state tax the ships of another state;
- spend money without passing a law to make it legal; spend money without keeping good records;
- give titles, such as king and queen, to anyone; allow federal workers to accept gifts or titles from foreign governments.

5. Why do you think the writers included the last clause of Section 9?

_____

_____

_____

_____

_____

Section 10: Powers Denied to the States

After listing what Congress is not allowed to do, the Constitution tells what powers are denied to the states.

State governments do not have the power to
- make treaties with foreign countries; print money; do anything that Section 9 of the Constitution says the federal government cannot;
- tax goods sent into or out of a state unless Congress agrees;
- keep armed forces or go to war; make agreements with other states or foreign governments unless Congress agrees.

6. What problems might arise if one state went to war with a foreign country?

_____

_____

_____

_____

_____

Article 2 describes the executive branch.

Section 1. Office of President and Vice President

The President has power to execute, or carry out, the laws of the United States.

Electors from each state choose the President. Today, these electors are called the Electoral College and are chosen by the voters.

Before 1804, the person with the most electoral votes became President. The person with the next-highest number became Vice President. The Twelfth Amendment changed this way of electing Presidents.

3. No State shall, without the Consent of Congress, lay any Duty of Tonnage, keep Troops, or Ships of War in time of Peace, enter into any Agreement or Compact with another State, or with a foreign Power, or engage in War, unless actually invaded, or in such imminent Danger as will not admit of delay.

ARTICLE II

Section 1.

1. The executive Power shall be vested in a President of the United States of America. He shall hold his Office during the Term of four Years, and, together with the Vice President, chosen for the same Term, be elected as follows:

2. Each State shall appoint, in such Manner as the Legislature thereof may direct, a Number of Electors, equal to the whole Number of Senators and Representatives to which the State may be entitled in the Congress: but no Senator or Representative, or Person holding an Office of Trust or Profit, under the United States, shall be appointed an Elector.

3. The Electors shall meet in their respective States, and vote by Ballot for two Persons, of whom one at least shall not be an Inhabitant of the same State with themselves. And they shall make a List of all the Persons voted for, and of the Number of Votes for each; which List they shall sign and certify, and transmit sealed to the Seat of the Government of the United States, directed to the President of the Senate. The President of the Senate shall, in the Presence of the Senate and House of Representatives, open all the Certificates, and the Votes shall then be counted. The Person having the greatest Number of Votes shall be the President, if such Number be a majority of the whole Number of Electors appointed; and if there be more than one who have such Majority, and have an equal Number of Votes, then, the House of Representatives shall immediately choose by Ballot one of them for President; and if no Person have a Majority, then from the five highest on the List the said House shall in like Manner choose the President. But in choosing the President, the Votes shall be taken by States, the Representatives from each State having one Vote; a quorum for this Purpose shall consist of a Member or Members from two thirds of the States, and a Majority of all the States shall be necessary to a Choice. In every Case, after the Choice of the President, the Person having the greatest Number of Votes of the Electors shall be the Vice President. But if there should remain two or more who have equal Votes, the Senate shall choose from them by Ballot the Vice President.

4. The Congress may determine the Time of choosing the Electors, and the Day on which they shall give their Votes; which Day shall be the same throughout the United States.

5. No Person except a natural born Citizen, or a Citizen of the United States, at the time of the Adoption of this Constitution, shall be eligible to the Office of President; neither shall any person be eligible to that Office who shall not have attained to the Age of thirty-five Years, and been fourteen Years a Resident within the United States.

6. In Case of the Removal of the President from Office, or of his Death, Resignation, or Inability to discharge the Powers and Duties of the said Office, the Same shall devolve on the Vice President, and the Congress may by Law provide for the Case of Removal, Death, Resignation or Inability, both of the President and Vice President, declaring what Officer shall then act as President, and such Officer shall act accordingly, until the Disability be removed, or a President shall be elected.

7. The President shall, at stated Times, receive for his Services, a Compensation, which shall neither be increased nor diminished during the Period for which he shall have been elected, and he shall not receive within that Period any other Emolument from the United States, or any of them.

8. Before he enter on the Execution of his Office, he shall take the following Oath or Affirmation: "I do solemnly swear (or affirm) that I will faithfully execute the Office of President of the United States, and will to the best of my Ability, preserve, protect and defend the Constitution of the United States."

Section 2.

1. The President shall be Commander in Chief of the Army and Navy of the United States, and of the Militia of the several States, when called into the actual Service of the United States; he may require the Opinion, in writing, of the principal Officer in each of the executive Departments, upon any Subject relating to the Duties of their respective Offices, and he shall have Power to Grant Reprieves and Pardons for Offences against the United States, except in Cases of Impeachment.

Congress decides when electors are chosen and when they vote for President. Americans now vote for the electors on Election Day, the Tuesday after the first Monday in November.

To become President, a person must be born in the United States and be a citizen. Presidents also have to be at least 35 years old and have lived in the United States for at least 14 years.

If a President dies or leaves office for any reason, the Vice President becomes President. If there is no Vice President, Congress decides on the next President. (In 1967, the Twenty-fifth Amendment changed how these offices are filled.)

7. Why is it important to agree on how to replace the President or Vice President if one should die or leave office?

_____

_____

_____

_____

The President's salary cannot be raised or lowered while he is in office. The President cannot accept other money or gifts while in office. Before taking office, the President must swear to preserve, protect, and defend the Constitution.

Section 2. Powers of the President

The President controls the armed forces and National Guard, and can ask for advice of those who run government departments. (These advisers to the President are members of the Cabinet.) The President can pardon, or free, people convicted of federal crimes.

The President can make treaties, but two thirds of the Senate must approve them. The President, with Senate approval, can name Supreme Court judges, ambassadors, and other important officials.

8. What is the Senate's ability to approve or reject treaties an example of?

_____

_____

Section 3. Duties of the President

From time to time, the President must talk to Congress about the condition of the nation. (Today, we call this speech the State of the Union address. It is given once a year in late January.) In an emergency, the President can call on Congress to meet. The President also meets with foreign leaders, makes sure the nation's laws are carried out, and signs the orders of military officers.

Section 4. Removal From Office

The President, Vice President, and other high officials can be impeached. If proved guilty, they are removed from office.

2. He shall have Power, by and with the Advice and Consent of the Senate, to make Treaties, provided two thirds of the Senators present concur; and he shall nominate, and by and with the Advice and Consent of the Senate, shall appoint Ambassadors, other public Ministers and Consuls, Judges of the supreme Court, and all other Officers of the United States, whose Appointments are not herein otherwise provided for, and which shall be established by Law: but the Congress may by Law vest the Appointment of such inferior Officers, as they think proper, in the President alone, in the Courts of Law, or in the Heads of Departments.

3. The President shall have Power to fill up all Vacancies that may happen during the Recess of the Senate, by granting Commissions which shall expire at the End of their next Session.

Section 3.

He shall from time to time give to the Congress Information of the State of the Union, and recommend to their Consideration such Measures as he shall judge necessary and expedient; he may, on extraordinary Occasions, convene both Houses, or either of them, and in Case of Disagreement between them, with Respect to the Time of Adjournment, he may adjourn them to such Time as he shall think proper; he shall receive Ambassadors and other public Ministers; he shall take Care that the Laws be faithfully executed, and shall Commission all the Officers of the United States.

Section 4.

The President, Vice President and all Civil Officers of the United States, shall be removed from Office on Impeachment for and Conviction of, Treason, Bribery, or other high Crimes and Misdemeanors.

Section 1.

The judicial Power of the United States, shall be vested in one supreme Court, and in such inferior Courts as the Congress may from time to time ordain and establish. The Judges, both of the supreme and inferior Courts, shall hold their Offices during good Behavior, and shall, at stated Times, receive for their Services, a Compensation, which shall not be diminished during their Continuance in Office.

Section 2.

1. The judicial Power shall extend to all Cases, in Law and Equity, arising under this Constitution, the Laws of the United States, and Treaties made, or which shall be made, under their Authority;— to all Cases affecting Ambassadors, other public ministers, and Consuls;— to all Cases of Admiralty and maritime Jurisdiction;— to Controversies to which the United States shall be a Party;— to Controversies between two or more States;— between a State and Citizens of another State;— between Citizens of different States;— between Citizens of the same State claiming Lands under Grants of different States, and between a State, or the Citizens thereof, and foreign States, Citizens, or Subjects.

2. In all Cases affecting Ambassadors, other public Ministers and Consuls, and those in which a State shall be a Party, the supreme Court shall have original Jurisdiction. In all the other Cases before mentioned, the supreme Court shall have appellate Jurisdiction, both as to Law and Fact, with such Exceptions, and under such Regulations as the Congress shall make.

3. The trial of all Crimes, except in Cases of Impeachment, shall be by Jury; and such Trial shall be held in the State where the said Crimes shall have been committed; but when not committed within any State, the Trial shall be at such Place or Places as the Congress may by Law have directed.

Article 3 deals with the judicial branch.

Section 1. Federal Courts
The judges of the Supreme Court and other federal courts have the power to make decisions in courts of law. If they act properly, federal judges hold their offices for life.

9. Do you think it's a good idea that federal judges hold their offices for life? Why?

_____

_____

_____

_____

_____

_____

Section 2. Powers of Federal Courts
Federal Courts have legal power over
- laws made under the Constitution
- treaties made with foreign nations
- cases occurring at sea
- cases involving the federal government
- cases involving states or citizens of different states
- cases involving foreign citizens or governments

Only the Supreme Court can judge cases involving ambassadors, government officials, or states. Other cases begin in lower courts, but they can be appealed, or reviewed, by the Supreme Court. In criminal cases other than impeachment, trials are held in the state in which the crime took place. A jury decides the case.

Section 3. Treason

Treason is waging war against the United States or helping its enemies. To be found guilty of treason, a person must confess to the crime; or, two people must have seen the crime committed.

10. Name the three branches of federal government described in Articles 1-3.

_____

_____

_____

Congress decides the punishment for a traitor. The traitor's family cannot be punished if innocent.

Article 4 deals with relationships between the states.

Section 1. Recognition by Each State

Each state must respect the laws and court decisions of the other states.

Section 2. Rights of Citizens in Other States

Citizens keep all their rights when visiting other states.

A person charged with a crime who flees to another state must be returned to the state in which the crime took place.

A slave who escapes to another state must be returned to his or her owner. (The Thirteenth Amendment outlawed slavery.)

Section 3. New States

Congress may let new states join the United States. New states cannot be formed from the land of existing states unless Congress approves.

Congress has the power to make laws to govern territories of the United States.

Section 3.

1. Treason against the United States shall consist only in levying War against them, or in adhering to their Enemies, giving them Aid and Comfort. No Person shall be convicted of Treason unless on the Testimony of two Witnesses to the same overt Act, or on Confession in open Court.

2. The Congress shall have Power to declare the Punishment of Treason, but no Attainder of Treason shall work Corruption of Blood, or Forfeiture except during the Life of the Person attainted.

ARTICLE IV

Section 1.

Full Faith and Credit shall be given in each State to the public Acts, Records, and judicial Proceedings of every other State. And the Congress may by general Laws prescribe the Manner in which such Acts, Records and Proceedings shall be proved, and the Effect thereof.

Section 2.

1. The Citizens of each State shall be entitled to all Privileges and Immunities of Citizens in the several States.

2. A Person charged in any State with Treason, Felony, or other Crime, who shall flee from justice, and be found in another State, shall on Demand of the executive Authority of the State from which he fled, be delivered up, to be removed to the State having Jurisdiction of the Crime.

3. No Person held to Service or Labor in one State, under the Laws thereof, escaping into another, shall, in Consequence of any Law or Regulation therein, be discharged from Service or Labor, but shall be delivered up on Claim of the Party to whom such Service or Labor may be due.

Section 3.

1. New States may be admitted by the Congress into this Union; but no new State shall be formed or erected within the Jurisdiction of any other State; nor any State be formed by the Junction of two or more States, or Parts of States, without the Consent of the Legislatures of the States concerned as well as of the Congress.

2. The Congress shall have Power to dispose of and make all needful Rules and Regulations respecting the Territory or other Property belonging to the United States; and nothing in this Constitution shall be so construed as to Prejudice any Claims of the United States, or of any particular State.

Section 4.

The United States shall guarantee to every State in this Union a Republican Form of Government, and shall protect each of them against Invasion; and on Application of the Legislature, or of the Executive (when the Legislature cannot be convened) against domestic Violence.

ARTICLE V

The Congress, whenever two thirds of both Houses shall deem it necessary, shall propose Amendments to this Constitution, or, on the Application of the Legislatures of two thirds of the several States, shall call a Convention for proposing Amendments, which, in either Case, shall be valid to all Intents and Purposes, as Part of this Constitution, when ratified by the Legislatures of three fourths of the several States, or by Conventions in three fourths thereof, as the one or the other Mode of Ratification may be proposed by the Congress; Provided that no Amendment which may be made prior to the Year One thousand eight hundred and eight shall in any Manner affect the first and fourth Clauses in the Ninth section of the first Article; and that no State, without its Consent, shall be deprived of its equal Suffrage in the Senate.

ARTICLE VI

Section 1.

All Debts contracted and Engagements entered into, before the Adoption of this Constitution, shall be as valid against the United States under this Constitution, as under the Confederation.

Section 2.

This Constitution, and the Laws of the United States which shall be made in Pursuance thereof; and all Treaties made, or which shall be made, under the Authority of the United States, shall be the supreme Law of the Land; and the Judges in every State shall be bound thereby, anything in the constitution or Laws of any State to the Contrary notwithstanding.

Section 4. Guarantees to the States

The federal government guarantees that each state has the right to elect its leaders. The federal government will also protect the states from invasion and violent disorders.

11. There were only thirteen states when the Constitution was written. Do you think the framers expected the United States to grow in size? Why?

_____

_____

_____

_____

_____

Article 5 describes the two ways the Constitution can be amended. Two thirds of the Senate and House of Representatives can suggest an amendment, or two thirds of the state legislatures can have a special convention to suggest an amendment. Once an amendment has been suggested, three fourths of the state legislatures or three fourths of the special conventions must approve the amendment.

Article 6 deals with national law and the national debt. The federal government promises to pay all its debts and keep all agreements made under the Articles of Confederation.

The Constitution and federal laws are the highest laws in the land. If state laws disagree with them, the federal laws must be obeyed.

Section 3. Supporting the Constitution

Federal and state officials must promise to support the Constitution. A person's religion cannot disqualify him or her from holding office. Nine of the thirteen states must approve the Constitution for it to become the law of the land.

Article 7 deals with ratifying the Constitution. On September 17, 1787, twelve years after the Declaration of Independence, everyone at the Constitutional Convention agreed that the Constitution was complete.
The delegates to the Constitutional Convention signed their names below the Constitution to show they approved of it.

12. "The power under the Constitution will always be in the people," wrote George Washington in 1787. Explain what you think he meant.

_____

_____

_____

_____

_____

_____

Section 3.

The Senators and Representatives before mentioned, and the Members of the several State legislatures, and all executive and judicial Officers, both of the United States and of the several States, shall be bound by Oath or Affirmation, to support this Constitution; but no religious Test shall ever be required as a Qualification to any Office or public Trust under the United States.

ARTICLE VII

The ratification of the Conventions of nine States, shall be sufficient for the Establishment of this Constitution between the States so ratifying the same.

Done in Convention by the Unanimous Consent of the States present the Seventeenth Day of September in the Year of our Lord one thousand seven hundred and Eighty-seven and of the Independence of the United States of America the twelfth. In witness whereof We have hereunto subscribed our Names.

Attest:
William Jackson,
Secretary
George Washington,
President and Deputy from Virginia

New Hampshire
John Langdon
Nicholas Gilman

Massachusetts
Nathaniel Gorham
Rufus King

Connecticut
William Samuel
  Johnson
Roger Sherman

New York
Alexander Hamilton

New Jersey
William Livingston
David Brearley
William Paterson
Jonathan Dayton

Pennsylvania
Benjamin Franklin
Thomas Mifflin
Robert Morris
George Clymer
Thomas FitzSimons
Jared Ingersoll
James Wilson
Gouverneur Morris

Delaware
George Read
Gunning Bedford, Jr.
John Dickinson
Richard Bassett
Jacob Broom

Maryland
James McHenry
Dan of St. Thomas
  Jenifer
Daniel Carroll

Virginia
John Blair
James Madison, Jr.

North Carolina
William Blount
Richard Dobbs
  Spaight
Hugh Williamson

South Carolina
John Rutledge
Charles
  Cotesworth Pinckney
Charles Pinckney
Pierce Butler

Georgia
William Few
Abraham Baldwin

AMENDMENTS
Amendment 1

Congress shall make no law respecting an establishment of religion, or prohibiting the free exercise thereof, or abridging the freedom of speech, or of the press; or the right of the people peaceably to assemble, and to petition the Government for a redress of grievances.

Amendment 2

A well-regulated Militia being necessary to the security of a free State, the right of the people to keep and bear Arms, shall not be infringed.

Amendment 3

No Soldier shall, in time of peace be quartered in any house, without the consent of the Owner, nor, in time of war, but in a manner to be prescribed by law.

Amendment 4

The right of the people to be secure in their persons, houses, papers, and effects, against unreasonable searches and seizures, shall not be violated, and no Warrants shall issue, but upon probable cause, supported by Oath or affirmation, and particularly describing the place to be searched, and the persons or things to be seized.

Amendment 5

No person shall be held to answer for a capital, or otherwise infamous crime, unless on a presentment or indictment of a Grand Jury, except in cases arising in the land or naval forces, or in the Militia, when in actual service in time of War, or public danger; nor shall any person be subject for the same offence to be twice put in jeopardy of life or limb; nor shall be compelled in any criminal case to be a witness against himself, nor be deprived of life, liberty, or property, without due process of law; nor shall private property be taken for public use, without just compensation.

The first ten amendments to the Constitution are called the Bill of Rights.

First Amendment—1791
Freedom of Religion and Speech
Government cannot promote religion or set up an official religion or stop people from practicing a religion. Government cannot stop people or newspapers from saying what they want.

Second Amendment—1791
Right to Have Firearms
People have the right to own and carry guns.

Third Amendment—1791
Right Not to House Soldiers
During peacetime, citizens do not have to house soldiers.

Fourth Amendment—1791
Search and Arrest Warrant
People or homes cannot be searched without reason. A search warrant is needed to search a house.

Fifth Amendment—1791
Rights of People Accused of Crimes
Only a grand jury can accuse people of a serious crime. No one can be tried twice for the same crime if found not guilty. People cannot be forced to testify against themselves.

13. Write the amendment number that protects each right.

_____ to speak freely

_____ to be protected against unreasonable searches

_____ to not be put on trial twice for the same crime

Sixth Amendment—1791
Right to a Jury Trial
People have the right to a fast trial by a jury and to hear the charges and evidence against them. They also have the right to a lawyer and to call witnesses in their own defense.

Seventh Amendment—1791
Right to a Jury Trial in a Civil Case
In a civil, or noncriminal case, a person also has the right to a trial by jury.

Eighth Amendment—1791
Protection From Unfair Punishment
A person accused of a crime cannot be forced to pay a very high bail. A person convicted of a crime cannot be asked to pay an unfairly high fine or be punished in a cruel or unusual way.

Ninth Amendment—1791
Other Rights
People have other rights that are not specifically mentioned in the Constitution.

Tenth Amendment—1791
Powers of the States and the People
Some powers are not given to the federal government or denied to states. These rights belong to the states or to the people.

Eleventh Amendment—1795
Limits on Rights to Sue States
People from another state or foreign country cannot sue a state.

Amendment 6

In all criminal prosecutions, the accused shall enjoy the right to a speedy and public trial, by an impartial jury of the State and district wherein the crime shall have been committed, which district shall have been previously ascertained by law, and to be informed of the nature and cause of the accusation; to be confronted with the witnesses against him; to have compulsory process for obtaining witnesses in his favor, and to have the Assistance of Counsel for his defense.

Amendment 7

In Suits at common law, where the value in controversy shall exceed twenty dollars, the right of trial by jury shall be preserved, and no fact tried by a jury, shall be otherwise re-examined in any Court of the United States, than according to the rules of the common law.

Amendment 8

Excessive bail shall not be required, nor excessive fines imposed, nor cruel and unusual punishment inflicted.

Amendment 9

The enumeration in the Constitution, of certain rights, shall not be construed to deny or disparage others retained by the people.

Amendment 10

The powers not delegated to the United States by the Constitution, nor prohibited by it to the States, are reserved to the States respectively, or to the people.

Amendment 11

The Judicial power of the United States shall not be construed to extend to any suit in law or equity, commenced or prosecuted against one of the United States by Citizens of another State, or by Citizens or Subjects of any Foreign State.

Amendment 12

The Electors shall meet in their respective States and vote by ballot for President and Vice President, one of whom, at least, shall not be an inhabitant of the same State with themselves; they shall name in their ballots the person voted for as President, and in distinct ballots the person voted for as Vice President, and they shall make distinct lists of all persons voted for as President, and of all persons voted for as Vice President, and of the number of votes for each, which lists they shall sign and certify, and transmit sealed to the seat of the government of the United States, directed to the President of the Senate;— The President of the Senate shall, in the presence of the Senate and the House of Representatives, open all the certificates and the votes shall then be counted;— the person having the greatest Number of votes for President shall be the President, if such number be a majority of the whole number of Electors appointed; and if no person have such a majority, then, from the persons having the highest numbers not exceeding three on the list of those voted for as President, the House of Representatives shall choose immediately, by ballot, the President. But in choosing the President, the votes shall be taken by States, the representation from each State having one vote; a quorum for this purpose shall consist of a member or members from two thirds of the States, and a majority of all the States shall be necessary to a choice. And if the House of Representatives shall not choose a President whenever the right of choice shall devolve upon them, before the fourth day of March next following, then the Vice President shall act as President, as in case of death or other constitutional disability of the President. The person having the greatest number of votes as Vice President, shall be the Vice President, if such number be a majority of the whole number of Electors appointed, and if no person have a majority, then from the two highest numbers on the list, the Senate shall choose the Vice President; a quorum for the purpose shall consist of two thirds of the whole number of Senators, a majority of the whole number shall be necessary to a choice. But no person constitutionally ineligible to the office of President shall be eligible to that of Vice-President of the United States.

Twelfth Amendment—1804
Election of President and Vice President

This amendment changed the way the Electoral College chooses the President and Vice President. Before this amendment, candidates for President and Vice President ran separately, and each elector had two votes—one for President and one for Vice President. The candidate receiving the most votes became President, and the runner-up became Vice President.

Under this amendment, a candidate for President and a candidate for Vice President must run together. Each elector has only one vote, and the pair of candidates that receives more than half the electoral votes become the President and Vice President. If no one receives a majority of the electoral votes, the House of Representatives votes for the President from a list of the top three vote getters. In this situation, each state has one vote, and the candidate must receive more than half of the votes to become President.

If the Representatives fail to elect a President by March 4 (later changed to January 20), the Vice President serves as President. If no candidate receives at least half the electoral votes for Vice President, the names of the two top vote getters are sent to the Senate. The Senators then vote on the names, and the person receiving more than half the votes becomes Vice President.

Thirteenth Amendment—1865
Abolition of Slavery

The United States outlaws slavery. Congress can pass any laws that are needed to carry out this amendment.

Fourteenth Amendment—1868
Rights of Citizens

People born in the United States are citizens of both the United States and of the state in which they live. States must treat their citizens equally. States cannot deny their citizens the rights outlined in the Bill of Rights.

This section of the amendment made former slaves citizens of both the United States and their home state.

Based on its population, each state has a certain number of Representatives in Congress. The number of Representatives from a state might be lowered, however, if the state does not let certain citizens vote.

This section tried to force states in the South to let former slaves vote.

14. Why would a state not want to have its number of Representatives in Congress cut?

_____

_____

_____

_____

_____

Amendment 13

Section 1. Neither slavery nor involuntary servitude, except as a punishment for crime whereof the party shall have been duly convicted, shall exist within the United States, or any place subject to their jurisdiction.

Section 2. Congress shall have power to enforce this article by appropriate legislation.

Amendment 14

Section 1. All persons born or naturalized in the United States and subject to the jurisdiction thereof, are citizens of the United States and of the State wherein they reside. No State shall make or enforce any law which shall abridge the privileges or immunities of citizens of the United States; nor shall any State deprive any person of life, liberty, or property, without due process of law; nor deny to any person within its jurisdiction the equal protection of the laws.

Section 2. Representatives shall be apportioned among the several States according to their respective numbers, counting the whole number of persons in each State, excluding Indians not taxed. But when the right to vote at any election for the choice of electors for President and Vice President of the United States, Representatives in Congress, the Executive and Judicial officers of a State, or the members of the Legislature thereof, is denied to any of the male inhabitants of such State, being twenty-one years of age and citizens of the United States, or in any way abridged, except for participation in rebellion, or other crime, the basis of representation therein shall be reduced in the proportion which the number of such male citizens shall bear to the whole number of male citizens twenty-one years of age in such State.

Section 3. No person shall be a Senator or Representative in Congress, or elector of President and Vice President, or hold any office, civil or military, under the United States, or under any State, who, having previously taken an oath, as a member of Congress, or as an officer of the United States, or as a member of any State legislature, or as an executive or judicial officer of any State, to support the Constitution of the United States, shall have engaged in insurrection or rebellion against the same, or given aid or comfort to the enemies thereof. But Congress may, by a vote of two thirds of each House, remove such disability.

Section 4. The validity of the public debt of the United States, authorized by law, including debts incurred for payment of pensions and bounties for services in suppressing insurrection or rebellion, shall not be questioned. But neither the United States nor any State shall assume or pay any debt or obligation incurred in aid of insurrection or rebellion against the United States, or any claim for the loss or emancipation of any slave; but all such debts, obligations and claims shall be held illegal and void.

Section 5. The Congress shall have power to enforce, by appropriate legislation, the provisions of this article.

Amendment 15

Section 1. The right of citizens of the United States to vote shall not be denied or abridged by the United States or by any State on account of race, color, or previous condition of servitude.

Section 2. The Congress shall have power to enforce this article by appropriate legislation.

Officials who took part in the Civil War against the United States cannot hold federal or state office. Congress can remove this provision by a two-thirds vote.

The United States will pay back the money it borrowed to fight the Civil War. The money that the South borrowed to fight the Civil War will not be paid back to lenders. The former owners of slaves will not be paid for the slaves that were set free. Congress can pass any necessary laws to enforce this article.

15. List two ways in which the Fourteenth Amendment tended to punish those who rebelled against the United States.

_____

_____

_____

_____

_____

_____

_____

Fifteenth Amendment—1870 Voting Rights
The federal and state government cannot stop people from voting based on race or color. Former slaves must be allowed to vote.

Sixteenth Amendment—1913
Income Tax
Congress has the power to collect an income tax regardless of the population of a state. (Originally, Section 9 of Article 1 had denied this power to Congress.)

Seventeenth Amendment—1913
Direct Election of Senators
The voters of each state will elect their Senators directly. (Originally, Article 1, Section 3 said state legislatures would elect Senators.)

A state can hold a special election to fill an empty Senate seat. Until then, the governor can appoint a Senator to fill an empty seat.

Eighteenth Amendment—1919
Prohibition
Making, importing, or selling alcoholic drinks is illegal in the United States. This was called Prohibition because the amendment prohibited, or outlawed, alcohol.

Congress and the states can make any laws to prohibit alcohol.

This amendment becomes part of the Constitution if it is approved within seven years.

This amendment was repealed, or cancelled, in 1933 by the Twenty-first Amendment.

16. Write the amendment number that did each of the following:

_____ let the Federal Government collect income tax

_____ guaranteed voting rights for African Americans

_____ outlawed the sale of alcohol

_____ abolished slavery

_____ let voters elect their Senators

Amendment 16
The Congress shall have power to lay and collect taxes on incomes, from whatever source derived, without apportionment among the several States, and without regard to any census or enumeration.

Amendment 17
The Senate of the United States shall be composed of two Senators from each State, elected by the people thereof, for six years; and each Senator shall have one vote. The electors in each State shall have the qualifications requisite for electors of the most numerous branch of the State legislatures.

When vacancies happen in the representation of any State in the Senate, the executive authority of such State shall issue writs of election to fill such vacancies: Provided, That the legislature of any State may empower the executive thereof to make temporary appointments until the people fill the vacancies by election as the legislature may direct.

This amendment shall not be so construed as to affect the election or term of any Senator chosen before it becomes valid as part of the Constitution.

Amendment 18
Section 1. After one year from the ratification of this article the manufacture, sale, or transportation of intoxicating liquors within, the importation thereof into, or the exportation thereof from the United States and all territory subject to the jurisdiction thereof for beverage purposes is hereby prohibited.

Section 2. The Congress and the several States shall have concurrent power to enforce this article by appropriate legislation.

Section 3. This article shall be inoperative unless it shall have been ratified as an amendment to the Constitution by the legislatures of the several States, as provided in the Constitution, within seven years of the date of the submission hereof to the States by Congress.

Amendment 19

The right of citizens of the United States to vote shall not be denied or abridged by the United States or by any State on account of sex.

Congress shall have power to enforce this article by appropriate legislation.

Amendment 20

Section 1. The terms of the President and Vice President shall end at noon on the 20th day of January, and the terms of Senators and Representatives at noon on the 3d day of January, of the years in which such terms would have ended if this article had not been ratified; and the terms of their successors shall then begin.

Section 2. The Congress shall assemble at least once in every year, and such meeting shall begin at noon on the 3d day of January, unless they shall by law appoint a different day.

Section 3. If, at the time fixed for the beginning of the term of the President, the President elect shall have died, the Vice President elect shall become President. If a President shall not have been chosen before the time fixed for the beginning of his term, or if the President-elect shall have failed to qualify, then the Vice President elect shall act as President until a President shall have qualified; and the Congress may by law provide for the case wherein neither a President elect nor a Vice President elect shall have qualified, declaring who shall then act as President, or the manner in which one who is to act shall be selected, and such person shall act accordingly until a President or Vice President shall have qualified.

Section 4. The Congress may by law provide for the case of the death of any of the persons from whom the House of Representatives may choose a President whenever the right of choice shall have devolved upon them, and for the case of the death of any of the persons from whom the Senate may choose a Vice President whenever the right of choice shall have devolved upon them.

Section 5. Sections 1 and 2 shall take effect on the 15th day of October following the ratification of this article.

Section 6. This article shall be inoperative unless it shall have been ratified as an amendment to the Constitution by the legislatures of three fourths of the several States within seven years from the date of its submission.

Nineteenth Amendment—1920
Women's Right to Vote

No government can stop people from voting because of their sex. Congress can pass necessary laws to carry out this amendment.

Twentieth Amendment—1933
Terms of Office

The term of a new President begins on January 20. This date is called Inauguration Day. Members of Congress take office on January 3. (Originally their terms began on March 4.)

Congress must meet at least once a year. They should first meet on January 3, unless they choose a different day.

If a candidate for President does not win a majority of votes in the Electoral College and dies while the election is being decided in the House, Congress has the power to pass laws to resolve the problem. Congress has similar power if a candidate for Vice President dies while the election is being decided in the Senate.

Sections 1 and 2 of this amendment take effect on the fifteenth day of October after the amendment becomes part of the Constitution. This amendment has to be approved by three fourths of the states within seven years.

17. How long was the Eighteenth Amendment in effect in the United States?

_____

_____

18. Do you think a President should be limited to just two terms in office? Why or why not?

_____

_____

_____

_____

_____

_____

Amendment 21

Section 1. The eighteenth article of amendment to the Constitution of the United States is hereby repealed.

Section 2. The transportation or importation into any State, Territory, or possession of the United States for delivery or use therein of intoxicating liquors, in violation of the laws thereof, is hereby prohibited.

Section 3. This article shall be inoperative unless it shall have been ratified as an amendment to the Constitution by conventions in the several States, as provided in the Constitution, within seven years from the date of the submission hereof to the States by the Congress.

Amendment 22

Section 1. No person shall be elected to the office of the President more than twice, and no person who has held the office of President, or acted as President, for more than two years of a term to which some other person was elected President shall be elected to the office of the President more than once. But this Article shall not apply to any person holding the office of President, when this Article was proposed by the Congress, and shall not prevent any person who may be holding the office of President, or acting as President, during the term within which this Article becomes operative from holding the office of President or acting as President during the remainder of such term.

Section 2. This article shall be inoperative unless it shall have been ratified as an amendment to the Constitution by the legislatures of three fourths of the several states within seven years from the date of its submission to the States by the Congress.

Amendment 23

Section 1. The District constituting the seat of Government of the United States shall appoint in such manner as the Congress may direct:

A number of electors of President and Vice President equal to the whole number of Senators and Representatives in Congress to which the District would be entitled if it were a State, but in no event more than the least populous State; they shall be in addition to those appointed by the States, they shall be considered, for the purposes of the election of President and Vice President, to be electors appointed by a State; and they shall meet in the District and perform such duties as provided by the twelfth article of amendment.

Amendment 24

Section 1. The right of citizens of the United States to vote in any primary or other election for President or Vice President, for electors for President or Vice President, or for Senator or Representative in Congress, shall not be denied or abridged by the United States or any State by reason of failure to pay any poll tax or other tax.

Section 2. The Congress shall have power to enforce this article by appropriate legislation.

Amendment 25

Section 1. In case of the removal of the President from office or of his death or resignation, the Vice President shall become President.

Section 2. Whenever there is a vacancy in the office of the Vice President, the President shall nominate a Vice President who shall take office upon confirmation by a majority vote of both Houses of Congress.

Section 3. Whenever the President transmits to the President pro tempore of the Senate and the Speaker of the House of Representatives his written declaration that he is unable to discharge the powers and duties of his office, and until he transmits to them a written declaration to the contrary, such powers and duties shall be discharged by the Vice President as Acting President.

Twenty-third Amendment—1961 Presidential Elections for District of Columbia

People living in Washington, D.C., have the right to vote in presidential elections. Washington, D.C., can never have more electoral votes than the state with the smallest number of people.

Twenty-fourth Amendment—1964 Outlawing of Poll Tax

No one can be stopped from voting in a federal election because he or she has not paid a poll tax or any other kind of tax.

Congress can make laws to carry out this amendment.

Twenty-fifth Amendment—1967 Presidential Succession

If the President dies or resigns, the Vice President becomes President. If the office of Vice President is empty, the President appoints a new Vice President.

When the President is unable to carry out the duties of the office, Congress should be informed. The Vice President then serves as Acting President. The President may resume the duties of the office after informing Congress.

If the Vice President and half the President's top advisers, or Cabinet, inform Congress that the President cannot carry out his or her duties, the Vice President becomes Acting President. If the President informs Congress that he or she is able to carry out these duties, the President returns to office. However, after four days, if the Vice President and half the Cabinet again tell Congress that the President cannot carry out his or her duties, the President does not return to office. Instead, Congress must decide within 21 days whether the President is able to carry out his or her duties. If two thirds of Congress votes that the President cannot continue in office, the Vice President becomes Acting President. If two thirds do not vote in this way, the President remains in office.

Votes for Eighteen-Year-Olds

People who are 18 years old have the right to vote in federal and state elections.

Congress can pass laws to carry out this amendment.

Over the years, amendments to the Constitution have improved our democracy by expanding voting rights to more and more citizens.

19. Write the number of the amendment that:

_____ gave votes to women

_____ gave votes to citizens in Washington, D.C.

_____ gave votes to 18-year-old people

_____ outlawed taxes that blocked voting

Twenty-seventh Amendment—1992
Limits on Congressional Salary Changes

Laws that increase the salaries of Senators and Representatives do not take effect immediately. They take effect after the next election of the House of Representatives.

Section 4. Whenever the Vice President and a majority of either the principal officers of the executive departments or of such other body as Congress may by law provide, transmit to the President pro tempore of the Senate and the Speaker of the House of Representatives their written declaration that the President is unable to discharge the powers and duties of his office, the Vice President shall immediately assume the powers and duties of the office as Acting President.

Thereafter, when the President transmits to the President pro tempore of the Senate and the Speaker of the House of Representatives his written declaration that no inability exists, he shall resume the powers and duties of his office unless the Vice President and a majority of either the principal officers of the executive department or of such other body as Congress may by law provide, transmit within four days to the President pro tempore of the Senate and the Speaker of the House of Representatives their written declaration that the President is unable to discharge the powers and duties of his office. Thereupon Congress shall decide the issue, assembling within forty-eight hours for that purpose if not in session. If the Congress, within twenty-one days after receipt of the latter written declaration, or, if Congress is not in session, within twenty-one days after Congress is required to assemble, determines by two-thirds vote of both Houses that the President is unable to discharge the powers and duties of his office, the Vice President shall continue to discharge the same as Acting President; otherwise, the President shall resume the powers and duties of his office.

Amendment 26

Section 1. The right of citizens of the United States, who are eighteen years of age or older, to vote shall not be denied or abridged by the United States or by any State on account of age.

Section 2. The Congress shall have the power to enforce this article by appropriate legislation.

Amendment 27

No law varying the compensation for the services of the Senators and Representatives, shall take effect, until an election of Representatives shall have intervened.

The United States of America, Political

Washington
★ Olympia

Salem ★

Oregon

Boise ★

Idaho

Montana
Helena ★

North Dakota
★ Bismarck

Minnesot

South Dakota
Pierre ★

St. Paul

Wyoming

Cheyenne ★

Nebraska

Iow

Sacramento ★

Carson City ★

Salt Lake City ★

Lincoln ★

Nevada

Utah

Denver ★

California

Colorado

Topeka ★

Kansas

Arizona

Santa Fe ★

Oklahoma

M

Phoenix ★

New Mexico

Oklahoma City ★

Texas

Austin ★

Alaska

Juneau ★

Honolulu ★

Hawaii

New Hampshire

Vermont

Maine

Augusta

Montpelier

Concord

Massachusetts

Boston

Albany

New York

Providence

Hartford

Rhode Island

Connecticut

New Jersey

Pennsylvania

Harrisburg

Trenton

Annapolis

Dover

Delaware

Maryland

Washington, D.C.

nesota

t. Paul

Wisconsin

Michigan

Madison

Lansing

Iowa

Des Moines

Illinois

Indiana

Ohio

Columbus

West Virginia

Virginia

Springfield

Indianapolis

Charleston

Richmond

Jefferson City

Frankfort

Missouri

Kentucky

Raleigh

Nashville

North Carolina

Tennessee

Arkansas

Columbia

South Carolina

Little Rock

Alabama

Atlanta

Mississippi

Georgia

Louisiana

Jackson

Montgomery

Baton Rouge

Tallahassee

Florida

LEGEND

⊛ National capital

★ State capital

N
W E
S

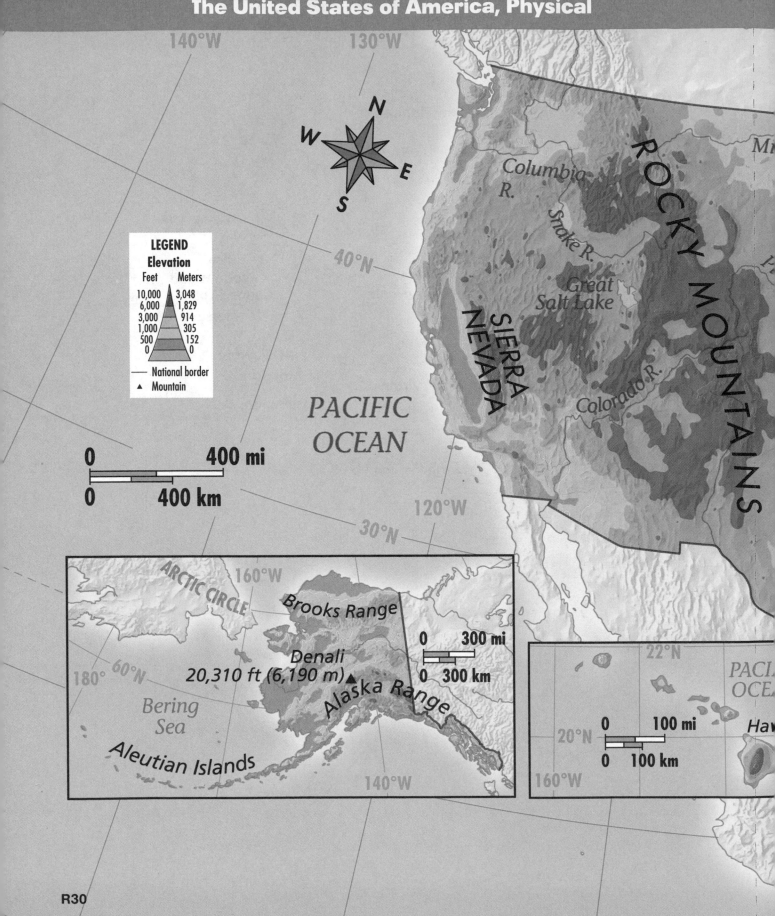

LEGEND
Elevation

Feet	Meters
10,000	3,048
6,000	1,829
3,000	914
1,000	305
500	152
0	0

— National border
▲ Mountain

N
W E
S

Columbia R.

ROCKY MOUNTAINS

Snake R.

Great Salt Lake

SIERRA NEVADA

Colorado R.

PACIFIC OCEAN

0   400 mi

0   400 km

ARCTIC CIRCLE

Brooks Range

Denali
20,310 ft (6,190 m)▲

Alaska Range

Bering Sea

Aleutian Islands

0   300 mi

0   300 km

PACI OCE

Haw

0   100 mi

0   100 km

Missouri R.

Lake
Superior

Great Lakes

Lake
Ontario

Lake
Huron

GREAT PLAINS

Platte R.

Lake
Michigan

Lake Erie

APPALACHIAN MOUNTAINS

CENTRAL
PLAINS

Ohio R.

ATLANTIC
OCEAN

Red R.

COASTAL PLAIN

Mississippi R.

80°W

70°W

NTAINS

Rio Grande

ACIFIC
OCEAN

Gulf of Mexico

Hawaii

90°W

TROPIC OF CANCER

20°N

154°W

map
area

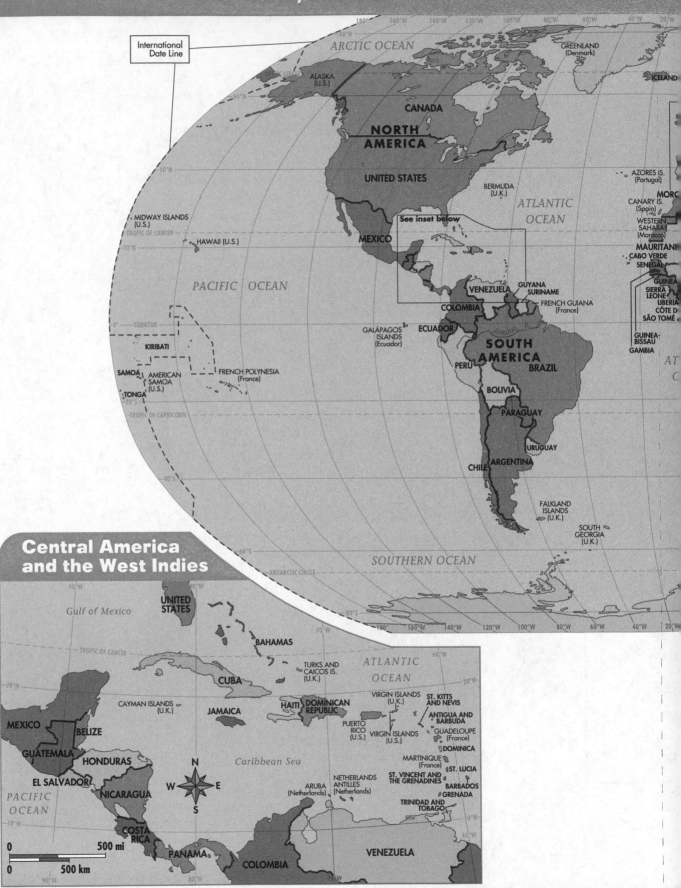

International Date Line

ARCTIC OCEAN

GREENLAND
(Denmark)

ICELAND

ALASKA
(U.S.)

CANADA

NORTH
AMERICA

UNITED STATES

BERMUDA
(U.K.)

ATLANTIC
OCEAN

AZORES IS.
(Portugal)

MOR

CANARY IS.
(Spain)

WESTERN
SAHARA
(Morocco)

MAURITANI

CABO VERDE

SENEGAL

See inset below

MEXICO

MIDWAY ISLANDS
(U.S.)

TROPIC OF CANCER

HAWAII (U.S.)

PACIFIC OCEAN

VENEZUELA

GUYANA
SURINAME

FRENCH GUIANA
(France)

GUINEA

SIERRA
LEONE

LIBERIA

CÔTE D

SÃO TOMÉ

COLOMBIA

GALÁPAGOS
ISLANDS
(Ecuador)

ECUADOR

SOUTH
AMERICA

GUINEA-
BISSAU

GAMBIA

AT

C

EQUATOR

KIRIBATI

PERU

BRAZIL

SAMOA

AMERICAN
SAMOA
(U.S.)

FRENCH POLYNESIA
(France)

BOLIVIA

TONGA

PARAGUAY

URUGUAY

CHILE

ARGENTINA

TROPIC OF CAPRICORN

FALKLAND
ISLANDS
(U.K.)

SOUTH
GEORGIA
(U.K.)

SOUTHERN OCEAN

ANTARCTIC CIRCLE

Central America
and the West Indies

Gulf of Mexico

UNITED
STATES

TROPIC OF CANCER

BAHAMAS

ATLANTIC
OCEAN

CUBA

TURKS AND
CAICOS IS.
(U.K.)

CAYMAN ISLANDS
(U.K.)

JAMAICA

HAITI

DOMINICAN
REPUBLIC

VIRGIN ISLANDS
(U.K.)

ST. KITTS
AND NEVIS

ANTIGUA AND
BARBUDA

MEXICO

BELIZE

GUATEMALA

HONDURAS

EL SALVADOR

PACIFIC
OCEAN

NICARAGUA

PUERTO
RICO
(U.S.)

VIRGIN ISLANDS
(U.S.)

GUADELOUPE
(France)

DOMINICA

MARTINIQUE
(France)

ST. LUCIA

Caribbean Sea

NETHERLANDS
ANTILLES
(Netherlands)

ST. VINCENT AND
THE GRENADINES

ARUBA
(Netherlands)

BARBADOS

GRENADA

TRINIDAD AND
TOBAGO

COSTA
RICA

PANAMA

COLOMBIA

VENEZUELA

0   500 mi

0   500 km

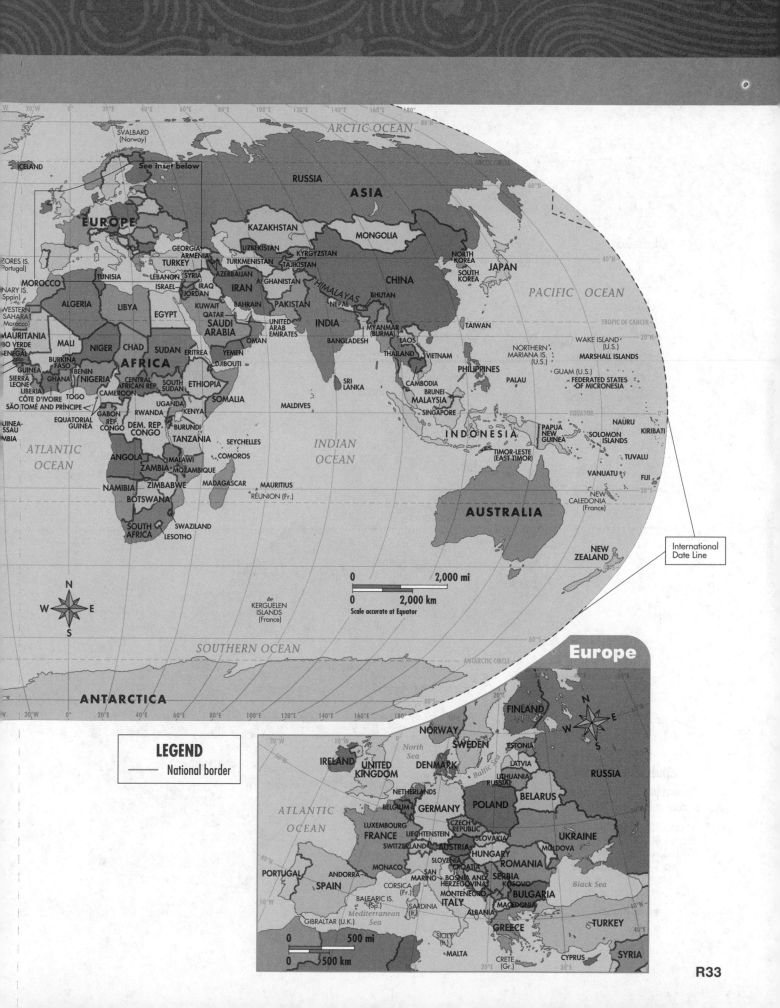

ARCTIC OCEAN

SVALBARD
(Norway)

See inset below

ICELAND

EUROPE

ASIA

RUSSIA

KAZAKHSTAN

MONGOLIA

UZBEKISTAN

KYRGYZSTAN

NORTH
KOREA

JAPAN

PACIFIC OCEAN

GEORGIA
ARMENIA

TURKEY

TURKMENISTAN

TAJIKISTAN

CHINA

SOUTH
KOREA

40°N

AZORES IS.
(Portugal)

MOROCCO

TUNISIA

LEBANON
ISRAEL

SYRIA

IRAQ
JORDAN

IRAN

AZERBAIJAN

AFGHANISTAN

HIMALAYAS

BHUTAN

TAIWAN

TROPIC OF CANCER

WAKE ISLAND
(U.S.)

20°N

CANARY IS.
(Spain)

ALGERIA

LIBYA

EGYPT

KUWAIT

BAHRAIN

QATAR

SAUDI
ARABIA

PAKISTAN

NEPAL

INDIA

LAOS

MYANMAR
(BURMA)

THAILAND

VIETNAM

NORTHERN
MARIANA IS.
(U.S.)

MARSHALL ISLANDS

WESTERN
SAHARA
(Morocco)

MAURITANIA

MALI

NIGER

CHAD

SUDAN

ERITREA

YEMEN

OMAN

UNITED
ARAB
EMIRATES

BANGLADESH

GUAM (U.S.)

PALAU

FEDERATED STATES
OF MICRONESIA

CABO VERDE

SENEGAL

AFRICA

DJIBOUTI

SRI
LANKA

CAMBODIA

PHILIPPINES

GUINEA

BURKINA
FASO

BENIN

GHANA

NIGERIA

CENTRAL
AFRICAN REP.

SOUTH
SUDAN

ETHIOPIA

SOMALIA

BRUNEI

MALAYSIA

SIERRA
LEONE

TOGO

CÔTE D'IVOIRE

LIBERIA

CAMEROON

SINGAPORE

EQUATOR

NAURU

SÃO TOMÉ AND PRÍNCIPE

UGANDA

KENYA

MALDIVES

INDONESIA

GUINEA-
BISSAU

EQUATORIAL
GUINEA

GABON

REP.
CONGO

DEM. REP.
CONGO

RWANDA

BURUNDI

PAPUA
NEW
GUINEA

SOLOMON
ISLANDS

KIRIBATI

GAMBIA

ATLANTIC
OCEAN

TANZANIA

SEYCHELLES

INDIAN
OCEAN

TIMOR-LESTE
(EAST TIMOR)

TUVALU

ANGOLA

ZAMBIA

MALAWI

MOZAMBIQUE

COMOROS

VANUATU

FIJI

NAMIBIA

ZIMBABWE

MADAGASCAR

MAURITIUS

RÉUNION (Fr.)

NEW
CALEDONIA
(France)

20°S

BOTSWANA

AUSTRALIA

SWAZILAND

SOUTH
AFRICA

LESOTHO

International
Date Line

N
W E
S

NEW
ZEALAND

KERGUELEN
ISLANDS
(France)

0   2,000 mi
0   2,000 km
Scale accurate at Equator

SOUTHERN OCEAN

ANTARCTIC CIRCLE

60°S

ANTARCTICA

20°W   0   20°E   40°E   60°E   80°E   100°E   120°E   140°E   160°E   180°

LEGEND
——— National border

Europe

FINLAND

NORWAY

SWEDEN

ESTONIA

N
W E
S

IRELAND

UNITED
KINGDOM

North
Sea

DENMARK

Baltic Sea

LATVIA

LITHUANIA

RUSSIA

RUSSIA

NETHERLANDS

BELARUS

ATLANTIC
OCEAN

BELGIUM

GERMANY

POLAND

LUXEMBOURG

CZECH
REPUBLIC

UKRAINE

FRANCE

LIECHTENSTEIN

SWITZERLAND

AUSTRIA

SLOVAKIA

HUNGARY

MOLDOVA

SLOVENIA

CROATIA

ROMANIA

PORTUGAL

ANDORRA

MONACO

SAN
MARINO

BOSNIA AND
HERZEGOVINA

SERBIA

KOSOVO

Black Sea

SPAIN

CORSICA
(Fr.)

MONTENEGRO

BULGARIA

BALEARIC IS.
(Sp.)

SARDINIA
(It.)

ITALY

MACEDONIA

TURKEY

GIBRALTAR (U.K.)

Mediterranean
Sea

ALBANIA

GREECE

SICILY
(It.)

MALTA

CYPRUS

SYRIA

CRETE
(Gr.)

0   500 mi
0   500 km

R33

California, Political and Population

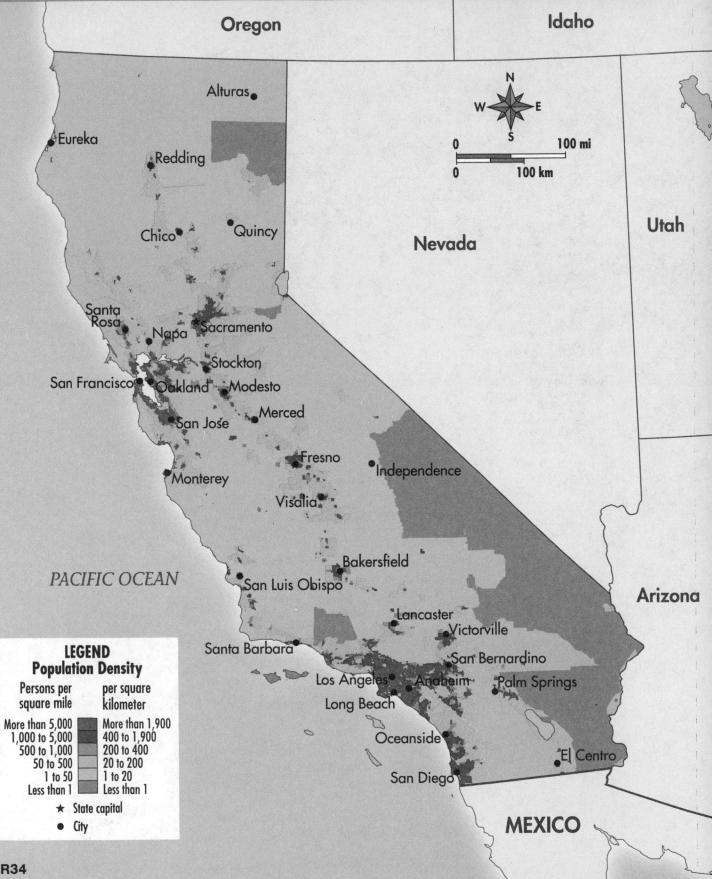

Oregon

Idaho

Alturas

Eureka

Redding

Nevada

Utah

Chico

Quincy

Santa Rosa

Napa ★Sacramento

Stockton

San Francisco Oakland Modesto

San Jose Merced

Fresno

Independence

Monterey

Visalia

Bakersfield

PACIFIC OCEAN

San Luis Obispo

Arizona

Lancaster

Victorville

Santa Barbara

San Bernardino

Los Angeles Anaheim Palm Springs

Long Beach

Oceanside

El Centro

San Diego

MEXICO

LEGEND
Population Density

Persons per square mile	per square kilometer
More than 5,000	More than 1,900
1,000 to 5,000	400 to 1,900
500 to 1,000	200 to 400
50 to 500	20 to 200
1 to 50	1 to 20
Less than 1	Less than 1

★ State capital
● City

0   100 mi
0   100 km

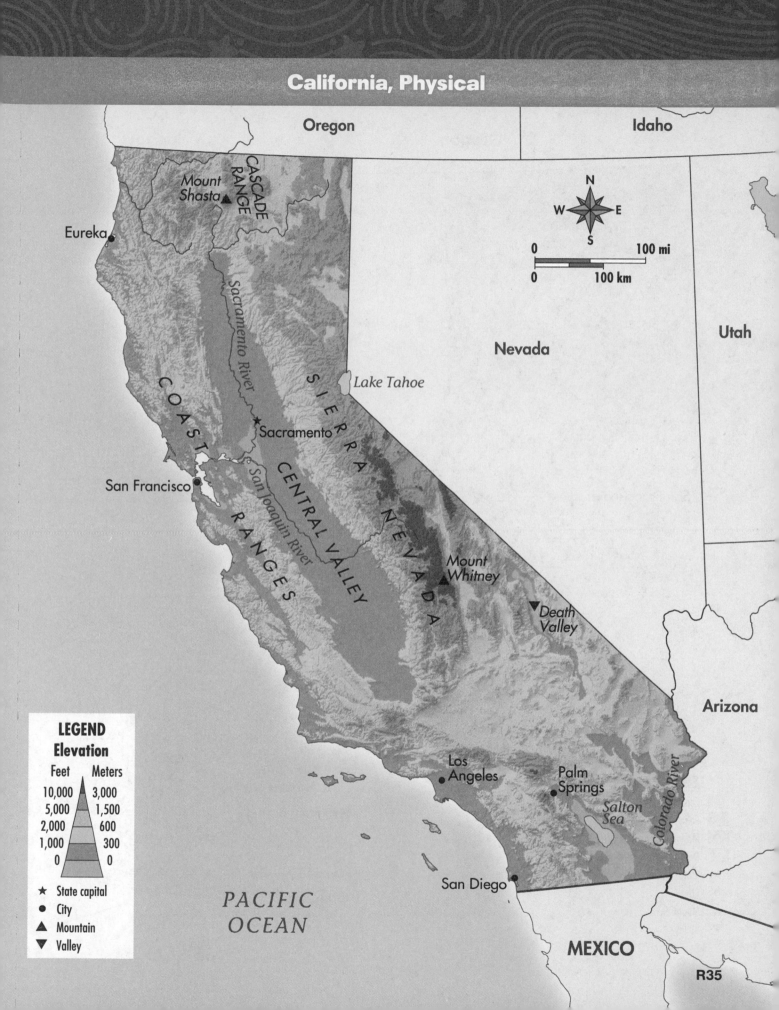

California, Physical

Oregon

Idaho

Nevada

Utah

Arizona

MEXICO

CASCADE RANGE

Mount Shasta

Eureka

COAST RANGES

Sacramento River

San Joaquin River

Sacramento

San Francisco

SIERRA NEVADA

Lake Tahoe

CENTRAL VALLEY

Mount Whitney

Death Valley

Los Angeles

Palm Springs

Salton Sea

Colorado River

San Diego

PACIFIC OCEAN

N
W E
S

| 0 | | 100 mi |
| 0 | | 100 km |

LEGEND
Elevation

Feet	Meters
10,000	3,000
5,000	1,500
2,000	600
1,000	300
0	0

★ State capital
● City
▲ Mountain
▼ Valley

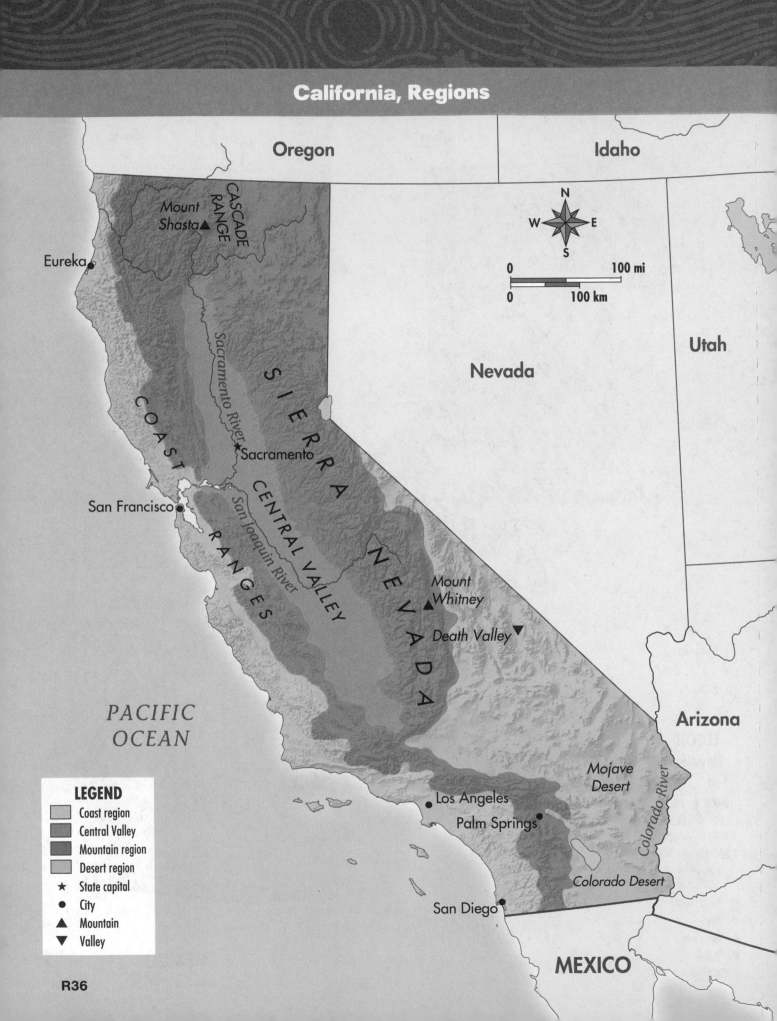

California, Regions

Oregon

Idaho

Nevada

Utah

Arizona

MEXICO

Mount Shasta▲

CASCADE RANGE

Eureka•

Sacramento River

C O A S T   R A N G E S

San Joaquin River

S I E R R A

★ Sacramento

C E N T R A L   V A L L E Y

San Francisco•

N E V A D A

Mount Whitney ▲

Death Valley ▼

PACIFIC OCEAN

Mojave Desert

Colorado River

Los Angeles•

Palm Springs•

Colorado Desert

San Diego•

N
W   E
S

0   100 mi
0   100 km

LEGEND

- Coast region
- Central Valley
- Mountain region
- Desert region
- ★ State capital
- • City
- ▲ Mountain
- ▼ Valley

Glossary

A

absolute location (AB suh loot loh KAY shun) The exact location of a place on Earth.

accessible (ak SES uh bul) Available.

activist (AK tihv ihst) Someone who works hard for change.

adapt (uh DAPT) To change or adjust.

advocate (AD vuh kayt) To speak in favor of.

aerospace (AIR oh spays) The industry that makes airplanes, spacecraft, rockets, and other things that fly.

agree (uh GREE) to have the same opinion

agriculture (AG rih kul chur) Farming.

amendment (uh MEND munt) A change made to the Constitution.

aqueduct (AK wuh dukt) A pipe or other system that moves water from one place to another.

architecture (AHR kuh tek chur) Building design.

article (AHRT ih kul) A section of a law or constitution

authority (uh THOR uh tee) A person in control of a place.

B

bill (bihl) A proposal for a new law.

biography (by AH gruh fee) A book about a person's life that is written by someone else.

boomtown (BOOM toun) A town that suddenly grows.

boycott (BOI kaht) Refusing to buy something in order to make a point.

budget (BUJ iht) A plan for spending money.

C

Californio (kal ih FOR nee oh) A person living in early California descended from Spanish settlers.

campus (KAM pus) The land and buildings of a school.

challenge (CHAL unj) Something that is hard to do.

checks and balances (cheks and BAL un ses) A system in our government in which each branch is allowed to check, or limit, the powers of the others.

circumnavigate (sur kum NAV uh gayt) To travel completely around.

city council (SIHT ee KOUN sul) A group of people who make laws for a city.

civil rights (SIHV ul ryts) Rights of all citizens to freedom and equality.

civil war (SIHV ul wor) A war between two sides within the same country.

claim (klaym) The official right to own something, such as an area of land.

climate (KLY mut) A place's average weather over time.

colony (KAHL uh nee) Land controlled by another nation.

commerce (KAHM urs) Business.

commercial agriculture (kuh MURSH ul AG rih kul chur) Farming for profit, rather than to eat what you grow.

communicate (kuh MYOO nih kayt) To share information.

community (kuh MYOO nuh tee) A group of people who live in the same area.

compass rose (KUM pus rohz) A symbol that shows the cardinal directions of north, south, east, and west; may also show the intermediate directions of northeast, northwest, southeast, and southwest.

compromise (KAHM pruh myz) Each side in a disagreement giving up something to reach an agreement.

consequence (KAHN sih kwens) A result or effect.

constitution (kahn stuh TOO shuyn) A written plan for government.

constitutional convention (kahn stuh TOO shun ul kun VEN shun) A special meeting to create a constitution.

contribute (kun TRIHB yoot) To give something to a larger whole.

convert (kun VIHRT) To change from one religion to another.

corruption (kuh RUP shun) Dishonest and illegal behavior by those in power.

create (kree AYT) To cause something to happen.

cultivate (KUL tuh vayt) To prepare and use land for growing plants.

culture (KUL chur) The beliefs and ways of living shared by a group of people.

current (KUR unt) A continuous movement of water in the same direction.

D

defense industry (dih FENS IHN dus tree) Businesses that make supplies for the military.

delegate (DEL uh giht) A person chosen to make decisions about government.

democracy (dih MAHK ruh see) A political system in which the power of government comes from the people.

deny (dee NY) To refuse.

deport (dee PORT) To send someone back to their home country.

depression (dee PRESH un) A period of time when business activity slows down.

describe (dih SKRYB) To explain something.

develop (dih VEL up) To grow or expand.

discover (dih SKUV ur) To find.

discrimination (dih skrihm ih NAY shun) Unfair treatment of people based on their race, gender, age, or other characteristic.

district (DIHS trikt) A part of the government set up to run a certain thing in a specific area.

diverse (duh VURS) Different.

draft (draft) To make an early version or plan of something.

drought (drout) A time of very little rain.

E

economy (ih KAHN uh mee) The way a region produces resources, goods, and services in order to meet its needs and wants.

elevation (el uh VAY shun) A place's height above sea level.

encounter (en KOUN tur) To meet.

engineer (en juh NEER) A person who designs things such as roads, bridges, or machines.

entrepreneur (ahn truh pruh NOOR) Someone who starts a new business.

environment (en VY run munt) The natural surroundings in an area, or the natural world in general.

equator (ee KWAYT ur) An imaginary line that runs around the center of Earth.

erode (ee ROHD) To gradually destroy.

exclusion (eks KLOO zhun) The act of keeping a person or group out of something.

executive branch (eg ZEK yoo tihv branch) The branch of government responsible for enforcing laws.

expedition (eks puh DIHSH un) An organized journey.

export (EKS port) Something sold or traded to another country.

F

federalism (FED ur ul ihz um) The constitutional principle that says that power is shared between the national government and state governments.

foreigner (FOR un ur) A person from another country.

former (FOR mur) In the past; before.

Franciscan (fran SIHS kun) A member of the Franciscan Order, a Roman Catholic religious group.

freeway (FREE way) A highway that does not cost money to use.

fugitive (FYOO jih tiv) A person who is trying to escape something, such as slavery.

G

galleon (GAL ee un) A type of large sailing ship.

geography (jee AHG ruh fee) The study of the location, people, places, and natural features of an area.

glacier (GLAY shur) A large sheet of ice.

H

hemisphere (HEM ih sfeer) Half of Earth.

heritage (HAIR uh tihj) Customs and history.

higher education (HY ur ej oo KAY shun) Education beyond high school.

historical map (hihs TAWR ih kul map) A map that shows events from the past.

Hollywood (HAHL ee wood) An area of Los Angeles that is the center of filmmaking in the United States.

humid (HYOO mihd) Wet and warm.

hunter-gatherer (HUNT ur GATHH ur ur) A person who collects plants and hunts wild animals for food.

hydroelectric power (hy droh ee LEK trihk pou ur) Electricity created by the force of falling water.

I

immigrate (IHM uh grayt) To come to another country to live.

independence (ihn dee PEN duns) Freedom from the rule of another person, country, or government.

indigenous (ihn DIHJ uh nus) Native to a place.

individual (ihn duh VIHJ oo ul) Single; separate.

industry (IHN dus tree) The businesses that make one kind of product or offer one kind of service.

influence (IHN floo uns) An effect or impact.

inhabitant (ihn HAB ih tunt) A person who lives in a certain place.

initiative (ih NIHSH uh tihv) A process in which voters vote on a proposed new law.

intent (ihn TENT) A goal or purpose.

internment camp (ihn TURN munt kamp) A place where people are held against their will, often during a war.

invasion (ihn VAY zhun) A military attack to take control of a place.

investor (ihn VEST ur) A person who gives money to a company in exchange for part of what that company earns later.

involve (ihn VAHLV) To take part in; include.

irrigation (ihr uh GAY shun) Bringing water to crops using canals, ditches, and pipes.

isolate (EYE suh layt) To separate or set apart from other things.

J

judicial branch (joo DIHSH ul branch) The branch of government responsible for interpreting laws.

K

kinship (KIHN shihp) Relationship.

L

land grant (land grant) An official document that gives someone the right to own an area of land.

landform (LAND form) A natural physical feature of Earth's surface.

latitude (LAT uh tood) Lines on a map that measure distance north or south of the equator.

legislative branch (LEJ ihs lay tihv branch) The branch of government responsible for making laws.

levee (LEV ee) A barrier built to keep water from overflowing onto the land.

limit (LIHM iht) To control.

locator map (LOH kay tur map) A simple map that shows the location of an area within a country or in the world.

lode (lohd) A deposit of gold or other metal or mineral trapped in a rock.

longitude (LAHN juh tood) Lines on a map that measure distance east or west of the prime meridian.

M

map legend (map LEJ und) A box that explains the symbols on the map.

mayor (MAY ur) The leader of a city or town.

migrant worker (MY grunt WUR kur) A person who regularly moves from place to place for work.

miner (MYN ur) A person who digs in the ground for minerals and metals, like gold.

mineral (MIHN ur ul) A nonliving, natural thing that does not come from plants or animals.

mission (MIHSH un) A kind of settlement with the goal of spreading a religion.

mountain man (MOUNT un man) A man who worked as a trapper and guided others in the west.

mountain pass (MOUNT un pas) A low area in a mountain range that a road or path can run through.

movement (MOOV munt) A group of people who work together to achieve a goal.

O

objective (ub JEK tihv) A goal or purpose.

occupy (AHK yoo py) To take control of a place.

opposition (ahp uh ZIHSH un) Organized disagreement.

oral (AWR ul) Spoken.

P

pastoral economy (PAS tur ul ih KAHN uh mee) An economy based on raising animals.

persist (pur SIHST) To continue to exist.

petition (puh TIHSH un) A written request.

physical map (FIHZ ih kul map) A map that shows information such as landforms and bodies of water.

plan (plan) To think about before something happens.

political map (puh LIHT ih kul map) A map that shows information such as state or national borders.

popular culture (PAHP yuh lur KUL chur) Cultural products aimed at everyday people, including movies, books, television programs, video games, and pop music.

population (pahp yuh LAY shun) The number of people who live in a place.

population density (pahp yuh LAY shun DEN suh tee) The average number of people living in an area in relation to the size of that area.

port (port) A place where ships load and unload goods for trade.

poverty (PAHV ur tee) The state of being poor and in need of resources.

preamble (PREE am bul) An introduction.

precipitation (pree sihp uh TAY shun) Rain or snow.

prejudice (PREJ uh dihs) Dislike or unjust behavior towards others based on untrue opinions.

presidio (prih SIHD ee oh) A military fort in Spanish America.

previously (PREE vee us lee) At an earlier time; before.

primary source (PRY mair ee sors) A source that is made or written by a person who witnessed an event firsthand.

prime meridian (prym muh RIHD ee un) The line of longitude marked as 0°.

private school (PRY vut skool) A school paid for by private groups or individuals, rather than the government.

propose (pruh POHZ) To suggest.

prospector (PRAHS pek tur) Someone who looks for a natural resource.

public school (PUB lihk skool) A school paid for by the government.

pueblo (PWEB loh) A town in Spanish America.

R

racism (RAY sihz um) The belief that people of other races are not as good as those of your race.

rancheria (ran chuh REE uh) A small piece of land set aside by the government for Indian families.

rancho (RAN choh) A large area of land used for raising cattle, sheep, and horses.

rationing (RASH un ing) When the government limits the amount of food or supplies people can buy.

recall (rih KAWL) To remove and replace a government official.

reform (rih FORM) To make changes and improvements to something.

refugee (REF yoo jee) A person who leaves his or her own country for safety, running away from war or violence.

region (REE jun) A large area of land that has similar features.

relative location (REL uh tihv loh KAY shun) Where a place is in relation to another place.

represent (re pri ZENT) To speak for someone.

republic (rih PUB lihk) A type of government run by elected leaders.

research (REE surch) The deep study of a particular subject.

reservation (rez ur VAY shun) An area of land controlled by a sovereign American Indian group.

reservoir (REZ ur vwahr) A place where water is collected and stored for use.

resource (REE sors) Something that is useful.

responsible (rih SPAHN suh bul) Being the cause of something.

revenue (REV uh noo) Money made by a business.

revolt (rih VOHLT) A violent attack on people in power.

rule of law (rool uv law) The constitutional principle that says that everyone must follow the law, including government leaders.

rural (ROOR ul) An area made up up of small towns and open space.

S

scale (skayl) A symbol that shows how distance on the map compares to distance in the real world.

school board (skool bord) A group of people who manage schools in an area.

seal (seel) An official symbol of a place, group, or political office.

secondary source (SEK un dair ee sors) A source that was written or created by someone who did not witness an event.

secularize (SEK yuh luh ryz) To take away from religious control.

secure (sih KYOOR) To get hold of or take possession of.

segregation (seg ruh GAY shun) The forced separation of people.

service (SUR vihs) Work that involves helping other people, rather than producing goods or products.

settler (SET lur) Someone who moves to a new place to live.

shaman (SHAY mun) Word used by historians to describe a man or woman who had a special religious role for California Indians.

slavery (SLAY vur ee) The practice of buying and selling people like property and forcing them to work without pay.

solar plant (SOH lur plant) A power plant that uses solar panels to take energy from the sun and change it into electricity.

speculate (SPEK yoo layt) To think about an idea and make guesses about it.

spiritual (SPIHR ih choo ul) Religious.

stock (stahk) A share, or portion, of ownership in a company.

strike (stryk) The refusal to do a job until demands are met.

subject (SUB jekt) A person who is ruled by a king or queen.

suburb (SUB urb) A community located near a city.

superintendent (soo pur ihn TEN dunt) The top executive in a school district.

support (suh PORT) To help.

system (SIHS tum) An established way of doing something.

T

tax (taks) Money paid to a government.

technology (tek NAHL uh jee) The use of scientific knowledge to solve problems.

telegraph (TEL uh graf) A machine that uses signals to send messages instantly from place to place using wires.

title (TYT ul) On a map, the words that tell its topic.

tourism (TOOR ihz um) Traveling to a place for fun.

trade school (trayd skool) A school that teaches technical skills required for a specific job.

traditional (truh DIHSH un ul) Based on long-standing customs, beliefs, and ways of doing things.

trailblazer (TRAYL blay zur) Someone who finds or makes a new path between places.

transfer (TRANS fur) To change hands, or to move from one place to another.

transportation system (trans pur TAY shun SIHS tum) A system that can move people or goods from place to place.

trend (trend) An idea that is popular or fashionable.

tribal council (TRY bul KOUN sul) The legislative branch of many California Indian groups.

typically (TIHP ih kul ee) Ordinarily, usually.

U

unemployed (un em PLOYD) Without a job.

unique (yoo NEEK) Not like other things; special, unusual.

university (yoo nuh VER suh tee) an educational institution designed for advanced learning.

urban (UR bun) Having to do with a city.

urbanization (ur buh nih ZAY shun) When people move from rural areas to towns and cities.

V

valley (VAL ee) A low area of land found between mountains.

veto (VEE toh) To reject.

viceroy (VYS roi) A governor in the Spanish empire.

village (VIHL uj) A small community.

vision (VIZH un) An idea or goal formed in one's mind.

W

wagon train (WAG un trayn) A group of covered wagons that traveled together over a long distance.

wildlife (WYLD lyf) Animals living in nature.

Glosario

A

absolute location/ubicación absoluta La ubicación exacta de un lugar en la Tierra.

accessible/accesible Disponible.

activist/activista Alguien que trabaja mucho para lograr un cambio.

adapt/adaptarse Cambiar o acostumbrarse.

advocate/defender Hablar a favor de algo.

aerospace/aeroespacial La industria que fabrica aviones, cohetes y otros objetos voladores.

agree/estar de acuerdo tener la misma opinión.

agriculture/agricultura Cultivo.

amendment/enmienda Cambio hecho a la Constitución.

aqueduct/acueducto Una tubería u otro sistema que lleva agua de un lugar a otro.

architecture/arquitectura Diseño de edificios.

article/artículo Sección de una ley o constitución.

authority/autoridad Persona que controla un lugar.

B

bill/proyecto de ley Propuesta para una nueva ley.

biography/biografía Libro sobre la vida de una persona escrito por otra persona.

boomtown/boomtown Ciudad que crece de golpe.

boycott/boicot Decidir no comprar algo para defender una idea.

budget/presupuesto Plan para gastar dinero.

C

Californio/californio Persona que vivía en la antigua California y era descendiente de colonos españoles.

campus/campus El terreno y los edificios de una escuela o universidad.

challenge/desafío Algo que resulta difícil.

checks and balances/sistema de controles y equilibrios Sistema de nuestro gobierno en el que cada poder tiene el permiso de controlar, es decir limitar, las capacidades de los otros poderes.

circumnavigate/circunnavegar Completar una vuelta navegando.

city council/concejo municipal Grupo de personas que crea leyes para una ciudad.

civil rights/derechos civiles Derechos de todos los ciudadanos a la libertad y la igualdad.

civil war/guerra civil Guerra entre dos bandos en un mismo país.

claim/reclamación El derecho oficial de poseer algo, como un terreno.

climate/clima El estado del tiempo promedio de un lugar a lo largo del tiempo.

colony/colonia Territorio controlado por otro país.

commerce/comercio Negocios.

commercial agriculture/agricultura comercial Cultivar para obtener ganacias, en lugar de quedarse con lo que se cosecha.

communicate/comunicarse Compartir información.

community/comunidad Grupo de personas que viven en la misma área.

compass rose/rosa de los vientos Símbolo que muestra los puntos cardinales norte, sur, este y oeste; también puede mostrar los puntos intermedios noreste, noroeste, sureste y suroeste.

compromise/llegar a un acuerdo Situación en la que cada lado de una disputa renuncia a algo para ponerse de acuerdo en una solución.

consequence/consecuencia Resultado o efecto.

constitution/constitución Plan escrito para el gobierno.

constitutional convention/convención constitucional Reunión especial para crear una constitución.

contribute/contribuir Dar algo para sumar a un todo que es mayor.

convert/convertirse Cambiar de una religión a otra.

corruption/corrupción Conducta deshonesta e ilegal de las personas que están en el poder.

create/crear Hacer que algo ocurra.

cultivate/cultivar Preparar y usar la tierra para hacer crecer plantas.

culture/cultura Modo de vida compartido por un grupo de personas, que incluye sus creencias y costumbres.

current/corriente Movimiento continuo de agua en la misma dirección.

D

defense industry/industria de defensa Empresas que producen provisiones para el ejército.

delegate/delegado Persona elegida para tomar decisiones de gobierno.

democracy/democracia Sistema político en el que el poder del gobierno proviene del pueblo.

deny/negar Rechazar.

deport/deportar Enviar a alguien de vuelta a su país de origen.

depression/depresión Período de tiempo en el que desacelera la actividad comercial.

describe/describir Explicar algo.

develop/desarrollar Hacer crecer o expandir.

discover/descubrir Hallar.

discrimination/discriminación Tratamiento injusto a las personas basado en la raza, el género, la edad u otras características.

district/distrito Parte del gobierno creada para hacer funcionar algo determinado en un área específica.

diverse/diverso Diferente.

draft/hacer un borrador Hacer una primera versión o plan de algo.

drought/sequía Tiempo de poca lluvia.

E

economy/economía La manera en que una región produce recursos, bienes y servicios para satisfacer sus necesidades y deseos.

elevation/elevación La altura de un lugar por encima del nivel del mar.

encounter/encontrar Conocer.

engineer/ingeniero Persona que diseña cosas como caminos, puentes o máquinas.

entrepreneur/empresario Alguien que crea una nueva empresa.

environment/medio ambiente El entorno natural de un área, o el mundo natural en general.

equator/ecuador Línea imaginaria que pasa alrededor del centro de la Tierra.

erode/erosionar Destruir gradualmente.

exclusion/exclusión Acción de mantener a una persona o grupo al margen.

executive branch/poder ejecutivo El poder del gobierno responsable de hacer cumplir las leyes.

expedition/expedición Viaje organizado.

export/exportación Algo que es vendido o intercambiado con otro país.

F

federalism/federalismo Principio constitucional que dice que el poder es compartido entre el gobierno nacional y estatal.

foreigner/extranjero Persona de otro país.

former/anterior En el pasado; de antes.

Franciscan/franciscano Miembro de la orden franciscana, un grupo religioso de la Iglesia católica romana.

freeway/carretera Una ruta que se puede usar sin pagar.

fugitive/fugitivo Persona que intenta escapar de algo, como por ejemplo la esclavitud.

G

galleon/galeón Un tipo de barco grande.

geography/geografía Estudio de la ubicación, personas, lugares y características naturales de un área.

glacier/glaciar Un gran bloque de hielo.

H

hemisphere/hemisferio La mitad de la Tierra.

heritage/herencia Costumbres e historia.

higher education/educación superior Educación que viene después de la escuela secundaria.

historical map/mapa histórico Mapa que muestra sucesos del pasado.

Hollywood/Hollywood Área de Los Ángeles que es el centro de la filmación de películas en los Estados Unidos.

humid/clima húmedo Con humedad y caluroso.

hunter-gatherer/cazador-recolector Persona que recolecta plantas y caza animales para alimentarse.

hydroelectric power/energía hidroeléctrica Electricidad creada por la potencia de agua que cae.

I

immigrate/inmigrar Llegar a otro país para vivir.

independence/independencia Libertad respecto del control de otra persona, país o gobierno.

indigenous/indígena Nativo de un lugar.

individual/individual Independiente; separado.

industry/industria Las empresas que producen un tipo de producto u ofrecen un tipo de servicio.

influence/influencia Efecto o impacto.

inhabitant/habitante Persona que vive en un lugar determinado.

initiative/iniciativa Proceso en el que los votantes votan una propuesta para una nueva ley.

intent/intención Meta o propósito.

internment camp/campo de internamiento Lugar donde las personas son detenidas contra su voluntad, generalmente durante una guerra.

invasion/invasión Ataque militar para tomar el control de un lugar.

investor/inversor Persona que da dinero a una empresa a cambio de una parte de las ganancias de la empresa en el futuro.

involve/involucrarse Participar en algo.

irrigation/irrigación Transporte de agua a los cultivos usando canales, zanjas y tuberías.

isolate/aislar Separar o colocar aparte de otras cosas.

J

judicial branch/poder judicial Poder del gobierno responsable de interpretar las leyes.

K

kinship/parentesco Relación.

L

land grant/cesión de tierra Documento oficial que da a alguien el derecho de poseer su propia extensión de tierra.

landform/accidente geográfico Característica física natural de la superficie de la Tierra.

latitude/latitud Líneas en un mapa que miden la distancia al norte o al sur del ecuador.

legislative branch/poder legislativo El poder del gobierno responsable de crear las leyes.

levee/dique Barrera construida para evitar que el agua inunde la tierra.

limit/limitar Controlar.

locator map/mapa localizador Mapa simple que muestra la ubicación de un área dentro de un país o en el mundo.

lode/veta Depósito de oro u otro metal o mineral atrapado en una roca.

longitude/longitud Líneas en un mapa que miden la distancia al este o al oeste del primer meridiano.

M

map legend/leyenda Recuadro que explica los símbolos que hay en un mapa.

mayor/alcalde Líder de una ciudad o un pueblo.

migrant worker/trabajador migratorio Persona que suele trasladarse de un lugar a otro para trabajar.

miner/minero Persona que cava en la tierra para buscar minerales y metales, como el oro.

mineral/mineral Algo natural y no viviente que no proviene de plantas ni animales.

mission/misión Un tipo de asentamiento con el objetivo de difundir una religión.

mountain man/montañés Hombre que trabajaba como trampero y guiaba a otros en el Oeste.

mountain pass/paso de montaña Área baja en una cordillera por la que puede pasar un camino o sendero.

movement/movimiento Grupo de personas que trabajan en conjunto para lograr una meta.

O

objective/objetivo Meta o propósito.

occupy/ocupar Tomar el control de un lugar.

opposition/oposición Desacuerdo organizado.

oral/oral Hablado.

P

pastoral economy/economía pastoral Economía basada en la cría de animales.

persist/persistir Seguir existiendo.

petition/petición Pedido escrito.

physical map/mapa físico Mapa que muestra información como los accidentes geográficos y las masas de agua.

plan/planificar Pensar en algo antes de que ocurra.

political map/mapa político Mapa que muestra información como las fronteras nacionales o estatales.

popular culture/cultura popular Productos culturales dirigidos a las personas comunes, incluyendo películas, libros, programas de televisión, videojuegos y música pop.

population/población La cantidad de personas que viven en un lugar.

population density/densidad de población La cantidad promedio de personas que viven en un área en relación con el tamaño de esa área.

port/puerto Lugar donde los barcos cargan y descargan bienes para el comercio.

poverty/pobreza El estado de ser pobre y necesitar recursos.

preamble/preámbulo Introducción.

precipitation/precipitación Lluvia o nieve.

prejudice/prejuicio Rechazo o comportamiento injusto hacia otros basado en opiniones que no son verdaderas.

presidio/presidio Fuerte militar en Hispanoamérica.

previously/previamente En un momento anterior; antes.

primary source/fuente primaria Fuente que fue escrita o hecha por alguien que presenció un suceso de primera mano.

prime meridian/primer meridiano La línea de longitud marcada como 0°.

private school/escuela privada Escuela financiada por grupos privados o por individuos, en lugar de por el gobierno.

propose/proponer Sugerir.

prospector/cateador Alguien que busca un recurso natural.

public school/escuela pública Escuela pagada por el gobierno.

pueblo/pueblo Pueblo en Hispanoamérica.

R

racism/racismo Creencia en que las personas de otras razas no son tan buenas como las personas de tu raza.

rancheria/ranchería Terreno pequeño reservado por el gobierno para familias indígenas.

rancho/rancho Terreno de gran tamaño usado para criar ganado vacuno, ovejas y caballos.

rationing/racionamiento Cuando el gobierno limita la cantidad de comida o provisiones que las personas pueden comprar.

recall/destituir Separar a un funcionario de su cargo y reemplazarlo.

reform/reformar Hacer cambios y mejoras a algo.

refugee/refugiado Persona que deja su país buscando seguridad, para escapar de un entorno de guerra o violencia.

region/región Gran área de tierra que tiene características similares.

relative location/ubicación relativa Dónde está un lugar en relación con otro lugar.

represent/representar Hablar en nombre de alguien.

republic/república Tipo de gobierno ejercido por líderes elegidos.

research/investigación El estudio en profundidad de un tema en particular.

reservation/reserva Territorio controlado por un grupo indígena soberano.

reservoir/embalse Lugar donde el agua es recogida y almacenada para su uso.

resource/recurso Algo que es útil.

responsible/responsable Que es la causa de algo.

revenue/ingreso Dinero ganado por una empresa.

revolt/rebelión Ataque violento contra las personas que están en el poder.

rule of law/imperio de la ley Principio constitucional que dice que todos deben obedecer la ley, incluso los líderes del gobierno.

rural/rural Área formada por pueblos pequeños y espacio abierto.

S

scale/escala Símbolo que muestra la relación entre la distancia en un mapa y la distancia en el mundo real.

school board/junta escolar Grupo de personas que dirige las escuelas de un área.

seal/sello Símbolo oficial de un lugar, un grupo o puesto político.

secondary source/fuente secundaria Fuente que fue escrita o creada por alguien que no presenció un suceso.

secularize/secularizar Hacer que algo no esté controlado por la religión.

secure/asegurar Apropiarse o tomar posesión de algo.

segregation/segregación Separación forzada de personas.

service/servicio Trabajo que implica ayudar a otras personas, en lugar de producir bienes o productos.

settler/colono Alguien que se traslada a vivir a un nuevo lugar.

shaman/chamán Palabra usada por los historiadores para describir a una persona que tenía una función religiosa especial para los indígenas californianos.

slavery/esclavismo La práctica de comprar y vender personas como si fueran propiedad y obligarlos a trabajar sin pagarles.

solar plant/planta de energía solar Planta de energía que usa paneles solares para extraer energía del sol y transformarla en electricidad.

speculate/especular Pensar acerca de una idea y hacer suposiciones.

spiritual/espiritual Religioso.

stock/acciones Partes de la propiedad de una empresa.

strike/huelga Rechazo a hacer un trabajo hasta que se cumplan ciertos pedidos.

subject/súbdito Persona que es gobernada por un rey o una reina.

suburb/suburbio Comunidad ubicada cerca de una ciudad.

superintendent/superintendente El ejecutivo de más alto nivel en un distrito escolar.

support/apoyar Ayudar.

system/sistema Una manera establecida de hacer algo.

T

tax/impuesto Dinero que se paga a un gobierno.

technology/tecnología Uso de conocimiento científico para resolver problemas.

telegraph/telégrafo Máquina que usa señales para enviar mensajes de un lugar a otro de forma instantánea mediante cables.

title/título En un mapa, las palabras que indican su tema.

tourism/turismo Viajar a un lugar por placer.

trade school/instituto de formación profesional Escuela que enseña las destrezas técnicas necesarias para un trabajo específico.

traditional/tradicional Basado en costumbres, creencias y modos de hacer las cosas que existen desde hace mucho tiempo.

trailblazer/pionero Alguien que encuentra o crea un nuevo camino para unir lugares.

transfer/transferir Cambiar de dueño, o llevar de un lugar a otro.

transportation system/sistema de transporte Sistema que puede trasladar personas o bienes de un lugar a otro.

trend/tendencia Idea que es popular o está de moda.

tribal council/consejo tribal Poder legislativo de muchos grupos indígenas californianos.

typically/típicamente Generalmente.

U

unemployed/desempleado Sin empleo.

unique/único Diferente a otras cosas, especial, inusual.

university/universidad Institución educativa diseñada para el aprendizaje avanzado.

urban/urbano Relacionado con una ciudad.

urbanization/urbanización Cuando las personas se mudan de áreas rurales a pueblos y ciudades.

V

valley/valle Área de tierra baja que se halla entre montañas.

veto/vetar Rechazar.

viceroy/virrey Gobernador en el imperio español.

village/aldea Una comunidad pequeña.

vision/visión Idea u objetivo que se forma en la mente de uno.

W

wagon train/caravana de carretas Grupo de carretas cubiertas que viajaban juntas y recorrían una gran distancia.

wildlife/fauna Animales que viven en la naturaleza.

Index

This index lists the pages on which topics appear in this book. Page numbers followed by *m* refer to maps. Page numbers followed by *p* refer to photographs. Page numbers followed by *c* refer to charts or graphs. Page numbers followed by *t* refer to timelines. The terms *See* and *See also* direct the reader to alternate entries.

Credits

Text Acknowledgments

Ansel Adams
The Portfolios of Ansel Adams by Ansel Adams. Copyright © Ansel Adams.

Greg Sarris
Greg Sarris Speech given during Pomo Heritage Week. Copyright © Greg Sarris

HarperCollins Publishers
Dragon's Gate by Laurence Yep. Copyright © HarperCollins Publishers.

Little, Brown and Company
By the Great Horn Spoon! by Sid Fleischmann. Copyright © Little, Brown and Company.

Los Angeles Time
Often Criticized, Serra Gets A Reappraisal From Historians from The Los Angeles Times, March 17, 2015 by Louis Sahagun. Copyright © Los Angeles Times

Naturegraph Publishers
Pomo Basketmaking: A Supreme Art for the Weaver by Elsie Allen. Copyright © Naturegraph Publishers.

The Nation
Dubious Battle in California from The Nation, September 12, 1936 by John Steinbeck. Copyright © The Nation.

The New York Times Company
A Farm-Bread Unionist from The New York Times, March 11, 1968. Copyright © The New York Times Company.

The Online Archive of California
Pattern of Life at the Mission by The Online Archive of California. Copyright © The Online Archive of California.

Pinoleville Pomo Nation
Mission Statement of Pinoleville Pomo Nation from www.pinolevillepomonation.org. Copyright © Pinoleville Pomo Nation.

University of California
Interview with Harold Zellerbach conducted by Harriet Nathan. Published by University of California, © 1971.

University of Oklahoma Press
Lands of Promise and Despair: Chronicles of Early California 1535-1846. Copyright © University of Oklahoma Press.

Wisconsin Historical Society.
American Journeys Collection: Relation of the Voyage of Juan Rodriquez Cabrillo, 1542-1543: document No. AJ-001 by Juan Rodriquez Cabrillo. Copyright © Wisconsin Historical Society.

Images

CVR: Mitch Diamond/Stockbyte/Getty Images; CA1B: Inge Johnsson/Alamy Stock Photo; CA1BC: Trekkerimages/Alamy Stock Photo; CA1C: Michael Nolan/Robertharding/Alamy Stock Photo; CA1T: The Natural History Museum/Alamy Stock Photo; CA1TC: Martin Shields/Alamy Stock Photo; CA2B: Cbies/Shutterstock; CA2T: Frank Bach/Alamy Stock Photo; CA3B: New York Daily News Archive/New York Daily News/Getty Images; CA3T: Michael Ochs Archives/Stringer/Getty Images; CA4T: Emily Riddell/Alamy Stock Photo; CA5: Courtesy of the Lester S. Levy Collection of Sheet Music, The Sheridan Libraries, The Johns Hopkins University; CA7B: Zuma Press, Inc./Alamy Stock Photo; CA7T: Ringo Chiu/Zuma Press, Inc./Alamy Stock Photo; CA9BL: Joakim Lloyd Raboff/Westend61 GmbH/Alamy Stock Photo; CA9BR: Pete Saloutos/Blend Images/Getty Images; CA9TL: Nik Wheeler/Alamy Stock Photo; CA9TR: Andy/Fotolia; CA13: Travel Stock/Shutterstock; CA19: Jeff J Daly/Alamy Stock Photo; CA20: Andrew J. Russell/Courtesy Kyle Watt Collection OR Oakland Museum of California; CA22: Asiseeit/E+/Getty Images; CA23: Alex Garcia/Los Angeles Times/Getty Images; CA25: California State Archives; CA27: Andrew J. Russell/Courtesy Kyle Watt Collection OR Oakland Museum of California; Copyright Page: Rachid Dahnoun/Aurora Open RF/Alamy Stock Photo; iii: Camarillo Dr. Albert M.; iii: Dr. James B. Kracht; iii: Dr. Kathy Swan; iii: Dr. Linda B. Bennett; iii: Elfrieda H. Hiebert; iii: Jim Cummins; iii: Kathy Tuchman Glass; iii: Paul Apodaca; iii: Steven Hackel; iii: Warren J. Blumenfeld; iii: Xiaojian Zhao; xv: SeBuKi/Alamy Stock Photo; xviiB: Michael Ochs Archives/Stringer/Getty Images; xviiT: Bettmann/Getty Images; xxix: Asiseeit/iStock/Getty Images; xxviiiL: Chuck Place/Alamy Stock Photo; xxviiiR: Monk/Relaximages/Alamy Stock Photo; xxx: Dana White/PhotoEditInc.; 001: Travel Stock/Shutterstock; 002: Rigucci/Shutterstock; 003BL: Nik Wheeler/Alamy Stock Photo; 003BR: Pete Saloutos/Blend Images/Getty Images; 003TL: Antonio Busiello/Robertharding/Alamy Stock Photo; 003TR: Witold Skrypczak/Alamy Stock Photo; 008B: Eye35.pix/Alamy Stock Photo; 008T: Claudio Del Luongo/Alamy Stock Photo; 010: Peter Horree/Alamy Stock Photo; 011: C.DANI/I.JESKE/De Agostini/Getty Images; 012: Nature and Science/Alamy Stock Photo; 018L: Lucky-photographer/Alamy Stock Photo; 018R: Julia Hiebaum/Alamy Stock Photo; 019: Maciej Bledowski/Alamy Stock Photo; 020: James Mattil/Shutterstock; 021: Robert Shantz/Alamy Stock Photo; 022: Gary Crabbe/Alamy Stock Photo; 024: Ansel Adams Publishing Trust; Digital Image The Museum of Modern Art/Licensed by SCALA/Art Resource, NY; 026L: Chuck Place/Alamy Stock Photo; 026R: Monk/Relaximages/Alamy Stock Photo; 028: Tracy Barbutes/Modesto Bee/ZUMA Press Inc/Alamy Stock Photo; 029: Michael Beiriger/Alamy Stock Photo; 033: A. Ramey/PhotoEdit; 034: Don Smetzer/PhotoEdit; 037: F8grapher/Alamy Stock Photo; 038B: Ingo